AF323786

OSCAR E. BERNINGHAUS
TAOS, NEW MEXICO

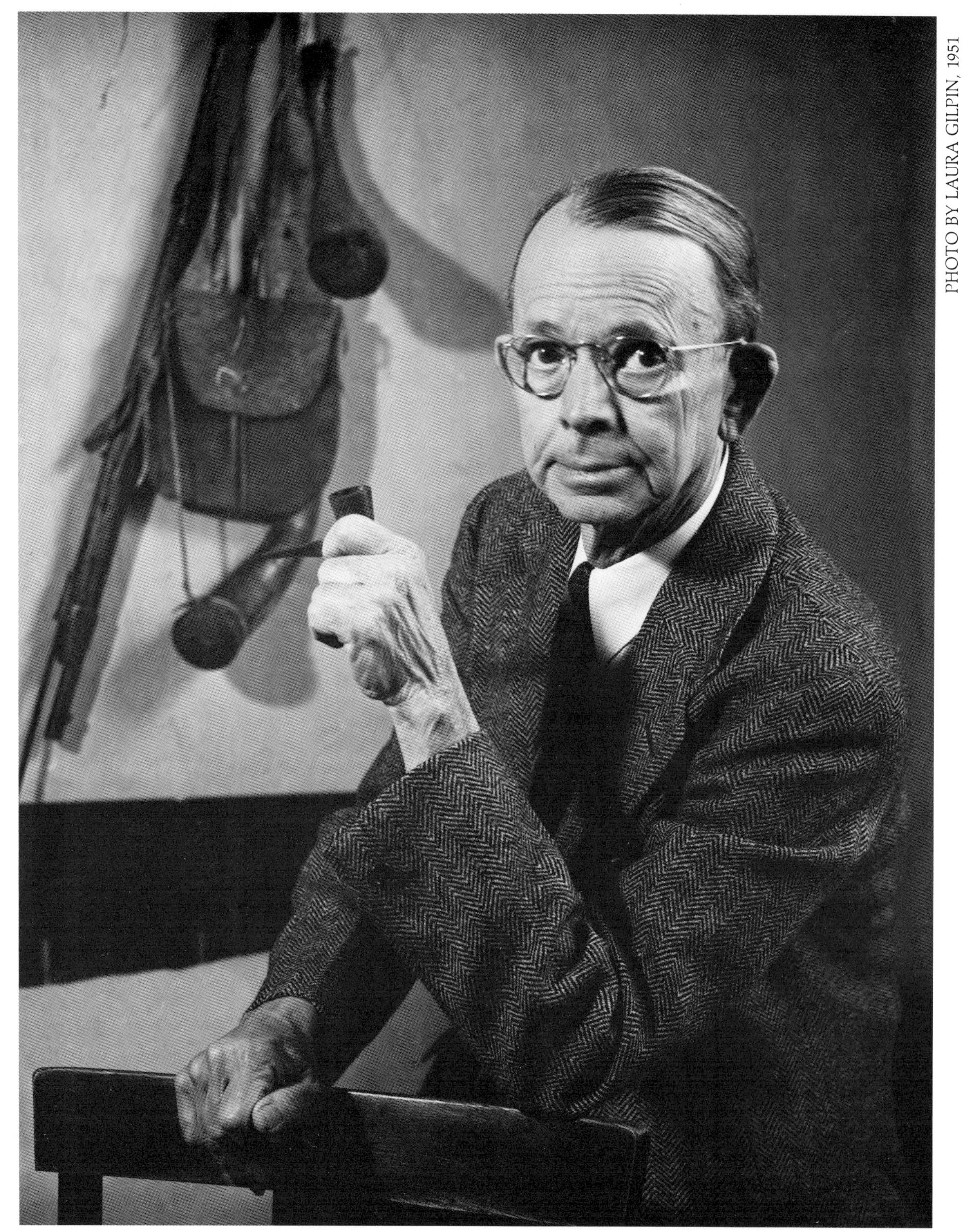

OSCAR E. BERNINGHAUS
TAOS, NEW MEXICO

MASTER PAINTER OF AMERICAN INDIANS AND THE FRONTIER WEST

By Gordon E. Sanders

Foreword by James D. Burke

TAOS HERITAGE PUBLISHING COMPANY

Library of Congress Cataloging-in-Publication Data
Sanders, Gordon E., 1927-
  Oscar E. Berninghaus, Taos, New Mexico: master painter of American Indians and the frontier west.
  Bibliography: p.
  Includes index.
  1. Berninghaus, Oscar E. (Oscar Edmund), 1874-1952. 2. West (U.S.) in art. 3. Indians of North America—Pictorial works. 4. Painters—United States—Biography. 5. Taos Society of Artists. I. Title.
ND237.B537S26 1985   759.13 [B]   85-25015
ISBN 0-9615177-1-9

Designed by Carl G. Grubb

Published by Taos Heritage Publishing Company
P.O. Box NNN, Taos, New Mexico 87571

Printed in the U.S.A. by Starline Printing, Inc.,
a JOURNAL company
Albuquerque, New Mexico

To Dorothy and Charles

ACKNOWLEDGMENTS:

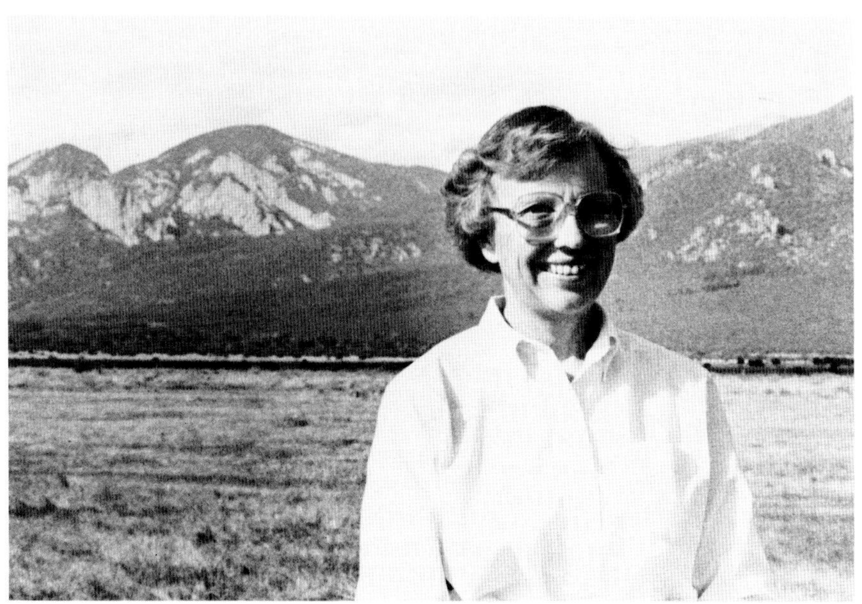

Hundreds of newspaper articles and items of memorabilia concerning the life of Oscar Berninghaus have been collected and carefully preserved by Barbara (Brandenburg) Brenner since her grandfather's death in 1952. She has spent years locating more than eight hundred paintings in museums, galleries and private collections with the idea of someday producing a book about "Papa." "It's amazing the number of pictures he turned out during his lifetime, and even now I feel we have uncovered only the tip of the iceberg. After the publication of this book, we will, perhaps, discover hundreds more. Doing a book on the life of my grandfather had been in the back of my mind for years, but it was my daughters, Marcia and Anne, who persuaded me to find an author and proceed with such a project. It has been a fascinating and rewarding experience." From her Taos, New Mexico, home Barbara Brenner has been the driving force needed to complete this book on Oscar Edmund Berninghaus.

Very special thanks to the following family members:

Jack and Dorothy (Berninghaus) Brandenburg, whose collection of mementos and memories of her father made this book possible.

J. Charles Berninghaus for his interest and recollections of his father.

John Brenner for a great deal of solid support.

Fred and Marcia (Brenner) Winter for their assistance with research and accounting.

Anne (Brenner) Sanders for her support and assistance in research.

Photo Credits:

J. Gordon Adams, Taos, New Mexico

Barbara Brenner, Taos, New Mexico

John O. Milmoe, Denver, Colorado

Gerald Peters, Santa Fe, New Mexico

Roy Madearis, Arlington, Texas

John Stebbins, Taos, New Mexico

The staff photographers of many museums

The help and cooperation of the following museums, galleries, organizations and individuals is greatly appreciated:

James Burke and Michael Shapiro, Saint Louis Art Museum, St. Louis, Missouri

Anne Morand, The Thomas Gilcrease Institute of American History and Art, Tulsa, Oklahoma

Chris Kallenberger, Philbrook Art Center, Tulsa, Oklahoma

Robert Lansdown, Woolaroc Museum, Bartlesville, Oklahoma

Linda Goldstein, Museum of Western Art, Denver, Colorado

Nelda Stark and Laura Bowler, Stark Museum of Art, Orange, Texas

Sandra D'Emilio, Museum of Fine Arts, Santa Fe, New Mexico

Anne Adams, Amon Carter Museum, Fort Worth, Texas

Elizabeth Cunningham, The Anschutz Collection, Denver, Colorado

Bill Vollmer, Anheuser-Busch Brewing Company, St. Louis, Missouri

National Academy of Design, New York, New York

Donald Brandin and Lisa Wangerin, Boatmen's National Bank, St. Louis, Missouri

The National Cowboy Hall of Fame, Oklahoma City, Oklahoma

David Witt, Harwood Foundation, Taos, New Mexico

University of New Mexico Art Department, Albuquerque, New Mexico

Karen Goering, Missouri Historical Society

Missouri Athletic Club, St. Louis, Missouri

St. Louis Artists' Guild, St. Louis, Missouri

Robert E. and Evelyn McKee Foundation, El Paso, Texas

Harrison Eiteljorg, Indianapolis, Indiana

Butler Institute of American Art, Youngstown, Ohio

Louise Young, San Antonio Art League, San Antonio, Texas

Norris Fergeson, McNay Art Museum, San Antonio, Texas

Clyde Jones, The West Texas Museum, Lubbock, Texas

Paul Benisek, Santa Fe Railway, Chicago, Illinois

Sverdrup, Parcel and Associates, St. Louis, Missouri

Samuel A. Salas, Cranbrook School, Bloomfield Hills, Michigan

Bruce B. Selkirk, Jr., Selkirk Galleries, St. Louis, Missouri

Martin Kodner, Gallery of the Masters, St. Louis, Missouri

William A. McAdoo, Carlsbad, New Mexico

Faye and Otto Noeding, Bent Gallery, Taos, New Mexico

Margaret Morris, Gerald Peters Gallery, Santa Fe, New Mexico

Jennifer H. McDonald, Fenn Galleries, Santa Fe, New Mexico

Walt Wiggins, Wiggins Gallery, Roswell, New Mexico

Maurice Sternberg, Galleries Sternberg, Chicago, Illinois

Stephen L. Good, Rosenstock Arts, Denver, Colorado

David Sherer, Taos Art Gallery, Taos, New Mexico

Woodrow Wilson Fine Arts, Santa Fe, New Mexico

James Berry-Hill, Berry-Hill Galleries, New York, New York

Patrick O'Connor, Hammer Galleries, New York, New York

Gerold Wunderlich, Wunderlich and Company, New York, New York

Jim Fowler's Period West Gallery, Scottsdale, Arizona

Michael Frost, Bartfield Gallery, New York, New York

Mr. Eugene B. Adkins, Tulsa, Oklahoma

Dr. and Mrs. David A. Baerreis

Mr. and Mrs. Marshall Thompson

Mrs. J.P. Whitehurst

Mr. and Mrs. Carl Ryberg

Mr. and Mrs. John Sands

Mr. Melvin Weimer

Mr. and Mrs. Charles O'Banion

And private collectors too numerous to mention

Oscar E. Berninghaus has enjoyed a very long term as a popular artist, with good reason. From his early and modest beginnings in St. Louis to his later success as one of the leaders of the Taos School in the 1920s and 1930s, his works were always accessible and direct. Whether illustrations or more formal easel paintings, museums and gallery visitors have quickly responded to his unfailing ability to depict events and places in the American scene in a manner ever fresh. His expert drawing and fine skill with the brush have clearly stood the test of time, for it would appear that the popular approval and strong market for his works continue, perhaps even more now than ever before.

Today, it seems almost incredible to note that this is the first monographic volume on Berninghaus to appear. The serious student of his works who would have found many examples of his paintings hanging in private collections, public museums, art galleries and auction rooms, could hardly make comparisons without hours spent in a major art reference library amid old periodicals. With this book, we have the opportunity to review Berninghaus anew, to see his life and works as a whole, to understand his works firsthand.

What will be his place in American art in the years to come? Will the rather artificial division between "Western art" (especially the Taos School) and the rest of American art in the period between the World Wars continue? How will Berninghaus fit into this often confusing period in American artistic life?

In retrospect, painting in the United States during these years now seems as diverse and pluralistic as in the turbulent 1960s and 1970s. Thus, we find Berninghaus in good company with many strongly varied yet professional talents in the many regions of the country. Nevertheless, for a sense of place, plein air, open spaces and expert incidental figures, Berninghaus has his own clear niche in the histories of our art today. Although these assessments are frequently more spoken than written, a new generation of writers and scholars on American art in the first half of the 20th century are now emerging. Their new ideas will certainly condition new approaches to these problematic discussions.

Berninghaus' long-standing reputation and popularity will make him as hard to ignore in the future as in the past. However, we should recall those qualities which have so firmly fixed his reputation—his great professionalism, dedication to art, sure skill and expertise with pen and brush, excellent use of materials and, most of all, the continuity of meaning in his art from the past to the present.

James D. Burke
Director, Saint Louis Art Museum
St. Louis, Missouri

CONTENTS

ST. LOUIS, STEAMBOATS AND WATERCOLORS

Oscar Edmund Berninghaus was the total artist. Painting was his vocation and his avocation. Starting as a small child with pencil and ink, he literally painted all his life. Self-taught for the most part, Berninghaus achieved international fame during his lifetime as one of America's great Western artists, an honor he shared with Frederic Remington and Charles Russell. For more than 50 years he was the subject of hundreds of newspaper articles in St. Louis, New York, Chicago, his adopted New Mexican home, Taos, and almost every other art center in the country. His paintings of the West at the turn of the century and of the Taos Indians were often the cover pieces of some of the nation's most prestigious publications. Oscar Berninghaus won almost every prize given for American art, including the Altman and Ranger prizes of the National Academy of Design.

In his *Self Portrait*, he appears as he did in life—no chaps, no spurs, no cowboy hat, no smock or tam—just a business suit and always a grey Borasalino hat! If you met him on the street, you never would have guessed he was an artist, and he would never have told you. "In fact," to quote him, "people could mistake me for an undertaker." He always let his paintings speak for themselves, and would have it no other way. Painting was his life—his business—his reason for being. He went to work every morning as any businessman would, not waiting for "inspiration," but knowing that inspiration came from hard work and diligent attention to his "job." In his usual orderly fashion, he arose each day, put on his white shirt and tie, and went to work, either in his studio or the high-mountain country around Taos.

Berninghaus was not a complaining man—sometimes he would spend hours before a canvas, only to look at it, not be satisfied, and scrape it all off with a palette knife. He would start anew and work without a word until he got the perfec-

tion he wanted—no tantrums, no outbursts, just determination and hard work—and of course, that incredible talent.

He loved Taos and everything it had to offer. He was a mainstay of the Taos Society of Artists, often settling disputes among the original six founders because of his even temper and detailed care of the Society's business affairs. Of art and Taos, he had an opinion: he believed that out of the

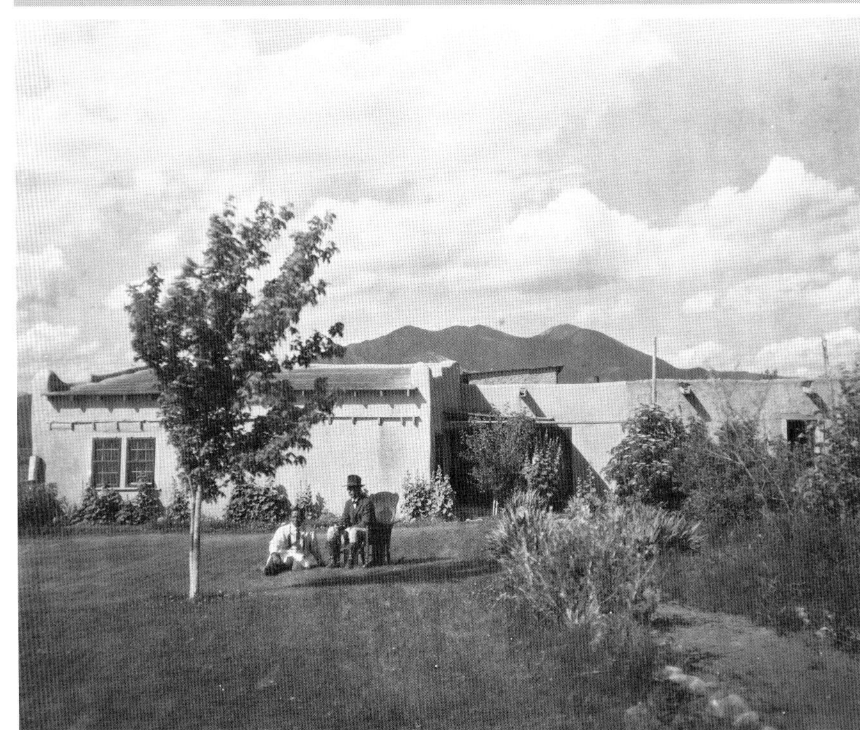

Oscar E. Berninghaus' home in Taos.

colony in Taos would come a distinctive art—American art. In an interview he told a reporter: "We have had French, Dutch, Italian and German art. Now we have American art. I feel that from Taos will come that art"—and it did.

Today, his paintings hang in the nation's most famous museums, and homes of private collectors all over the world. There is even a Berninghaus in the White House—selected from the Santa Fe Railroad Collection for President Reagan's study. Oscar Berninghaus was a vital part of American history, and his life began in 1874 in St. Louis, Missouri.

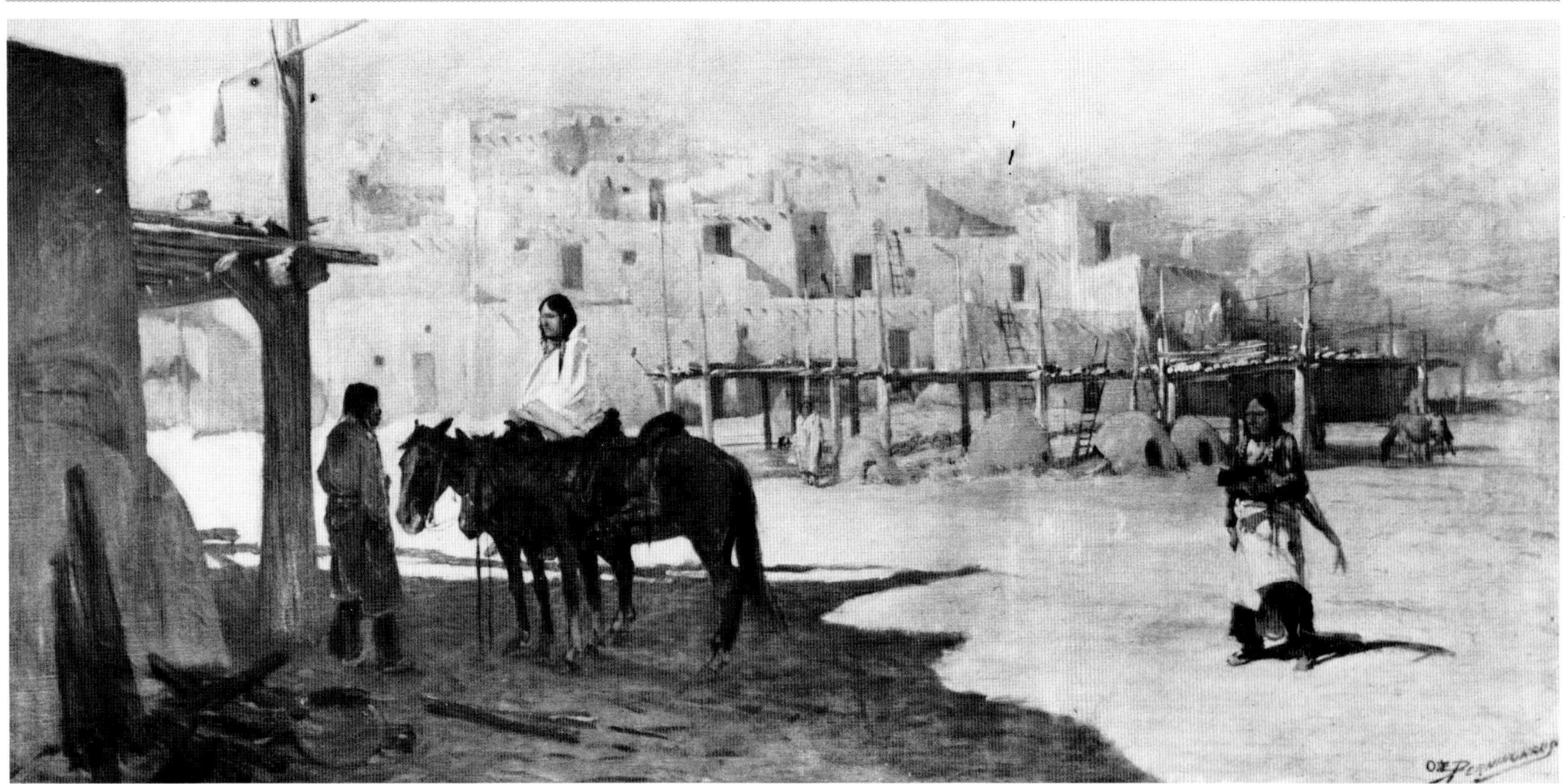

PUEBLO OF TAOS, 1914. 41x81 inches, oil on canvas. Santa Fe Collection of Southwestern Art, Santa Fe Railway.

"AMERICAN ART—
I Feel That From Taos
Will Come That Art."

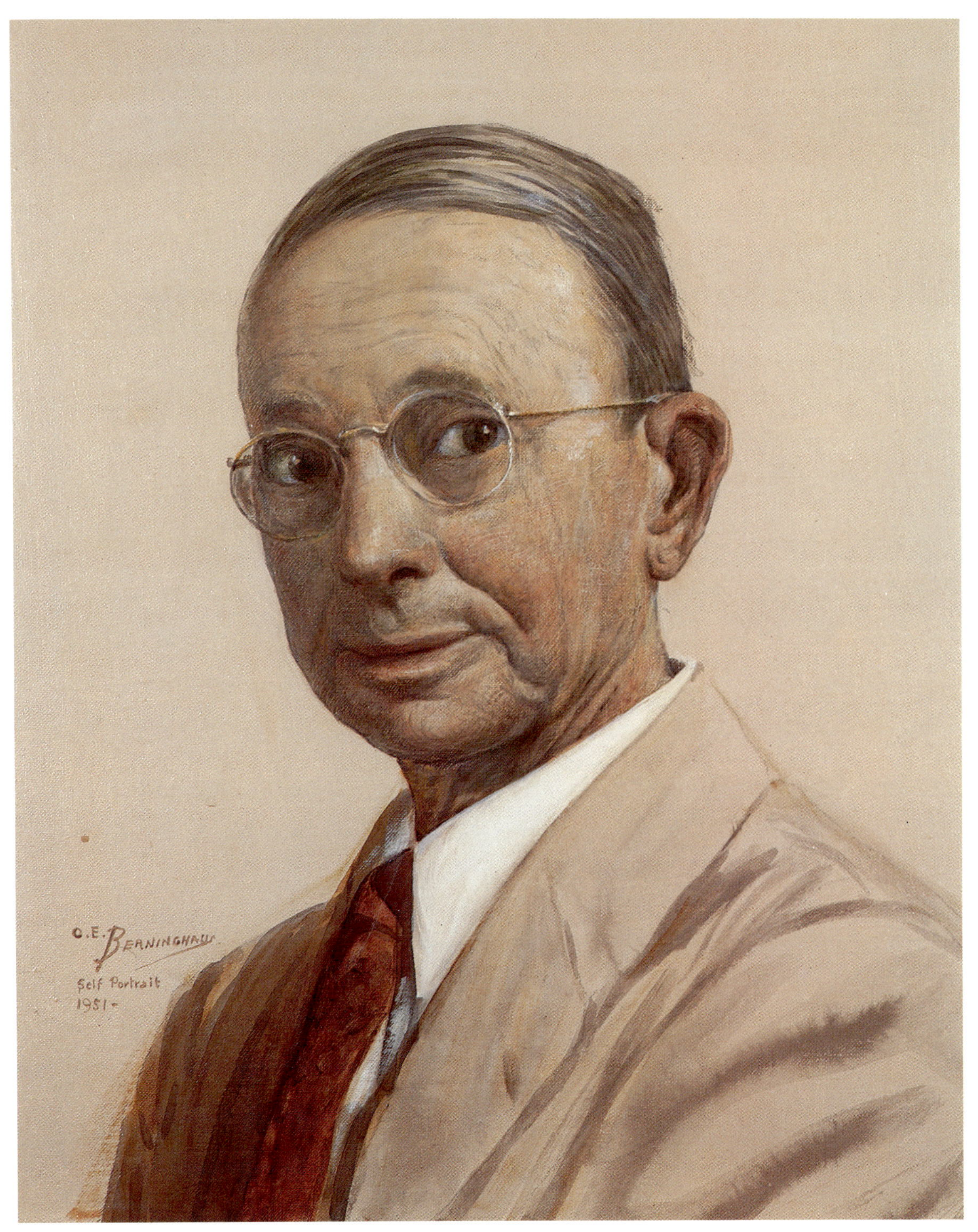

SELF PORTRAIT.
19¾ × 15¾ inches, oil on canvas.
Courtesy of The Thomas
Gilcrease Institute of
American History and Art,
Tulsa, Oklahoma.

During the last quarter of the 19th century, St. Louis, Missouri, was a hub of commerce. A population of more than 300,000 in the 1870s grew to more than a half million by the turn of the century. It was the fourth-largest city in the United States and considered the gateway to the West. Founded by Pierre Laclede and Auguste Chouteau in 1764, St. Louis had been a center for fur traders and trappers who used the city as a jumping-off point to search the mountains and streams of western territories for beaver. The city really began to boom in the mid-seventies with the spanning of the Mississippi River by the Eads Bridge in 1874—allowing both railroad and stage traffic to cross the river at greatly reduced toll fees.

St. Louis had the largest brewery in the world, Anheuser-Busch, which produced more than a million barrels a year. Adolphus Busch's interest in art led him to a "first" in advertising a product. He commissioned Cassidy Adams to paint *Custer's Last Stand,* then sent hundreds of thousands of prints to almost every bar in the country with the Anheuser-Busch Brewing Association label spread across the bottom of the print. His effort was so successful that to this day the company still commissions artists to paint works for their collection.

Oscar Berninghaus was born on October 2, 1874, of German-born parents, Edmund and Augusta Berninghaus. The family lived modestly but well, and received most of its income from the sale of lithographs. Family documents and letters indicate that Mr. Berninghaus kept a large selection of lithographs around the house and that young Oscar delighted in looking at them, and at a very early age tried his hand at drawing.

As Oscar Berninghaus grew up, he constantly drew, sketched and experimented with watercolors. Often he would go down to the riverfront to watch and sketch the boats, the river and the people. The levee was alive with tall stories of Indian adventure, and young Berninghaus was fascinated by these accounts of Western frontier life. His keen memory for detail was useful when he was commissioned to create the bygone days in *Commerce on the Levee.* The 8-foot

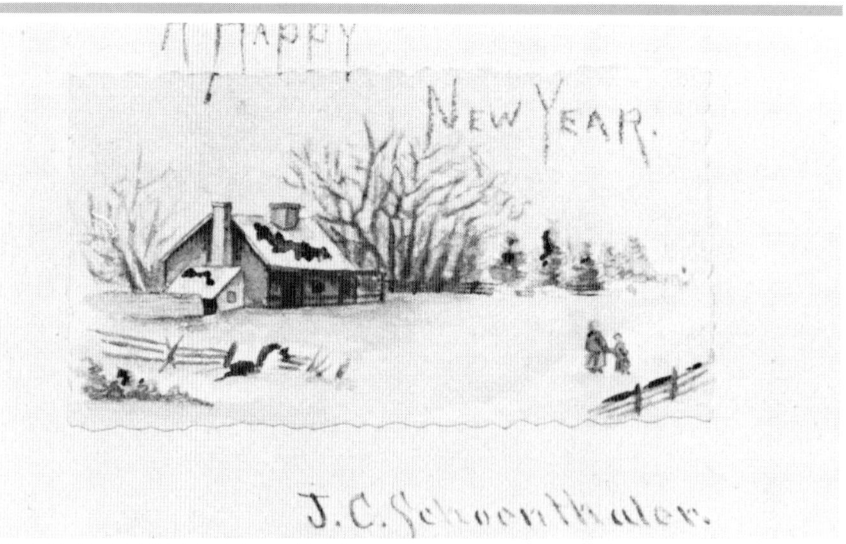

HAPPY NEW YEAR CARD, 1886.
1½ x 3 inches, watercolor. O.E. Berninghaus, age 12.
Private collection.

by 12-foot canvas was completed in 1936 at his studio in Taos, New Mexico, wrapped around a stovepipe, shipped to St. Louis, and installed in the lobby of the *St. Louis Star Times* on May 12. On that same day, the paper ran a four-column black-and-white reproduction of the canvas on the front page with a complete account of the work and an article about the artist—a young man who years ago had sketched and dreamed during the heyday of the Mississippi River trade.

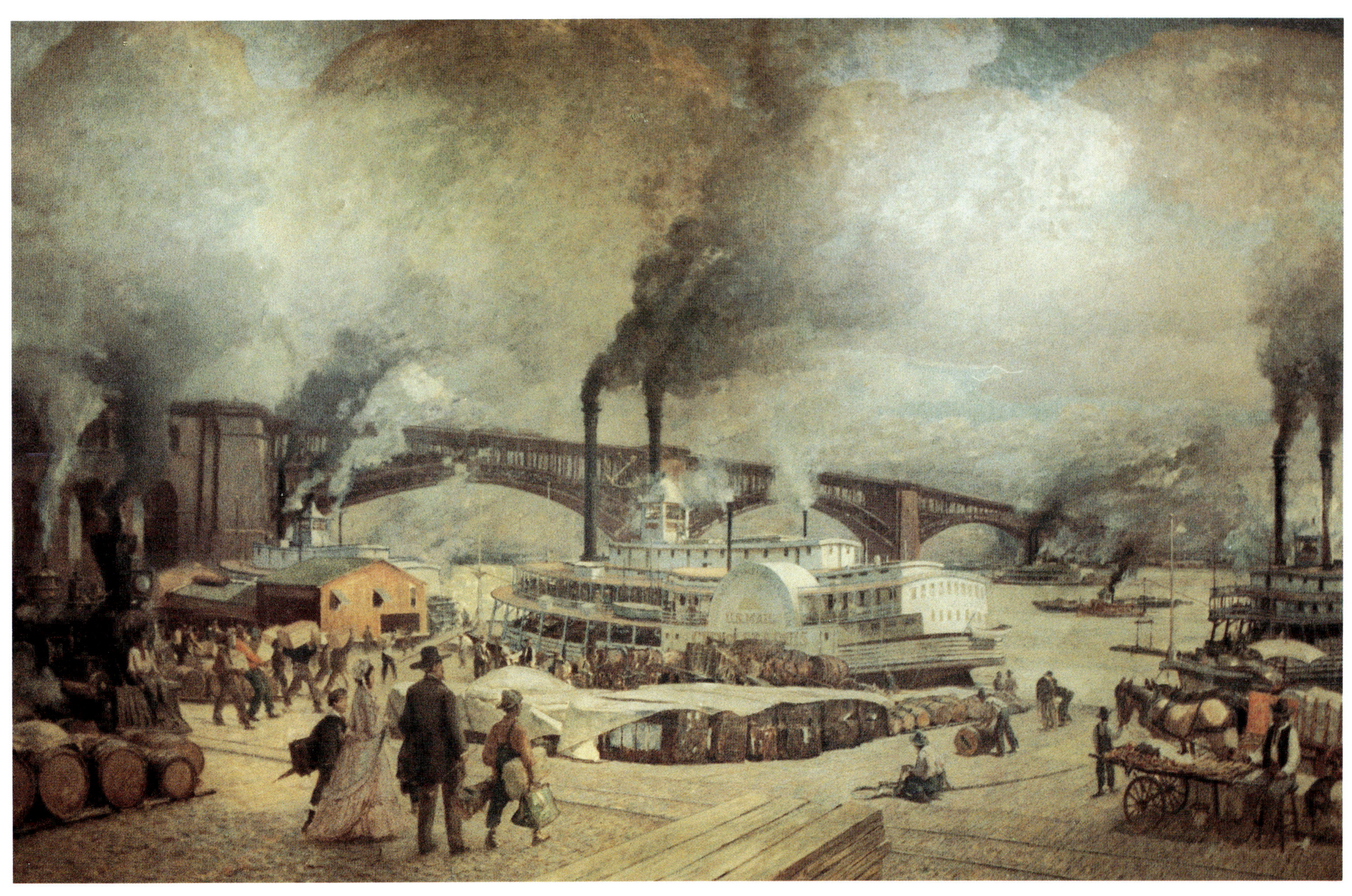

COMMERCE ON THE LEVEE IN THE EARLY 80s, 1936. 8x12 feet, oil on canvas. Courtesy of Sverdrup, Parcel and Associates, St. Louis, Missouri.

At age 10, young Berninghaus was quite accomplished in sketching local scenes. He spent hours practicing his drawing, and developed a clear, well-stated style that stayed with him all his life. By the time he was 12, he was deeply into watercolors, always advancing and perfecting his technique. He also showed early signs of being a good businessman. When there were important local events, Oscar would sketch the scene and offer the drawings for sale to interested groups, even to newspapers. For these efforts, he received a number of token fees—to the delight of his family. He was attending public school at this time, along with his sisters, Estella and Lydia, and brother, Julius. The youngest Berninghaus child, Hulda, was born in 1884.

Schools in St. Louis during the 1880s were very strict, thanks to the famous educator and philosopher William Torry Harris. His principal belief was that children must be disciplined early—in the first grade—or they would be lost to education. How much effect this had on Oscar is not known, but considering how orderly and totally dedicated he was during his life—not only as an artist, but also as a businessman and community leader—it would certainly suggest the system was not all that bad.

In 1890, at the age of 16 and with the consent of his parents, Oscar Berninghaus decided to end his public schooling and get a job. He was hired as an errand boy by Compton and Sons of St. Louis, and worked for the lithography company for the better part of three years. During this time he was further exposed to great art works, and picked up the technical knowledge of printing, lithography, color separation, poster art and engraving. All of his spare time was devoted to his own artistic interest—constantly improving his ability in drawing, lettering and use of watercolors, ink wash, and pen and ink. He had decided to become a commercial artist, and knew the importance of practice.

When Berninghaus was 19, he was accepted as an apprentice by Woodward and Tiernan, one of the country's largest printing companies. This was indeed a great learning experience for Oscar, who had picked up the nickname of

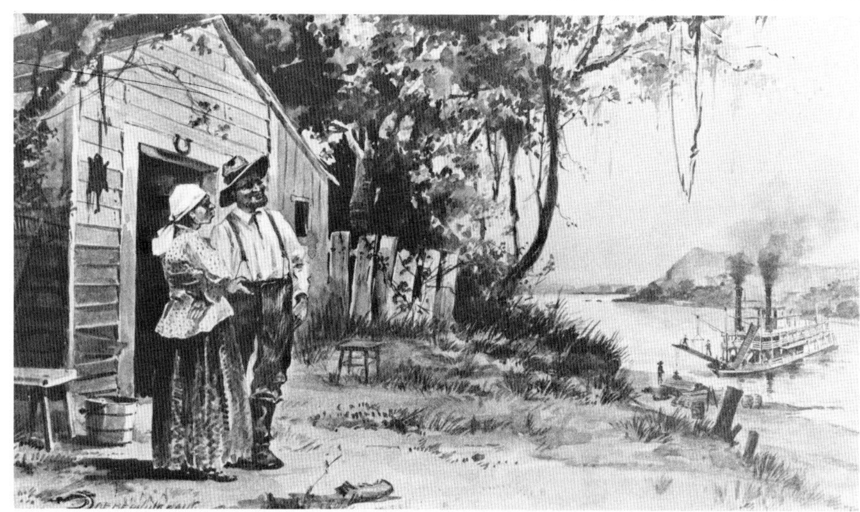

MISSISSIPPI RIVER SCENE, 1915, 6½ x 11 inches, ink wash. Private collection.

"Bern." For a number of years, he used this name to sign his work. Although his training with Woodward and Tiernan was excellent, he felt he needed something more. For three terms he attended night classes at the School of Fine Arts at Washington University in St. Louis while continuing his full-time job. All this, and a number of small commissions which he executed in his "spare time"!

And then came a commission which changed the entire course of his career.

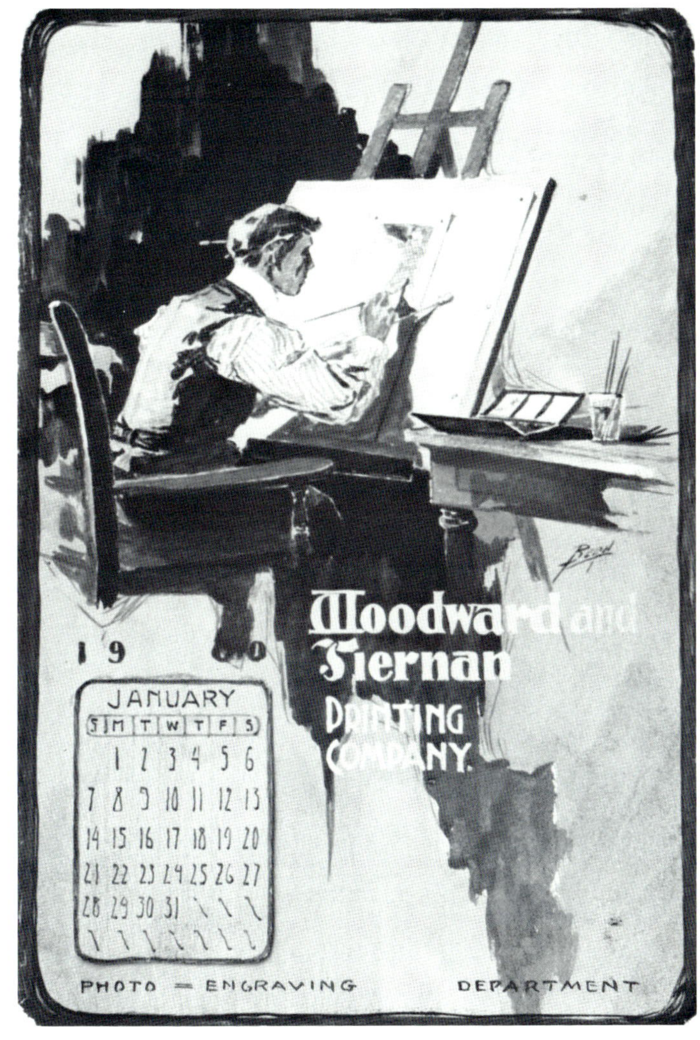

WOODWARD AND TIERNAN PRINTING CO.,
1900 Calendar. 10 x 7 inches, watercolor and pen.
Private collection.

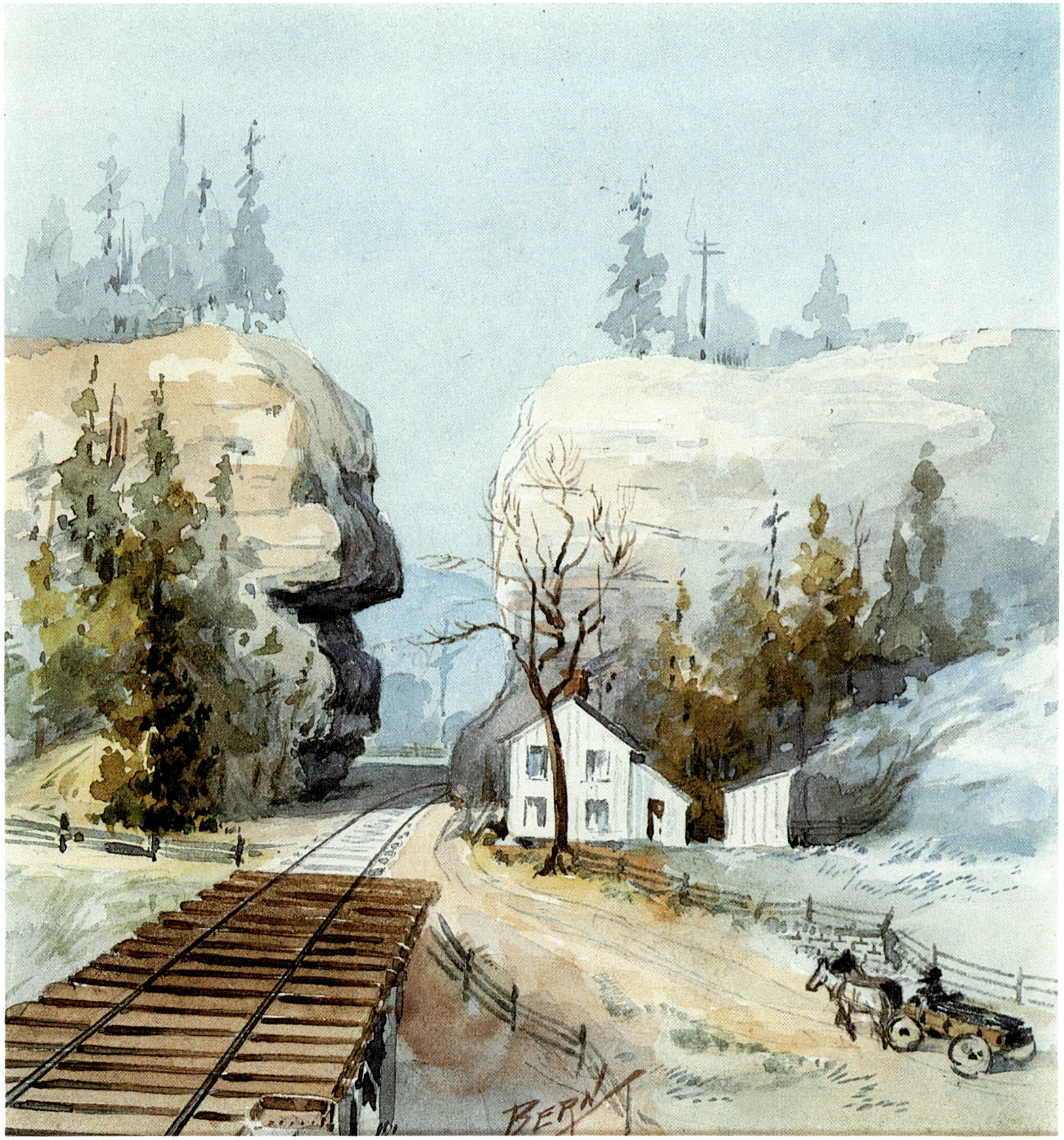

RAILROAD THROUGH ARKANSAS GAP, c. 1898.
$4\frac{1}{8}$ x $4\frac{1}{2}$ inches, watercolor. Private collection.

In 1899, it was good business for the Western states to attract Easterners to their part of the country, as they would bring families with skills and trades. The Denver and Rio Grande Railroad decided to advertise the beautiful unspoiled scenery of Colorado and New Mexico in eastern publications. With this decision, they hired Berninghaus to come west to sketch and produce watercolors of the mountain scenery, mining camps, people and villages. Thanks to some work he had done for the Missouri Pacific Railroad while working at Woodward and Tiernan, the railroad gave him a free pass from St. Louis to Denver—he was on his way!

After spending a day or so in Denver, he headed south to Antonito, Colorado, on the standard-gauge Denver and Rio Grande Railroad. In Antonito he switched over to the narrow-gauge spur of the D. and R.G. "Chili Line." The trip was exciting for the young artist and sketches he did along the way were similar to *Old Trading Post at Ignacio, Colorado*. This early watercolor gives us a glimpse of Berninghaus' technique and the subjects he painted all during his life. As he developed over the years, his horses would become more dominant, more active—the Indians more to the foreground. He was bursting with excitement, and the trip made such an impression on him that he remembered every detail for the rest of his life. In 1950, he wrote about his adventure more than a half century earlier:

For reasons unknown to me the little train would stop every few miles, perhaps to cool down the axle, take in fuel and water, or to remove some fallen boulder from the mountain side. This gave me pleasant opportunity to make sketches of such objects as sagebrush, pinon trees, rock formations, adobe shacks in the little Mexican villages along the line and animal life such as burros and others of which there were plenty.

The train crew, taking an interest in me and what I was doing, suggested I might ride the top of the freight car that I may better see the country as we rolled along, but not before I was securely strapped to the brakeman's iron guard rail that ran atop each car, standard equipment of the day.

As we stopped and passed Servilleta, a station now gone, the brakeman pointed out a certain mountain lying toward the east; this he called Taos Mountain, and told me of a little Mexican village of the same name and the Indian Pueblo lying at the foot of it. That it was one of the oldest towns in the United States (he knew) and gave me some of its history, describing it all so vividly that I started on a twenty-five mile wagon trek over what was comparatively a goat trail.

The trip took 10 hours, and the wild expanse of mountain and desert, the curious coyotes and pronged-horned antelopes that trotted along behind the coach or stood close-by while the conveyance passed, delighted me as did the little adobe town and the massive piles of the pueblo.

I found it all as the brakeman had described it and more so, a barren plaza with hitching rail around it, covered wagons of home seekers, cow and Indian ponies hitched to it. A few merchants and too many saloons made up the business section; there were comparatively few Anglos, some of these had mining interests, some were health seekers, and some perhaps fugitives from justice, as Taos might well be a good hide-out place at the time . . . I stayed here but a week, became infected with the Taos germ and promised myself a longer stay the following year.

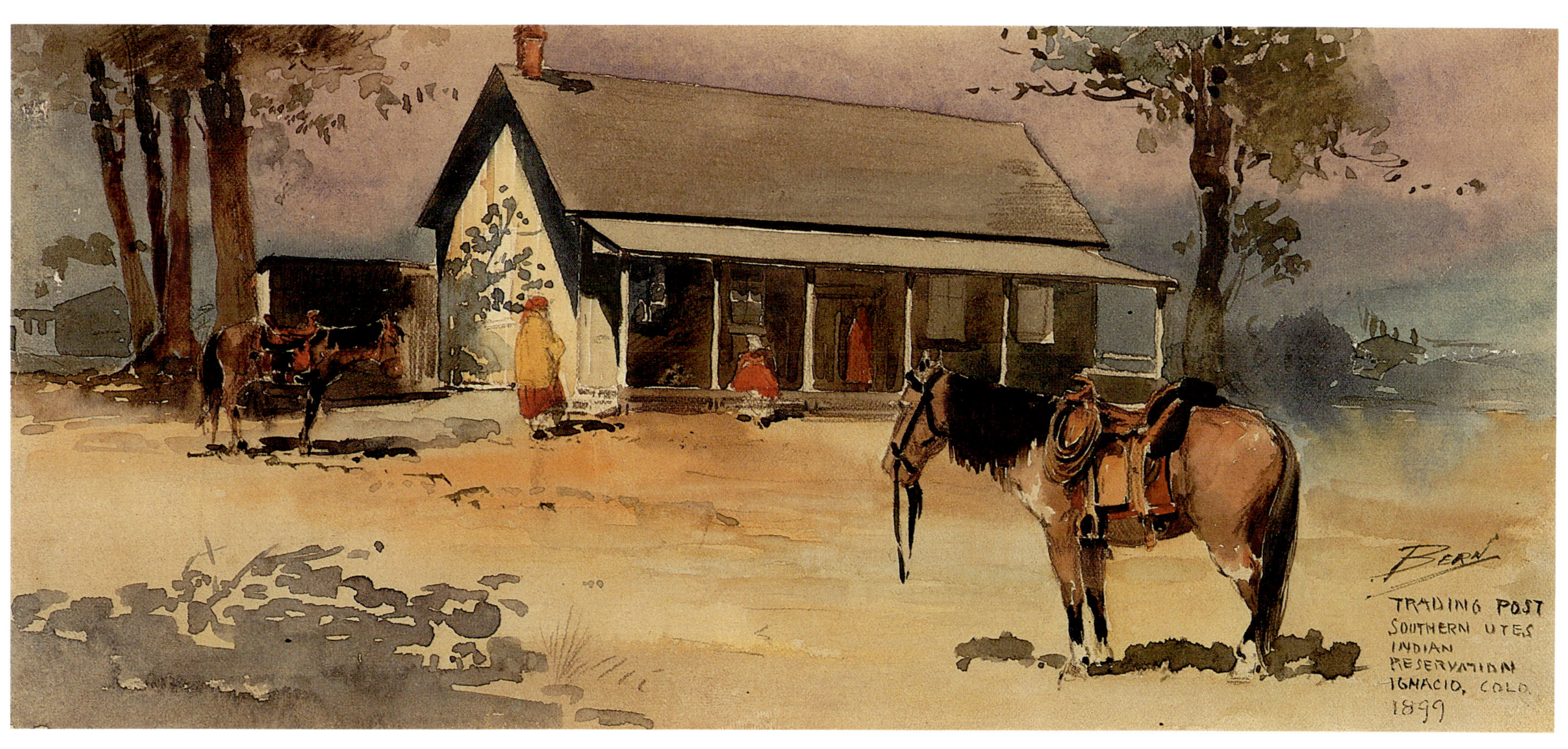

OLD TRADING POST AT IGNACIO, COLORADO, 1899. 5x10½ inches, watercolor. Private collection.

OSCAR E. BERNINGHAUS
TAOS COUNTRY, INDIANS AND OILS

And so, in the summer of 1899, Oscar Berninghaus had his first encounter with the magic of Taos. It was old, colorful and steeped in history. He visited the massive Pueblo to the north, talked with some of the Indians and went horseback riding in the mountains. He saw a thousand scenes he wanted to paint—mountains, skies, people, horses and buildings. It was all so different from the greens and grays of St. Louis. Here the sky was big, bright and blue—you could see for miles! The air was totally fresh—thin and crisp in the mornings—dry and warm in the evenings. The altitude of 7,000 feet above sea level assured cool, comfortable nights, and the low humidity was a welcome change from the Midwest. Taos was indeed a paradise, especially for an artist.

For eight days he wandered about the village and became acquainted with Bert Phillips, another artist who had come to Taos the previous year. Phillips was older and more travelled than Berninghaus, and was a great encouragement to the young artist. He was from New York and had studied in Paris and England along with Ernest Blumenschein and Joseph Sharp. Berninghaus and Phillips became good friends—a friendship that lasted their lifetimes.

While returning to St. Louis, Berninghaus thought over his experience in Taos, and many questions came to mind. Should he continue as a commercial artist, or should he become an independent artist, or could he be both? One thing he was sure of—he would have to master oils, as up to this point, watercolor was his main medium.

Taos country was big, wild, and certainly no place for an artist to make a living. He would have to master oils, for only then could he control the texture and mass of the Sangre de Cristo mountains. Watercolors were great for travel—they were lightweight and easy to manage. They were also comfortable for Berninghaus. He had mastered both transparent and gouache techniques. But they were not enough. In Taos he had seen a special light—a kind of atmospheric light between him and the mountains that was indeed puzzling. It was as though the air itself was filled with pigment, floating in tiny particles everywhere. Perhaps it was dust that had blown from the mountain slopes—from the plains, the sagebrush, the trees, or whatever. But it was there, and it was good. Taos was an independent universe of color. As an artist, he was fascinated with the way the sun and sky along with the mountains and buildings all seemed to blend together harmoniously. Even the Indians appeared to be made of the same pigments as their Pueblo, their horses, their fields of corn and pumpkins—it was glorious, and he promised he would return next year.

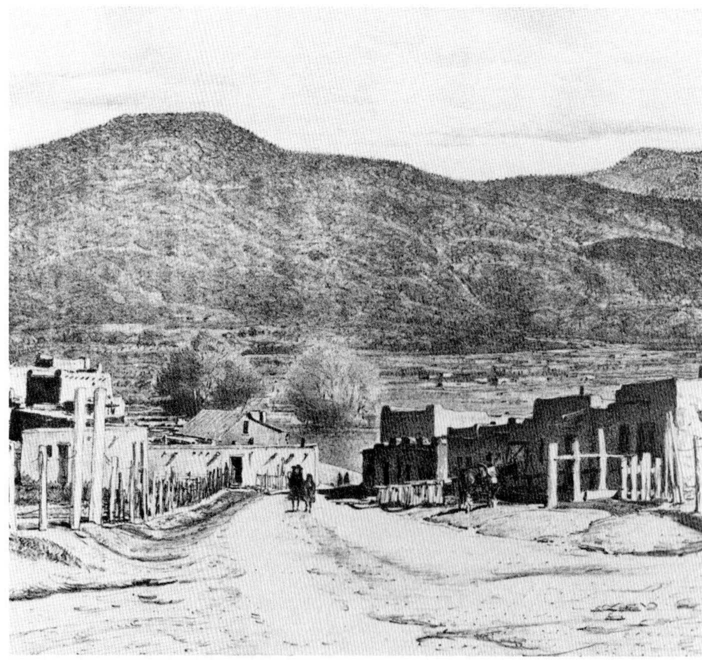

TAOS STREET SCENE. 12x12 inches, lithograph. Private collection.

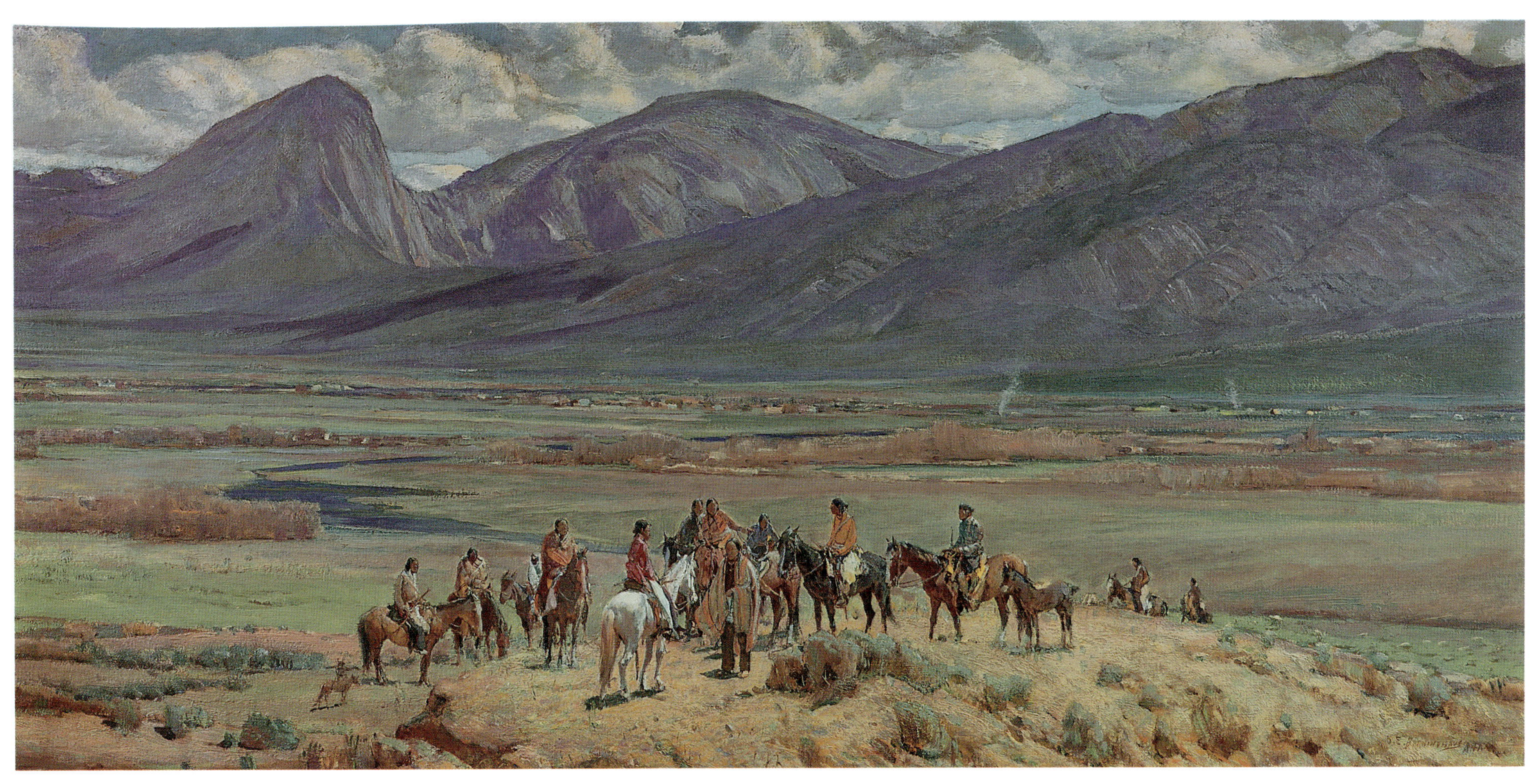

TAOS COUNTRY, 1938. 25 x 50 inches, oil on canvas. Courtesy of the Woolaroc Museum, Bartlesville, Oklahoma.

Back in St. Louis, Oscar Berninghaus spent the last few months of the 19th century developing his craft—painting. He had made dozens of sketches in and around Taos—the Indians with vast mountain backdrops, drawings of the Pueblo and town of Taos. He had decided to make a career as a painter, and especially a painter of the American Frontier— the Indians, the mountains and life in the West.

In November 1899, he received an exciting commission. The well-known photographer J.C. Strauss asked Berninghaus to paint an Indian for a decorative panel in his St. Louis photo studio. The young artist spent day after day on this early project. Twenty years later he was famous as a painter of Indians, as evidenced by *Santiago, The War Chief*, a fine canvas of color and depth. The old man is aided by a walking stick—a look of wisdom gleaned from a lifetime of experience. He stares back into time when he was a young warrior and rode the high plains for buffalo. He remembers fighting off intruding tribes and the glorious days and passions of youth. Now they are all gone—the buffalo, his enemies and his youth. But he is still proud and is much respected by the younger generation. At the Pueblo his storytelling delights all, and his advice is not taken lightly. During ceremonials, he is still called "War Chief"!

Berninghaus began the 20th century with his own one-man exhibition. Things were beginning to happen, and this showing at the Frank D. Healy Galleries in St. Louis was a step in the right direction. The show consisted of watercolors, two oils and several sketches and drawings—most of them from his brief visit to Taos. Not one to rest on his laurels, Berninghaus spent the winter and spring of 1900 diligently working to perfect his technique in oils and other media.

Not only did he work on his own art, but he read about art and visited a number of exhibitions featuring French art.

For some reason Berninghaus was never impressed with the world revolution taking place in art in the late 1800s. Of course he knew about the Impressionists and to a certain extent agreed with their concept that a picture did not have to portray a great event. Ordinary people and simple scenes could be works of art themselves. However, when it came to dropping detail for mood, and changing perspectives or distorting mass, that was quite a different matter. As for

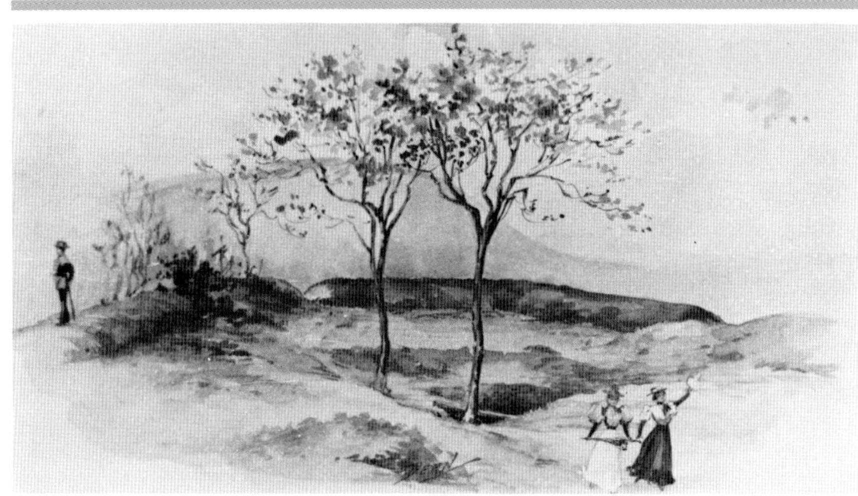

SUNDAY STROLL, c. 1898.
5x8 inches, watercolor. Private collection.

Georges Seurat and his pointillism, Berninghaus was somewhat taken with all those tiny dots. Looking at Seurat's *Sunday Afternoon on the Island of La Grande Jatte*, Berninghaus was reminded of the feeling he had about the air in Taos. Those little particles of pigment that permeated the atmosphere were fascinating, but it is not known whether he actually experimented with this technique at that time. During his lifetime, he did, in fact, paint a couple of pointillist skies—as did another Taos artist, Walter Ufer.

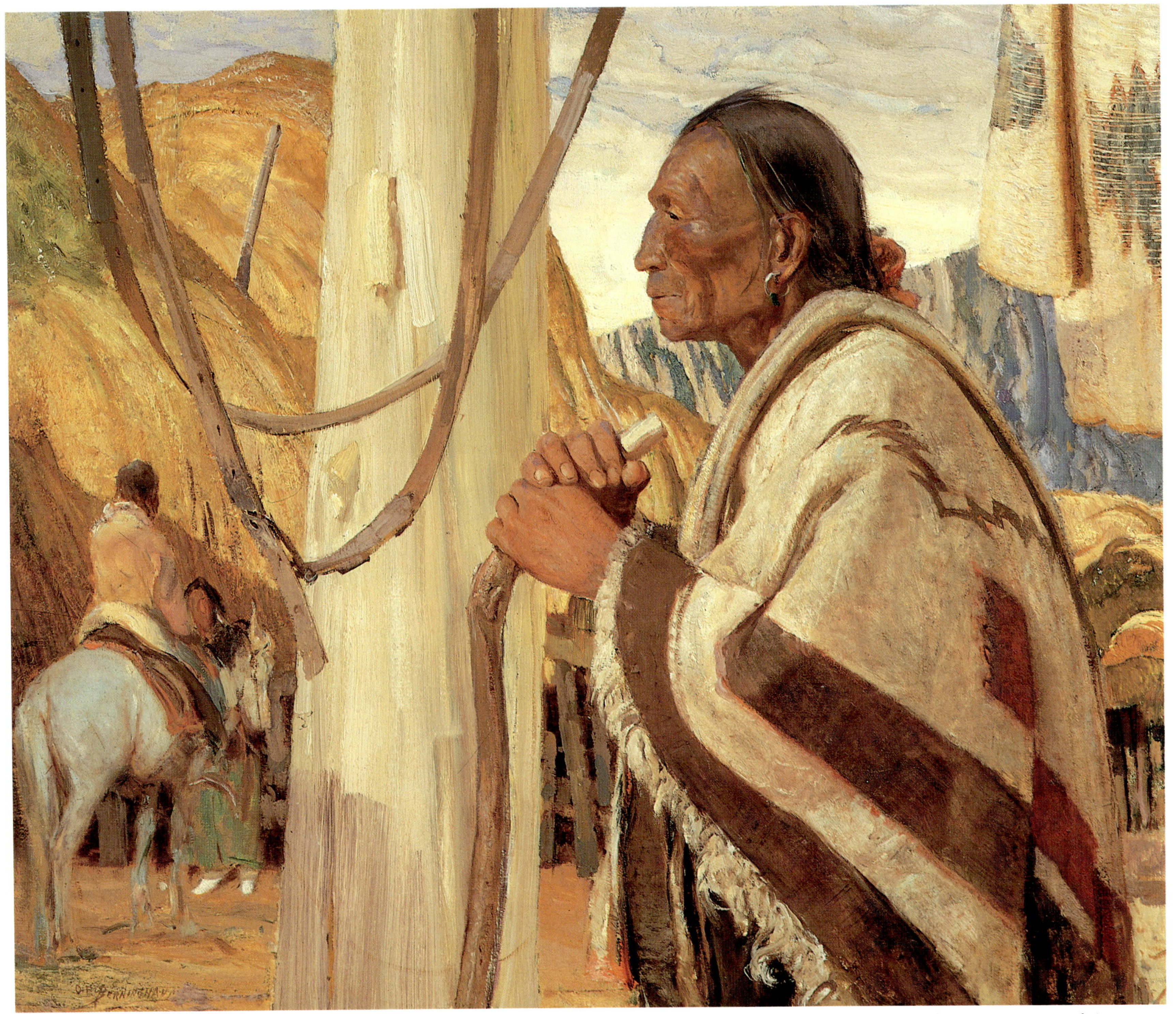

SANTIAGO, THE WAR CHIEF, c. 1930. 30x33 inches, oil on canvas. Courtesy of the Harwood Foundation Museum of Art, Taos, New Mexico.

13

The year 1900 was a great one for 26-year-old Berninghaus. Besides the one-man exhibition in St. Louis, he also made the trip back to Taos, where he spent the entire summer. For the first time in his life, he felt good about his career. This was what he wanted—Taos, New Mexico—the painter's paradise! He went on sketching trips to the high country east and north of Taos, and it was magnificent. You could see for 100 miles, so to speak, in any direction! The aspen trees that would turn saffron gold in the autumn were outstanding. There were streams and lakes and air so fresh it made you want to breathe consciously. Here indeed was an almost unspoiled wilderness that stirred something deep inside his being. How it would be to live here like the Indians, in harmony with nature. Somehow he must get it all on canvas and take it to the markets in St. Louis, Chicago and New York.

Berninghaus made many trips to the Pueblo to sketch the building, making careful notes about the colors, the structure itself, and its occupants, the Indians. He hired several to model for him, and worked in the hot sun with pencil and charcoal. These sketches he took back to his poorly lighted studio, and worked at night putting these images on paper and canvas with his oils and watercolors.

Often he would have dinner with Bert Phillips, who was the first of the six founding artists to actually live in Taos year round. In 1898, Phillips had come to Taos with Ernest Blumenschein, and decided at that time to make Taos his permanent home. Blumenschein, Phillips and Joseph Sharp had all studied in Paris under Jean Paul Laurens and Benjamin Constant. Sharp had visited Taos in 1893, and his Taos scenes won him an article in Harper's Weekly, which included a reproduction of his *Harvest Dance of the Pueblo Indians*. Back in Paris, his friends, Phillips and Blumenschein, at the Academie Julian were excited with his success and the

stories he told them about Taos. So—they came to Taos, with Phillips remaining and Blumenschein and Sharp returning to Paris before finally making a permanent move to Taos.

Oscar E. Berninghaus had had a great summer, and returned to St. Louis with a number of completed works. The *St. Louis Star Illustrated* was delighted with the paintings

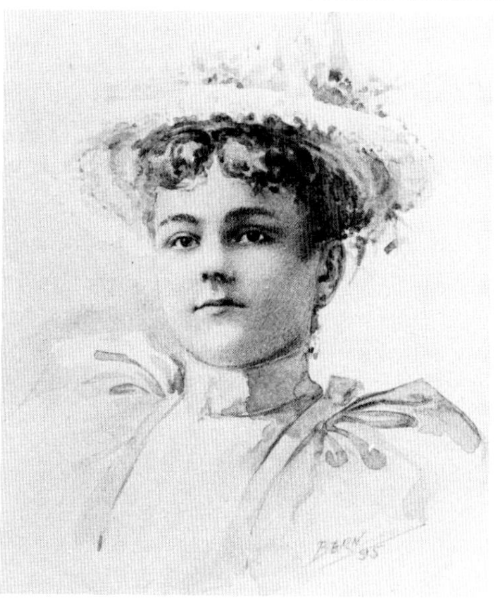

EMELIA MILLER, 1895.
4½ x 3 inches, watercolor, portrait of Berninghaus' wife. Private collection.

and reproduced *The Pursuit, Indian on Pony, Barroom Scene, Taos, N.M.*, and a large picture of the artist in their October 1900 issue. Of Berninghaus, the paper wrote: "Mr. O.E. Berninghaus, although a young man, has gained the reputation as a painter of American Indians. He ranks among the foremost of Indian painters of the country."

On November 8, 1900, Berninghaus married the beautiful woman he had been seeing for the past few years, Emelia Miller. He was 26, she 23. For "Bernie," as he was affectionately called, 1900, the beginning of a new century, was indeed a very good year!

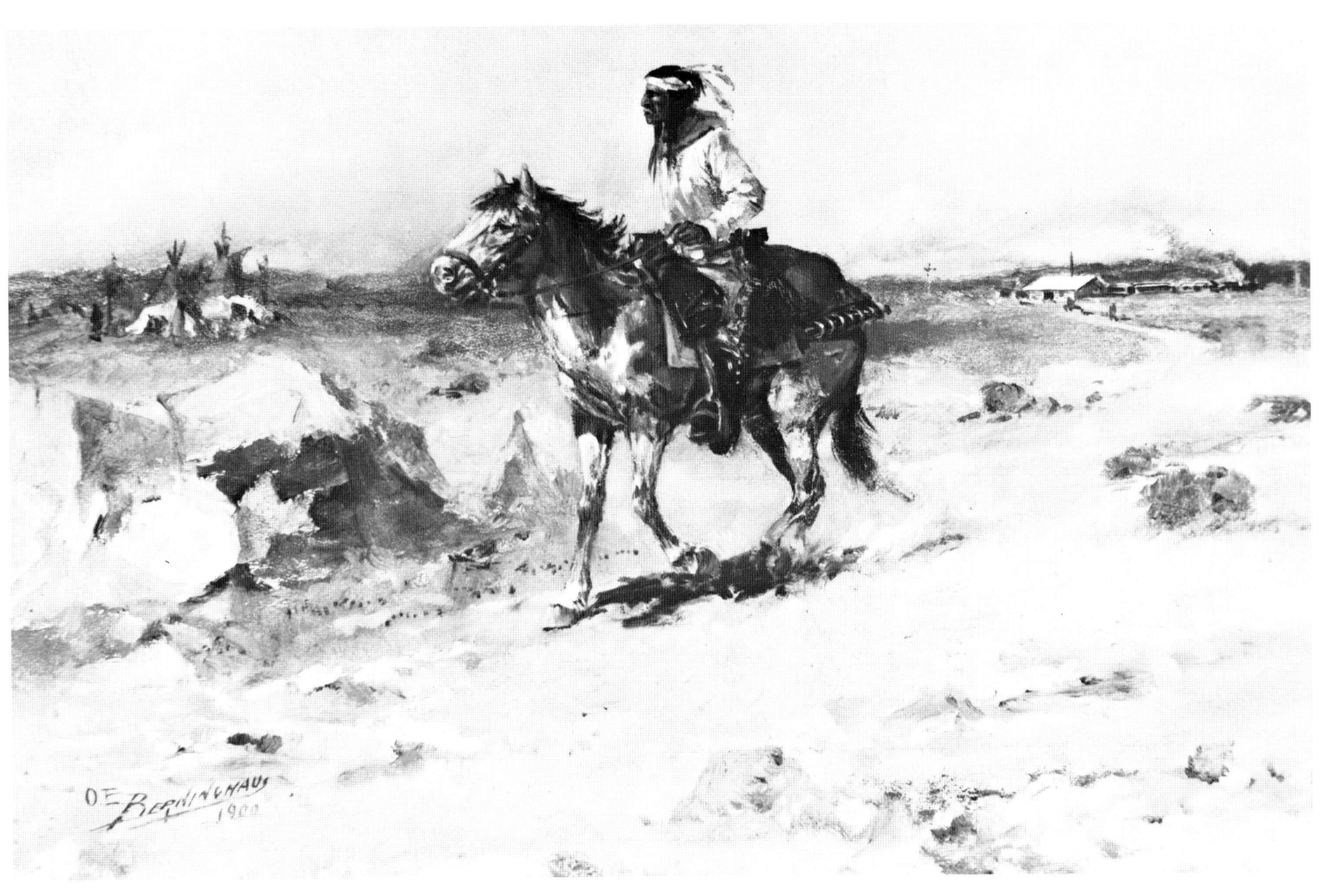

IGNACIO TRAIN DEPOT, 1900. 9 x 13 inches, oil on canvas. Courtesy of the Anschutz Collection, Denver, Colorado.

The first five years of the 20th century were busy ones for Oscar Berninghaus. Almost every summer now, he would say goodbye to his family and head for Taos to paint the Indians, their ponies and their way of life. In the winter he would return and pursue his commercial art career. He was achieving fame both as an illustrator and independent artist. His work was being mentioned with critical acclaim in newspaper art sections in such far away cities as New York, Chicago, Kansas City and San Francisco. Some writers were already comparing him to Frederic Remington. He had met Charles Russell with whom he would later share a studio.

The summer of 1902 was a blessed one for Bernie and his wife, Emelia, as Dorothy Lydia Berninghaus was born on July 8th. The name Lydia was in memory of Oscar's sister who had died in 1899 at the age of 18 of typhoid fever. Oscar Berninghaus was a man who loved his family, and the arrival of Dorothy was something to celebrate. He "celebrated" Dorothy's birth by spending the summer in St. Louis with his wife and child.

In 1903, St. Louis was alive with preparation for one of the greatest events ever to be witnessed by the people of the planet earth—The 1904 World's Fair! Artists from all over the world were submitting designs and concepts for the Exposition. In September of 1903, the *St. Louis Post-Dispatch* carried a small article saying: "O.E. Berninghaus, the advertising illustrator, has the proud distinction of having two of his designs for the World's Fair medals accepted in a competitive contest participated in by illustrators from all over the country." This was good news to Oscar, who had returned from another summer of painting in the hot sun of Taos County.

Berninghaus was beginning to realize that for him the Indians of Taos Pueblo were great subjects. He had come to love them and often stated his affection for their wisdom and farming ability. He saw these Indians as peaceful and productive. Later he would immortalize them in such masterpieces as *Autumn Days* which in 1924 won him the St. Louis Artists' Guild prize. The following is a quote from a news release at that time: "Our idea of the greatest picture in the Guild show is Oscar Berninghaus' big, dazzling, resonant "AUTUMN DAYS" that sings out in rich contralto. Its remarkable simplicity of actual subject—an Indian and a horse, tree trunks and foliage—so ardently handled as to almost inflate the canvas, shows the strength of his conception, its propelling force. The ease, the pleasure, the dexterity with which the idea was executed are so delightfully present in every square inch. Sympathy for the old white horse, interest in the weathered old Indian, respect for the gnarled old tree trunks combine to strengthen the effect of the pattern of the picture. It is semi-realistic, just the right amount of 'decorativeness' being maintained to distinguish it and place it among the 'unforgettable.'"

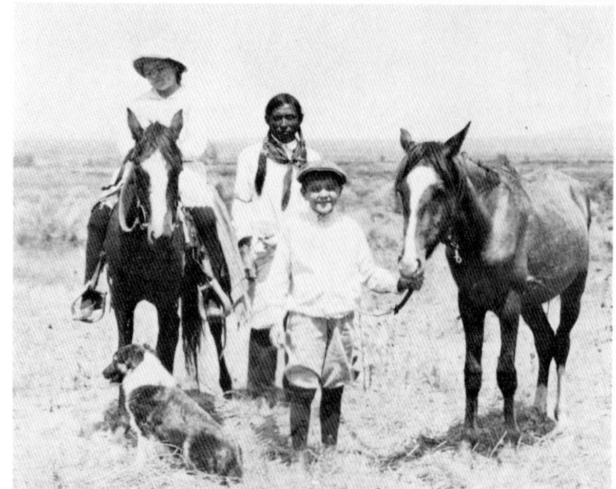

Charles and Dorothy with
Albert "Looking Elk," c. 1914.

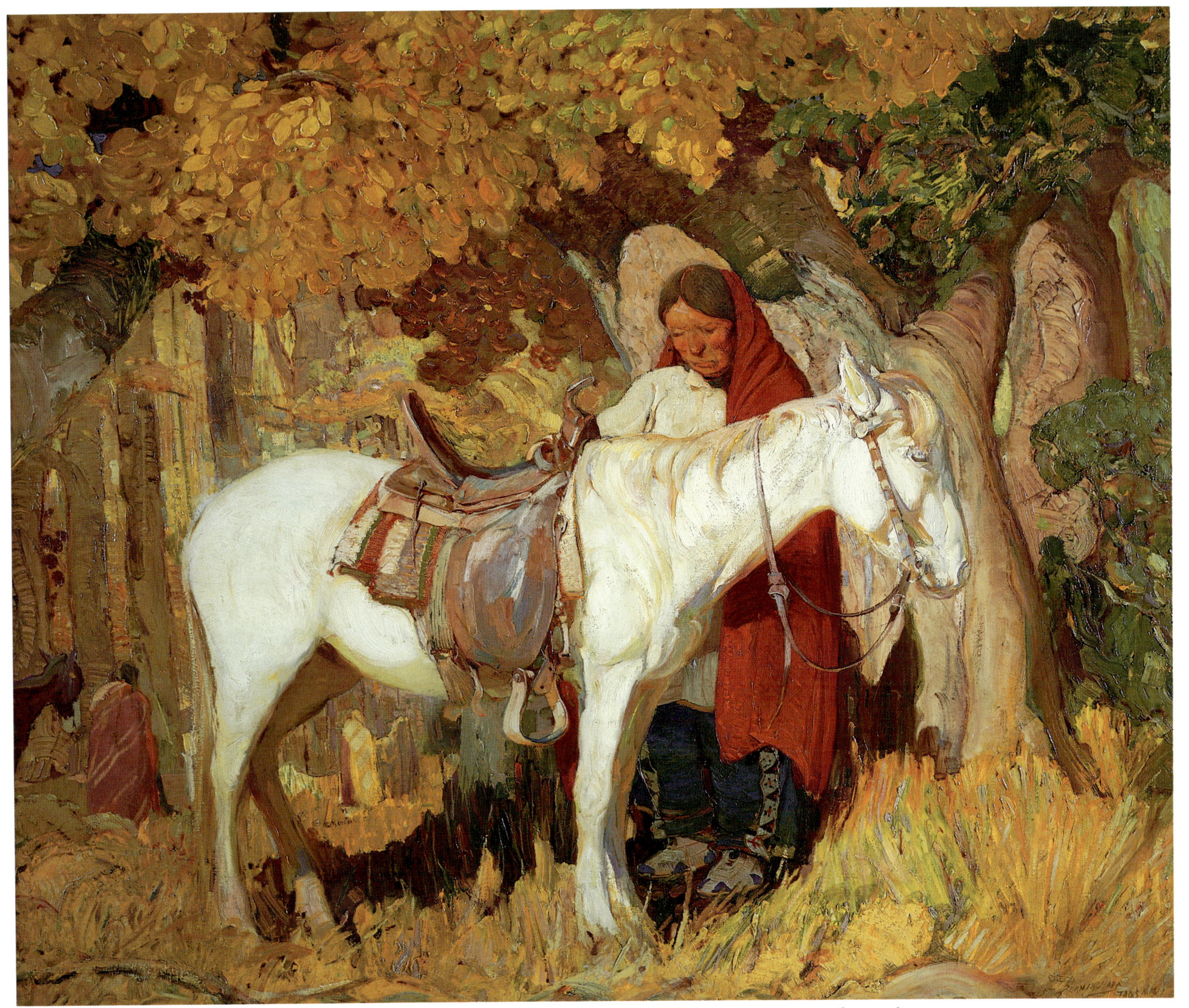

AUTUMN DAYS or *AUTUMN IN INDIAN COUNTRY*, 1924. 35½ x 40 inches, oil on canvas.
Courtesy of Galleries Maurice Sternberg, Chicago, Illinois. Grand Prize, St. Louis Art League, 1924.

In 1904, St. Louis, Missouri, became the absolute center of world attention! On April 30th, the Fair opened with dignitaries from all over the world attending, and the opening ceremony featured William Howard Taft, representing President Theodore (Teddy) Roosevelt. The Exposition President, D.R. Francis, shouted to the thousands gathered at the gates: "Enter Herein, Ye Sons of Men," and at the White House in Washington, President Roosevelt tripped a remote switch that started the Fair machinery rolling! The enormity of the 1904 Exposition is beyond description in anything less than a full book. Forty-three foreign countries and forty-five U.S. states had pavilions and exhibits. Berninghaus was there for the grand opening, and no doubt realized it would be a great event to paint—but he chose to return to Taos for that summer to follow the pattern he carried on over the next 20 years—sketching and painting during the summer months there and returning to his studio in St. Louis for the winters. This made sense to him even though the travel to and from was inconvenient. Taos was a great subject to paint, but the art markets with newspaper and magazine print capabilities were all back East. To build his reputation as an independent painter, he needed the critical review of these publications. It was also true that most of the big galleries were in the East, and that is where the paintings were bought and sold.

On May 19, 1905, Oscar and Emelia had another child, Julius Charles, who also grew to become a Taos artist. "Charles" helped his father during the years when Oscar was doing huge murals in public buildings throughout the country. "Father" would do the basic concepts and the drawings, and "son" would help with the painting-in tasks. Later, Charles gained his own recognition as a landscape painter—his favorite subjects being the mountain and desert scenes around Taos. Perhaps his best works are those that include the prolific hollyhock and other local flowers. Charles paints with only one brush, carefully wiping it clean after each color application. He says to paint the Taos landscape you have to be fast, or the light will change and the mood will vanish. As is apparent in *Daisies*, Charles was more influenced by the post-impressionists than his father.

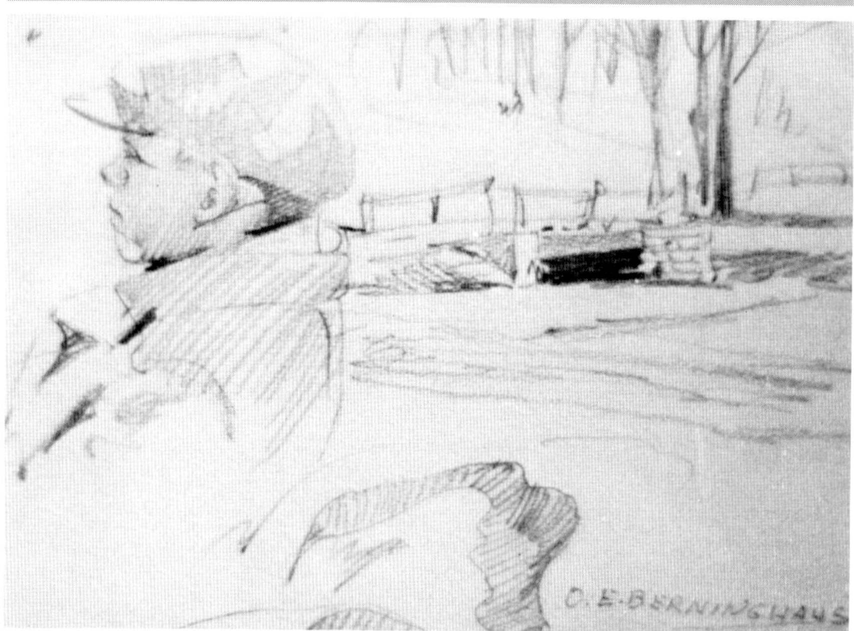

Pencil sketch of Charles at age 10. 5x7 inches. Private collection.

Oscar Berninghaus received a big boost in 1905, when the *St. Louis Post-Dispatch* put three paintings in its downtown window and held a contest to raise money for the poor children at Christmas. The Berninghaus canvas, *The First Christmas Day in St. Louis*, ran away with the prize. The huge canvas was reproduced in full color on the cover of the art section on December 10, 1905. Locally Berninghaus was praised for this work in the *Dispatch* and it helped him to become a favorite of St. Louis art lovers.

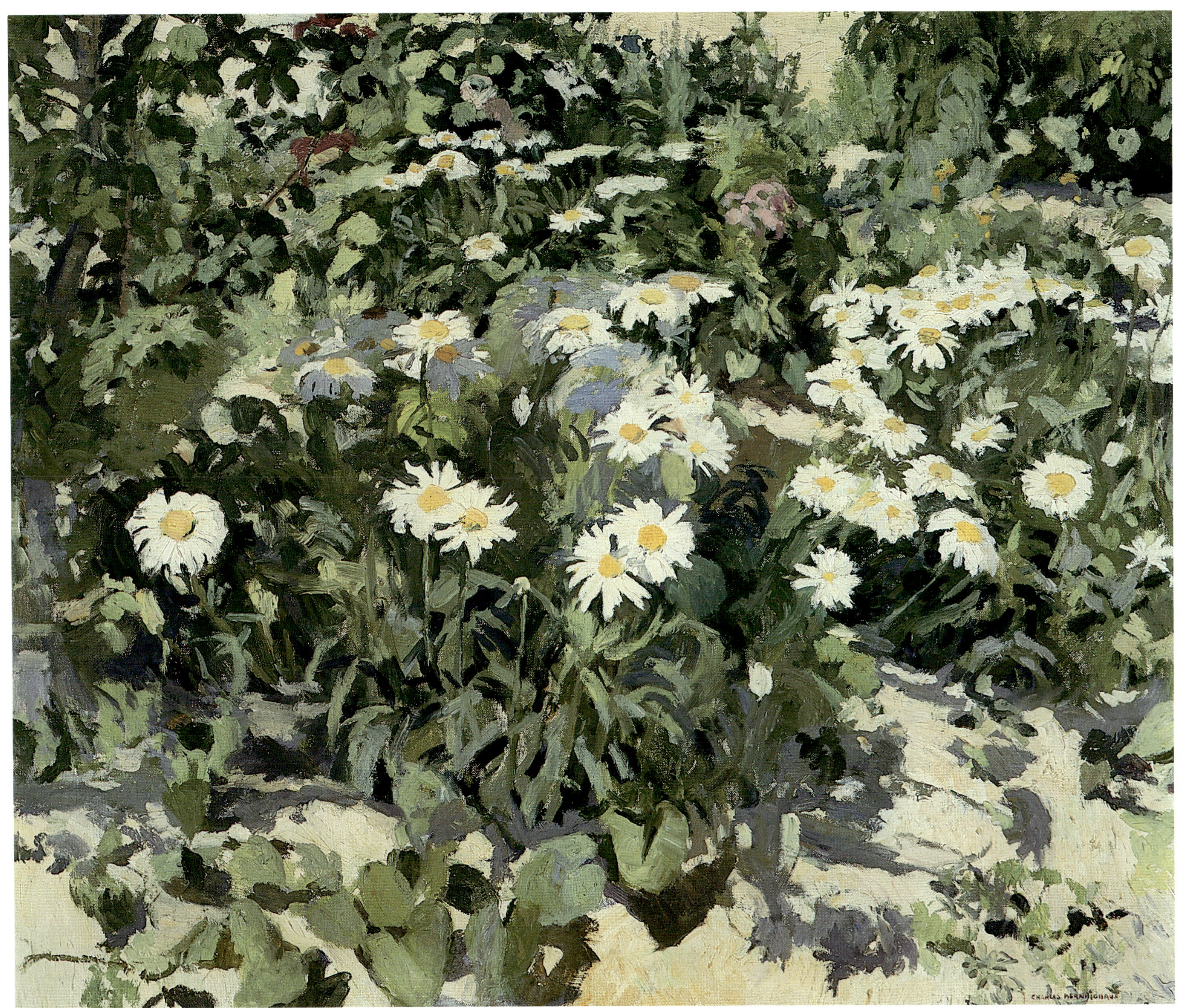

DAISIES. 35×40 inches, oil on canvas. By Charles Berninghaus. Private collection.

As a painter, Oscar Berninghaus was a very intense man. He had the ability to learn, to experiment, to improve—to listen, to observe. His research was impeccable—he had to know his subject, whether it be a mountain, an Indian or a tree. He studied the flora and fauna in and around Taos, and spent hours talking with cowboys, farmers and wagonmasters. Every detail, he wanted to know. He also had one of the finest traits that anyone who wants to know something can have—the ability to ask. He listened and learned, but he never copied. What he learned was evaluated, weighed and used to fortify his own style—his interpretation. Regardless of what he painted it always came out "Oscar E. Berninghaus." As an artist, his ego was always intact, never threatened by another artist's work or success. This inner calm and security made him a very popular person, not only with his family but also with his fellow painters. If indeed he had his moments of doubt, he never let on about them.

As a man, Berninghaus was a gentle person. Slightly built, not tall, weighing about 150 pounds, he smoked a pipe and enjoyed the sociability of his friends. He loved his wife and children, and enjoyed taking them to parks in St. Louis for picnics and Sunday musicals.

In 1906 he was a member of the St. Louis Artists' Guild, the Society of Western Artists, the Deuce Poker Club, and the Salamagundi Club. In 1907 the St. Louis Artists' Guild awarded him the coveted "Clifford M. Dolph" prize in its second annual competition. Early in 1908 the Noonan-Kocian Gallery exhibited fifty Berninghaus paintings of Taos and Western scenes. This kind of interest in Berninghaus by the St. Louis art community meant a long and profitable relationship between the Gallery and the artist.

That summer he took his wife, Emelia, and their two children to Taos. They took the Missouri and Pacific to Denver, then switched to the Denver and Rio Grande narrow gauge—

the same trip he had taken in 1899. When Berninghaus and his family arrived in Servilleta, New Mexico, they were met by "Long John Dunn." He was a colorful character who operated the stagecoach line to Taos, and owned the Dunn Bridge, which crossed the Rio Grande. Dorothy Berninghaus, who was six years old at the time, recalls that Dunn took them to Taos in an open buckboard with four horses. During the 30-mile trip they encountered an enormous

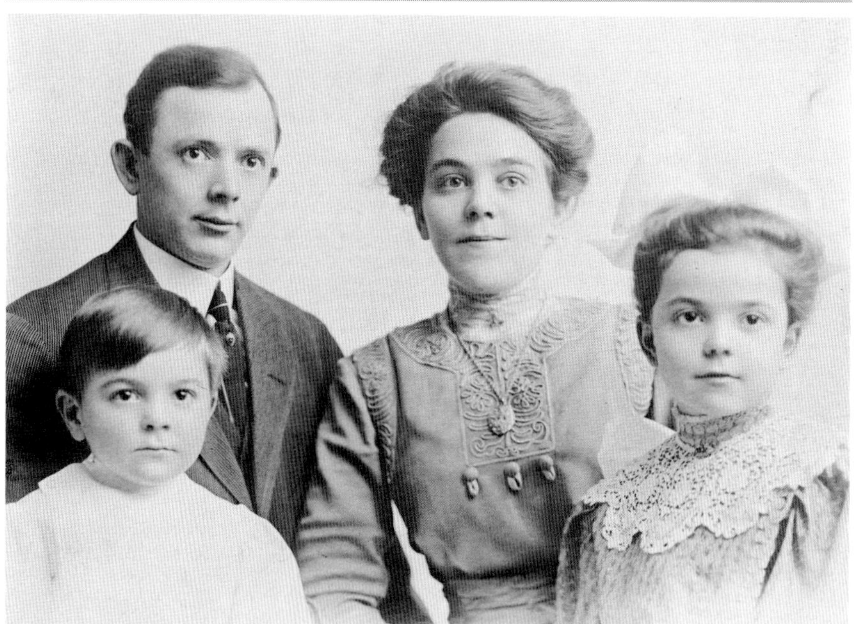

Charles Berninghaus, age 8; O.E. Berninghaus, Emelia Miller Berninghaus, Dorothy Berninghaus, age 11.

hailstorm and were pummeled by balls of ice as big as your thumb. Now at 82, and with a twinkle in her eye, she says those hailstones were somehow responsible for the brown spots on the back of her hands! When she tells this story her husband, Jack Brandenburg, just smiles and says: "Right, Dorothy, right!"

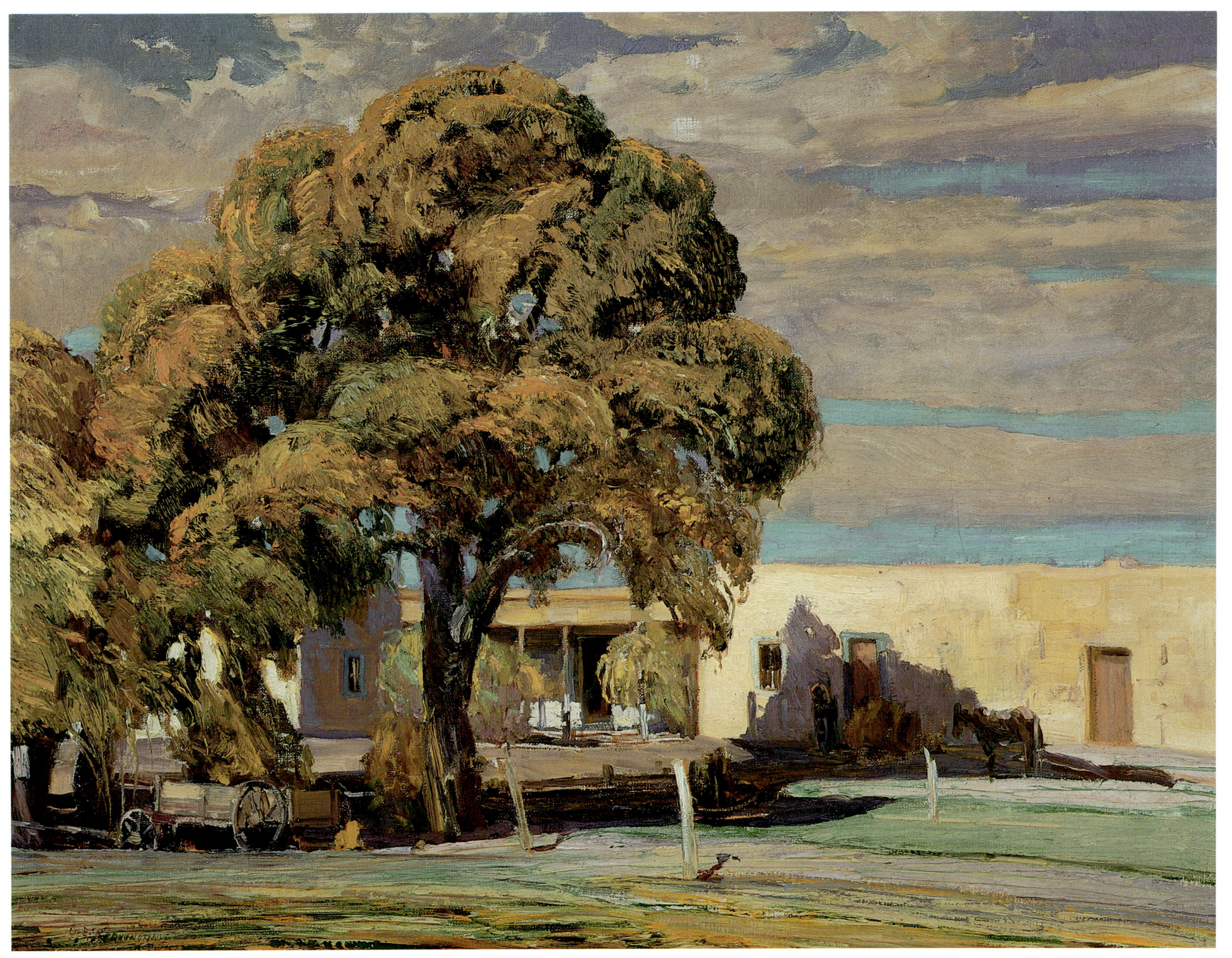

LOWER RANCHITOS HACIENDA, 1927. 21x27 inches, oil on canvas. Private collection.

Taos was rapidly becoming an art center, and was being painted by Bert Greer Phillips, Joseph Henry Sharp, Ernest L. Blumenschein, Eanger Irving Couse, W. Herbert Dunton and Oscar E. Berninghaus. The Eastern press considered Taos the Wild West—the frontier—and with some degree of accuracy as New Mexico was still a territory. This alone was reason for many a romantic write-up by art reviewers in the art sections of major newspapers.

The population of Taos was mainly Spanish-American—in fact in 1900 there were only 26 Anglo residents, possibly 100 by 1908. In the summer months, the overall population of the valley swelled above its normal 2,000 to 3,000 with the arrival of travelers and business traders. The annual "Fiesta" or trade fair brought together Indians from all over, and ranchers and buyers from large cities to the east. It was a time of family reunions and trade among the Spanish as well.

When Oscar Berninghaus and his family arrived in Taos in the summer of 1908 many of the other artists were already there. According to accounts in family papers, they would all meet whenever possible at one of the local hotels (there might have been two!) where there was food, drink and lots of talk about art.

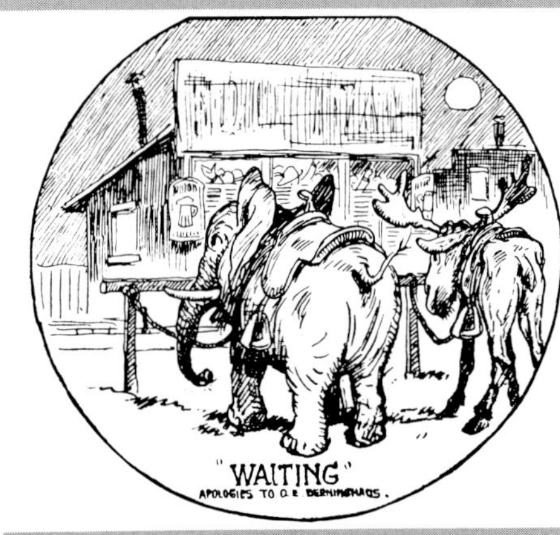

Newspaper clipping;
Elephant and donkey.
St. Louis Globe-Democrat,
June 8, 1916

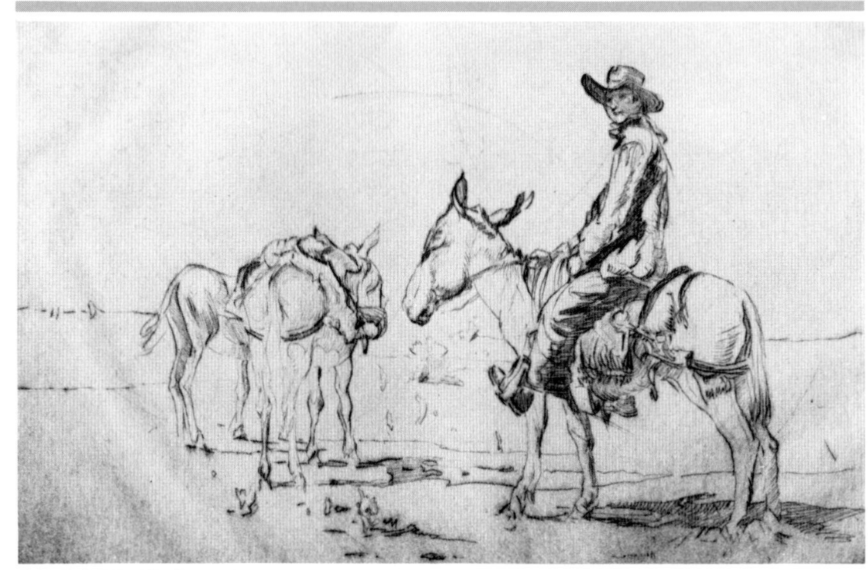

PROSPECTOR ON BURRO, c. 1920. 5x6 inches, etching.
Private collection.

All the artists were excellent riders, and used the horse not only as a model, but as necessary transportation. Berninghaus was probably the best among his peers when it came to painting horses—especially the Indian ponies. A favorite subject featured several horses waiting outside—sometimes in cold and snow. *The Long Wait* is typical of these canvases—each different from the other, but alike in their message and emotion. He achieved such success with the theme of waiting horses that during a political campaign in St. Louis, he was featured in a cartoon by the *St. Louis Globe-Democrat,* on June 8, 1916. It seems that while a certain meeting was taking place between local Republicans and Democrats, their "steeds" were left "waiting." Apologies were made to Oscar Berninghaus. This political satire certainly indicates Berninghaus was a well-known painter in St. Louis society.

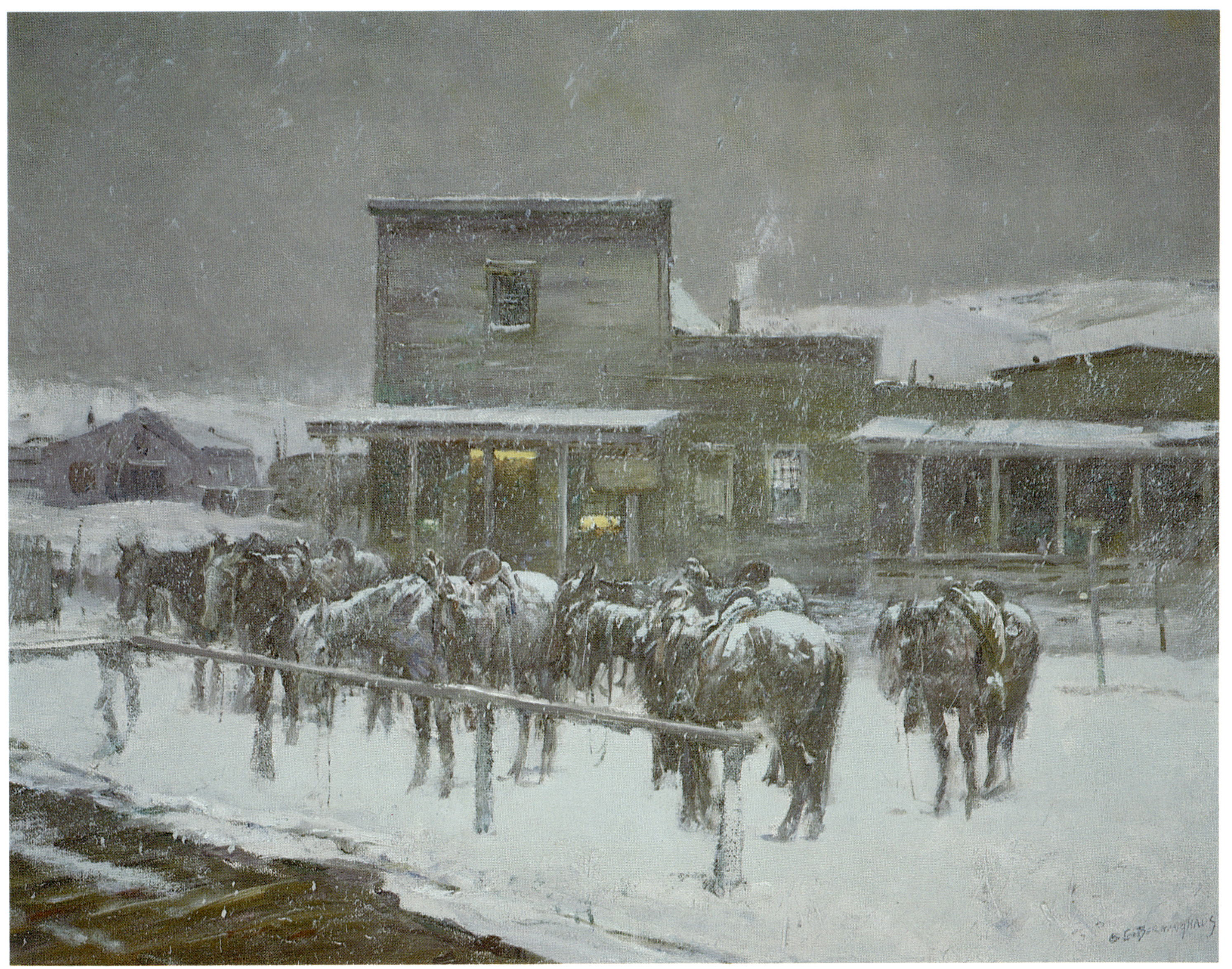

THE LONG WAIT, c. 1930. 16×20 inches, oil on board. Private collection.

New Mexico became a state in 1912, and the Taos Society of Artists was formed that same year. There were six founding members, Joseph Sharp, Bert Phillips, Ernest Blumenschein, Oscar Berninghaus, Irving Couse and Herbert Dunton. Until July 1915, the Society was informal and usually referred to as the Taos Art Colony. However, it is evident there was a verbal agreement among the painters, and that some organizing had previously been done by Bert Phillips. The *St. Louis Republic* ran a full-page cover story in its art section dated August 11, 1913, that featured reproductions of works by a number of the original six artists. The article also stated that Oscar Berninghaus had joined the Taos Art Colony. All of the paintings used in the pictorial section were dated 1912, lending credibility to the 1912 agreement theory. Berninghaus was quoted widely in the 1913 article. "This is splendid country for an artist because there are more varieties of atmosphere here than I have found in any other place. Up in the hills one can get the right setting for old trapping pictures. There are many varieties of sage and cactus for background, according to the elevation you choose." Of the Taos Indians he told the paper: "The Taos Indians are a splendid type—in fact the best I have ever seen, and if one wants to paint Mexico pictures, he can get a background near Taos, just as picturesque as any spot in old Mexico." The article also hailed Berninghaus as the legitimate successor to Frederic Remington, who died in 1909.

To say that Oscar Berninghaus was a busy man in 1912 would indeed be an understatement. He now had a studio in downtown St. Louis in a building at the corner of Jefferson and Washington avenues. His neighbor in this group of studios was Charles M. Russell, already an internationally famous artist. Since the 1880s, Russell had been painting the Indians and rugged mountains of Montana. Back in St. Louis he furthered his fame as a sculptor.

Berninghaus also had a studio in Taos, where he and his family spent the summer. Over the years their stays in Taos had become longer each year, and extended into the glorious autumn season.

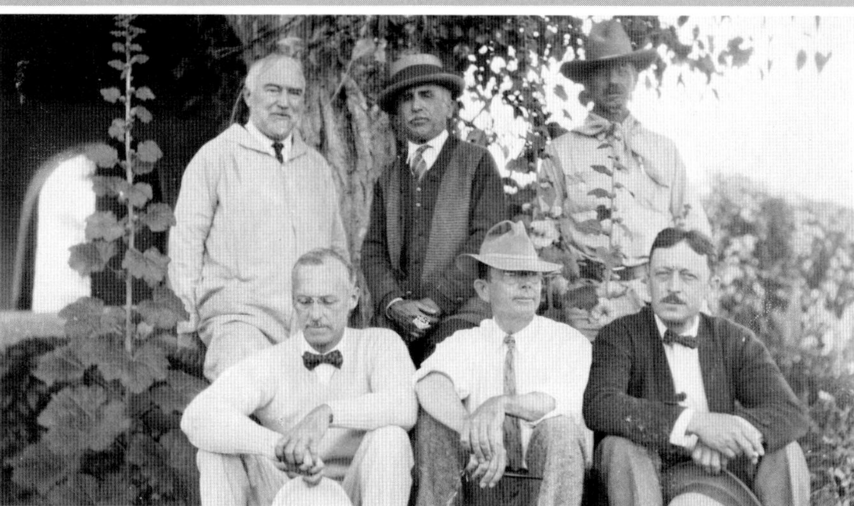

Six members of the Taos Society of Artists, 1927.
Back row: Irving Couse, Bert Phillips, Herbert Dunton.
Front row: Ernest Blumenschein, Oscar Berninghaus, Victor Higgins.

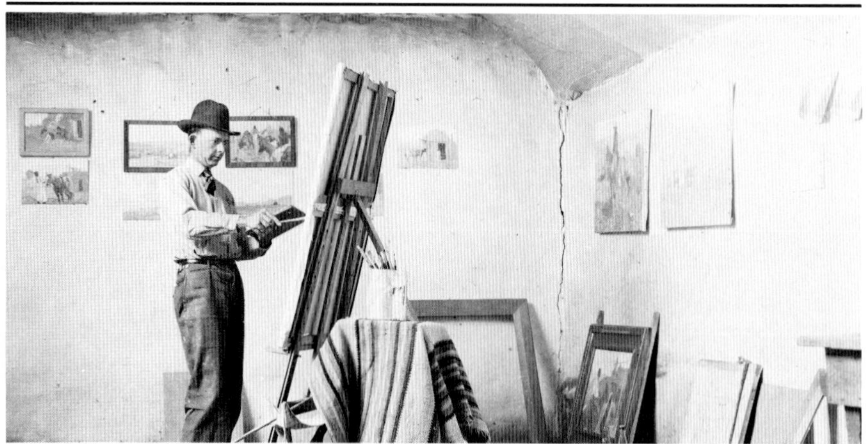

Berninghaus in his studio, c. 1915.

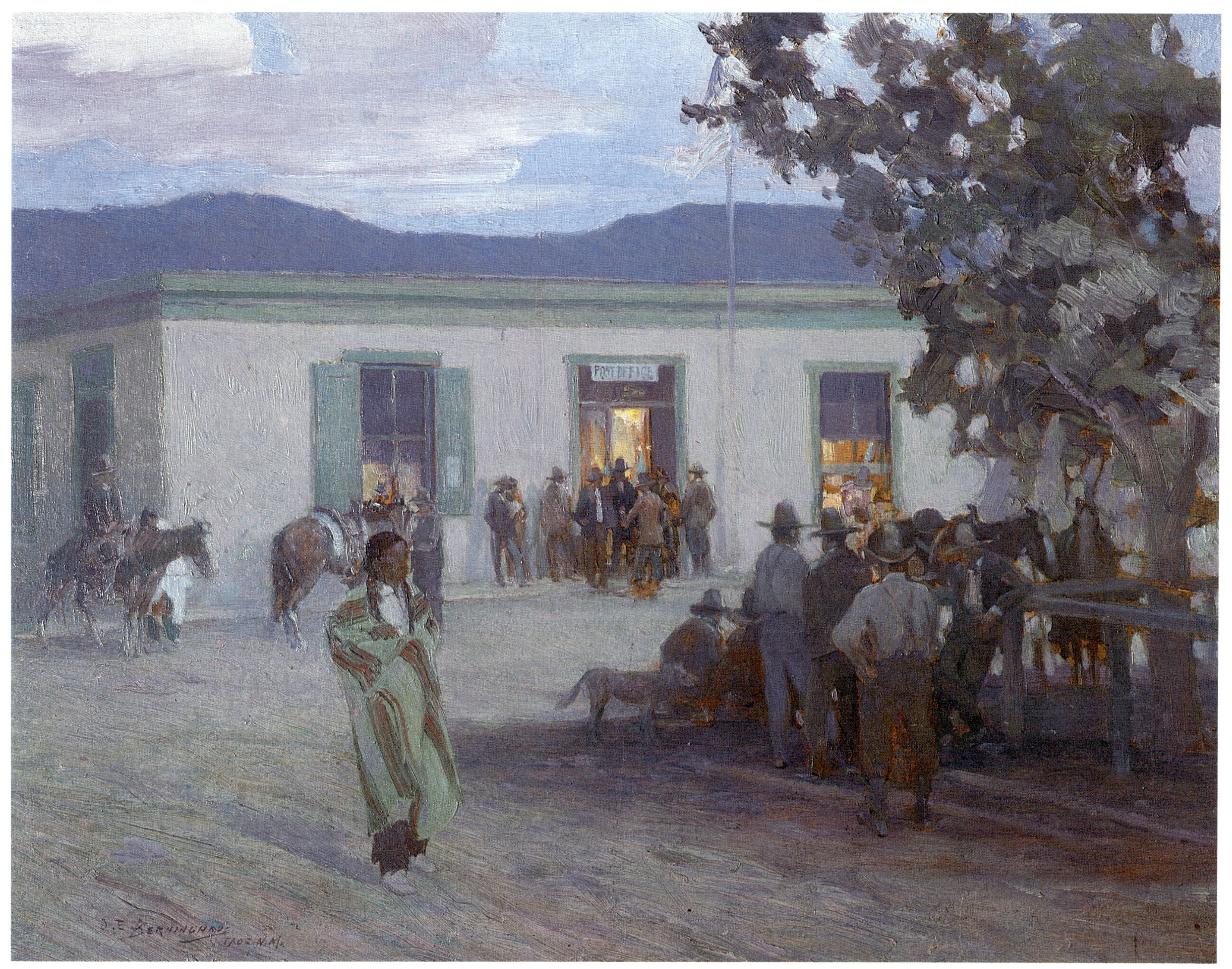

POST OFFICE, TAOS, NEW MEXICO, 1915. 16×20 inches, oil on canvas. Collection of Mr. and Mrs. Martin Kodner.
Gallery of the Masters, St. Louis, Missouri.

The year 1913 was bittersweet for Oscar Berninghaus. As an artist, his career was moving ahead by leaps and bounds. The Society of Western Artists awarded him the Chicago Fine Arts Building Prize. His works were being shown in the Noonan-Kocian Gallery in St. Louis almost year round, and he was busy on a huge commission from the Anheuser-Busch Brewery. In addition to commercial work, he continued painting as an independent artist.

All this was offset by the tragic death of his wife, Emelia. She had been seriously ill for some time and finally on August 2, 1913, succumbed, a victim of diabetes. For more than 20 years Oscar would remain single, and was both father and mother to his two children, Dorothy and Charles, who were only 11 and 8 at the time of their mother's death. Because of his heavy schedule of painting and travelling, his wife's sister, Anne Miller, and her mother moved into the Berninghaus home in St. Louis to look after the children while he went about his work. In the years ahead, however, when summer came Oscar packed up his children and headed for his beloved Taos.

Because of his orderly manner, Berninghaus was able to manage his children quite well during those summers in Taos—and fit in a full schedule of sketching and painting. Each spring, the family was met by Long John Dunn at the Denver and Rio Grande Station for the long stagecoach ride to Taos. Sometimes the passengers would stay all night at a small hotel built near the confluence of the Rio Grande and Rio Hondo. It, too, was owned by John Dunn, who seemed to have a monopoly on travel in the Taos area.

In the art world there have been many arguments about the differences between a "commercial artist" and an "independent artist." The purists maintain that doing illustrations is something less than noble. To be an unsuccessful "independent" is even worse, they say. But Oscar Berninghaus seemed to have mastered the best of both worlds. He gave dignity and beauty to his commissions from the leading corporations of St. Louis, and yet was a very successful independent painter. His biggest account and patron was the Anheuser-Busch family. The brewery wanted to show their beer being transported to all parts of the country, so Berninghaus was selected to paint the wagons, pack mules, boats and trains that were hauling Budweiser beer from place to place.

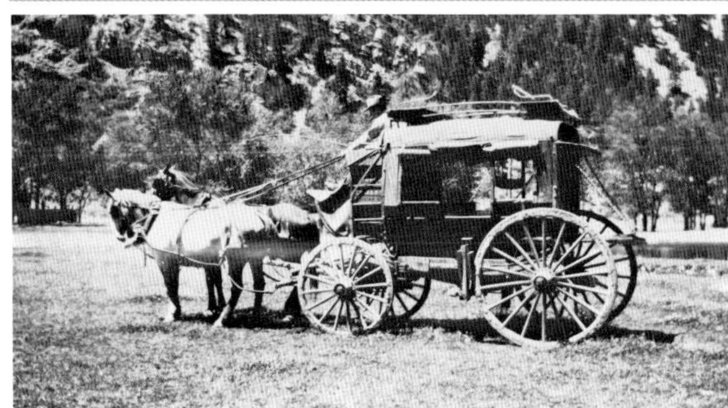

Stagecoach: Berninghaus' first visit to Taos, 1899.

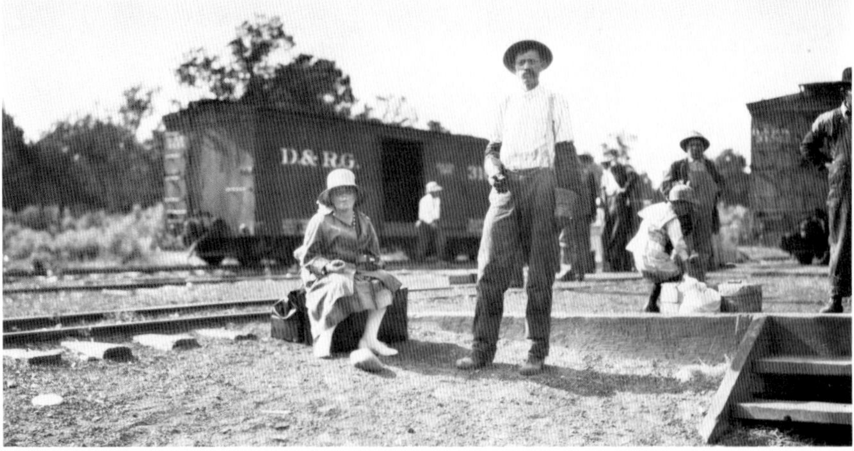

Dorothy Berninghaus and John Dunn at D. and R.G. Station, Taos Junction, c. 1915.

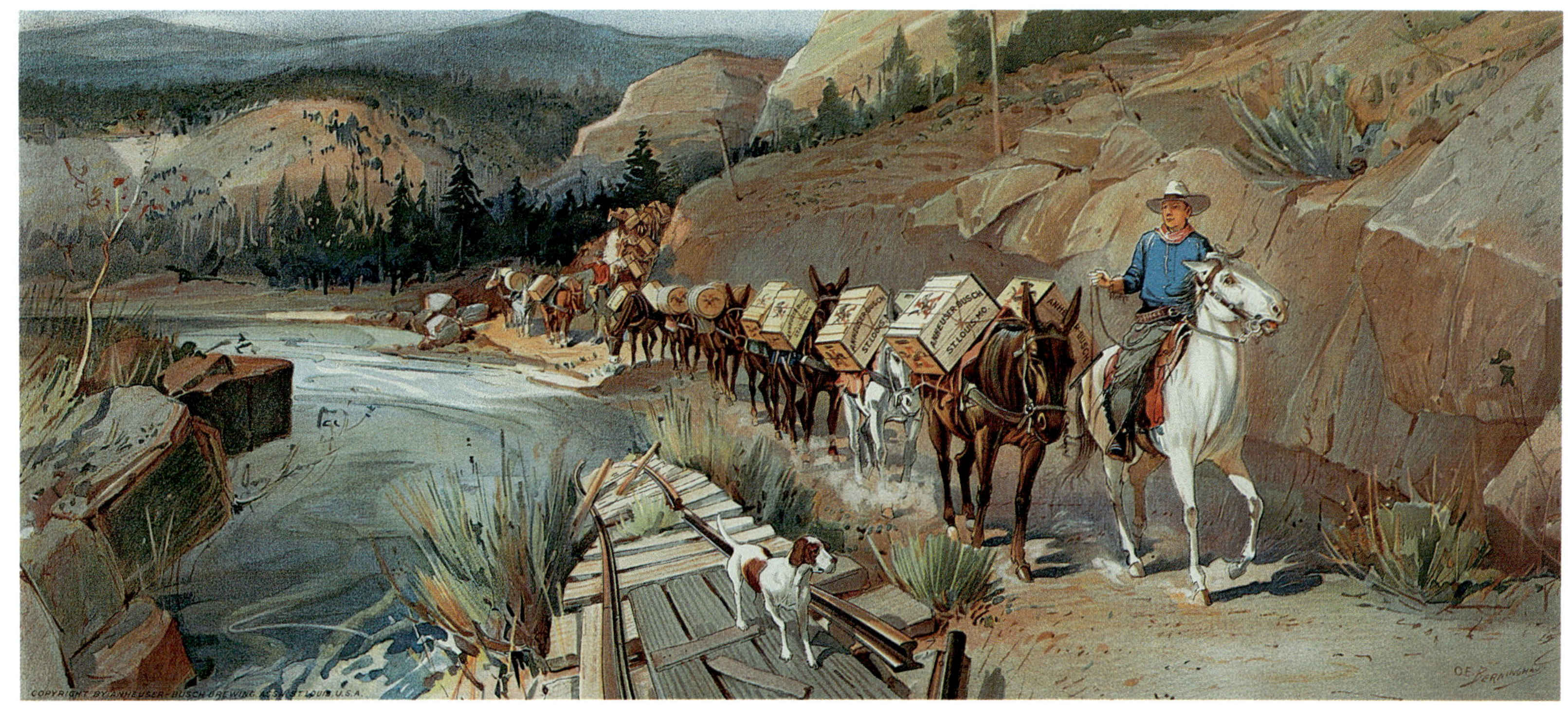

THE RELIEF TRAIN, c. 1912.
11 $^{5}/_{16}$ x 20 $^{1}/_{8}$ inches,
chromolithograph. Courtesy of
the Amon Carter Museum,
Fort Worth, Texas.

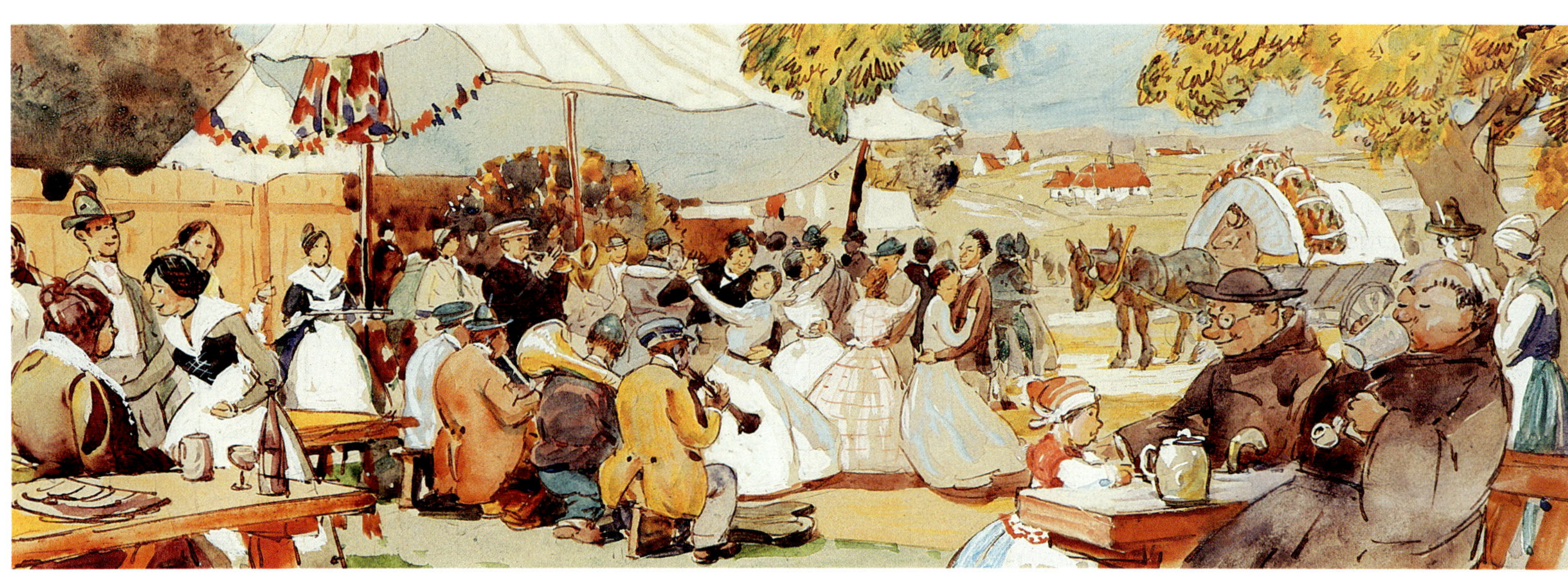

BEER GARDEN SCENE, c. 1920.
Study for mural in Lenox Hotel,
St. Louis. 6x16 inches,
watercolor. Private collection

In 1914 Anheuser-Busch published a booklet entitled "Epoch Marking Events of American History," a series of historical pictures painted by O.E. Berninghaus. The booklet was actually a compilation of a series of posters (billboards) Oscar had painted for the brewery. It featured ten, full-color paintings with historical information printed to the left of the picture, and no mention was made of beer as the booklet was presented to schools and other institutions of learning as an educational piece. Included were: *De Soto Discovering the Mississippi, Marquette Descending the Mississippi, Laclede Landing at Present Site of St. Louis, Progress of the Louis and Clark Expedition, Fremont the Pathfinder, St. Louis Levee in the Early Seventies, Indians Attacking an Overland Stage, West Bound Wagon Train on the Salt Lake Trail, Union Pacific Train in Western Kansas* and a painting of the Anheuser-Busch plant. The company now boasted a 142-acre site in St. Louis—an area equal to seventy city blocks. The plant was modern and the Busch family believed in worker comfort—toilet accommodations, washrooms and showers, locker and lunch rooms, plus a modern medical clinic for emergency cases. The plant employed 2,500 people and could produce 2 million bottles of beverage a day!

During his lifetime, Berninghaus painted scores of canvases for the Busch family, and was a frequent guest at the Busch estate, Grant's Farm. He painted for Adolphus Busch, the founder of the brewery; for August A. Busch, Sr., and was well remembered by August A. Busch, Jr. and his wife. In 1977 the Busch family gave a large number of Berninghaus paintings to the St. Louis Art Museum, a collection that is now valued at $5 million, and there is still a fine collection in the Busch family. When the paintings were presented to the Museum, August Busch, Jr. commented in an interview with the *St. Louis Globe-Democrat*: "My father always admired Berninghaus' paintings. He thought he was a great artist, but more than that, he admired and liked him as a person, as a friend. I remember Oscar as a perfect gentleman, a wonderful individual, as attractive as the devil."

Indians attacking an Overland Stage, 1860.

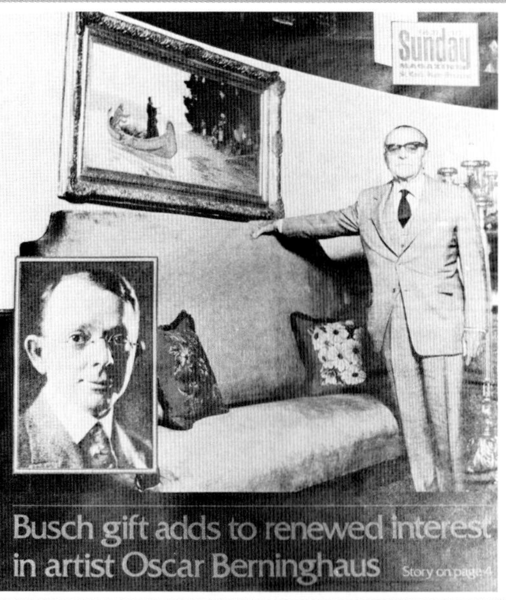

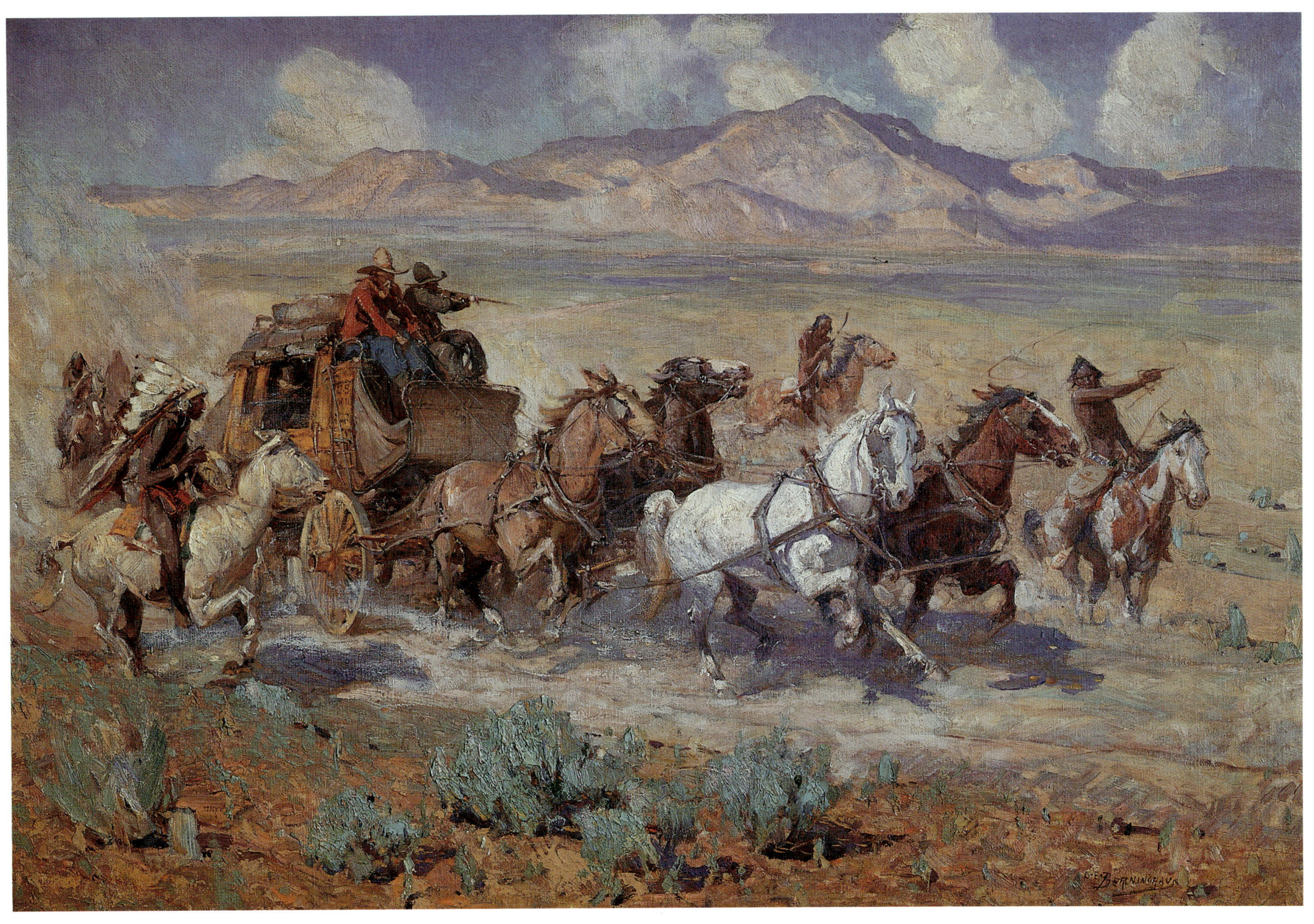

THE OVERLAND MAIL, 1930. 27½ x39⅝ inches, oil on canvas. Courtesy of Philbrook Art Center, Tulsa, Oklahoma.

The famous "Taos Society of Artists" was officially organized in the summer of 1915. Oscar Berninghaus was elected temporary chairman of the initial meeting in July at the home of Dr. T.P. Martin. E. Irving Couse was chosen as the first president, with Bert Phillips the secretary-treasurer. Only five of the six original members were present: J.H. Sharp, O.E. Berninghaus, W.H. Dunton, B.G. Phillips and E.I. Couse—E.L. Blumenschein was the missing member. The purpose of the Society was to promote the sale of paintings by its members. As there was no gallery in Taos at the time, this was done by means of travelling exhibitions sent to the big art galleries in New York, Chicago, St. Louis and other major art markets. The Society was an instant success and, to say the least, put Taos on the map.

In years to come, the Society would enlarge its membership to ten with the addition of Walter Ufer, Victor Higgins, E. Martin Hennings and Kenneth Adams. Actually, including associate memberships and honorary ones, the Society had a total of 21 members during its brief lifetime from 1915 to 1927, when it disbanded. As the name implied, the Society was a society of artists, not a school of art. It was made up of professionals who already knew what they wanted to paint and how to do it. There was no aesthetic theme as in post impressionism, fauvism, abstractionism, surrealism, etc. All the founding members were already well-known artists in their own right.

The actual business of the Society was somewhat mechanical—getting all the canvases together and nailing them up in wooden crates for shipment to the big galleries back East. After all this effort, they had to go by stage to Taos Junction, then on the Denver and Rio Grande railroad to Albuquerque or Denver to catch the Santa Fe or Missouri Pacific to take them to their ultimate destination. This was followed by re-shipment to other galleries on the exhibition tour. The other decision that had to be made was which members would accompany the tour and appear in person at the various galleries.

Most of the meetings were wild and wooly—especially when it came to electing a secretary for the coming year. It was like the "kiss of death" for the chosen one, and in many instances the "honor" was outright refused! All were busy with their own careers, and just the thought of all those letters and details sent many a member running for yet another cocktail!

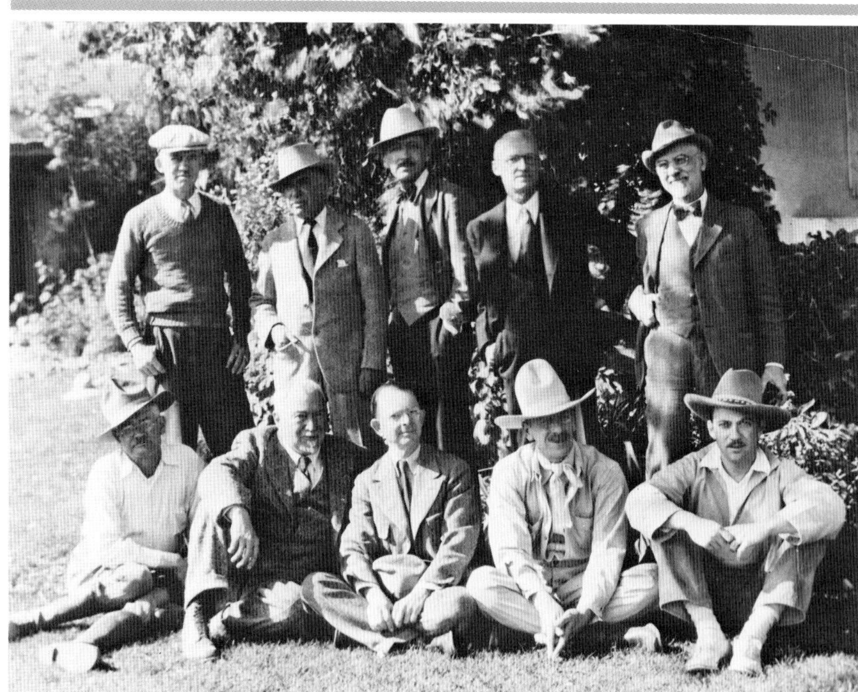

Front row: Walter Ufer, Irving Couse, Oscar Berninghaus, Herbert Dunton, Kenneth Adams.
Back row: Martin Hennings, Bert Phillips, Victor Higgins, Ernest Blumenschein, Joseph Sharp.

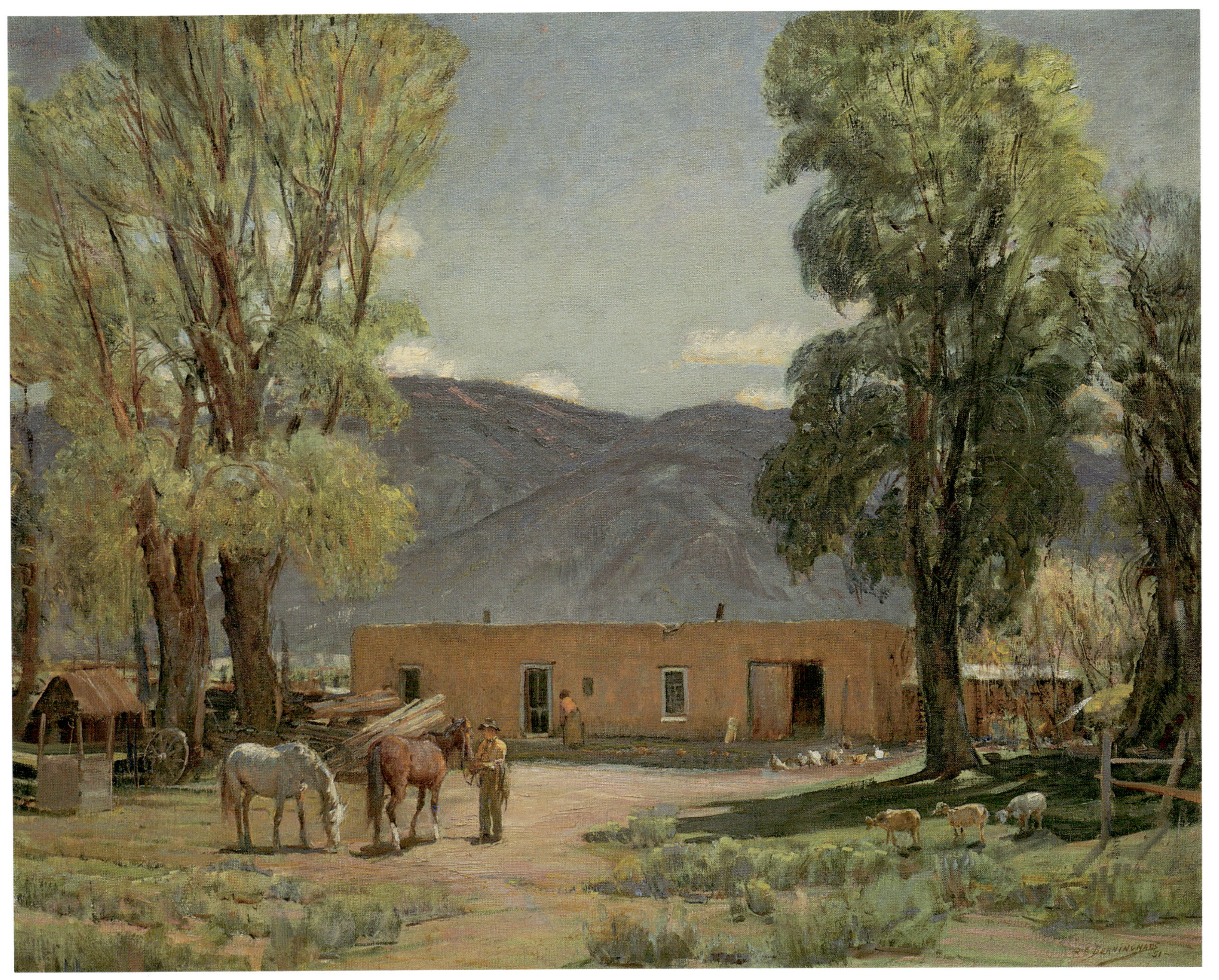

AN HACIENDA IN TAOS, 1951. 25x30 inches, oil on canvas. Private collection.

Much has been written about the Taos Society of Artists. Scholars have poured over the handwritten minutes of the annual meetings which are stored in the archives of the Library of the University of New Mexico in Albuquerque. Various books and articles have been written, some in great detail. Perhaps the best is the *Taos Society of Artists*, by Robert R. White, which was published in 1983 by the New Mexico Historical Society. Oscar Berninghaus was a vital part of the Society and often took the unwanted "secretary" position. Why the members did not simply hire an executive secretary is not known, but the fact is that they did not, and it remained a bone of contention. However, the total success of the organization was never a problem. The idea of a group of talented painters working together in the primitive surroundings of Taos had an enormous appeal to art writers and critics all over the world. As a matter of fact, Taos became one of the great art centers of the world, second only to Paris, France, according to a number of written accounts in the late teens and 1920s. Today its fame is even more widespread.

Taos attracted not only painters, but leading intellectuals who came to write and sculpt—and just to be in Taos. Mabel Dodge came in 1916, followed by D.H. Lawrence, Andrew Dasburg, Leon Gaspard, Nicolai Fechin, Dorothy Brett, Georgia O'Keeffe and dozens of others all caught up in the magic of Taos. Mabel Dodge commented in her book *Taos and Its Artists* that Taos brought out the best in everyone who came. "At no time has any notable artist come to Taos and been able to remain if his creative compulsion was to express hatred, vileness, or any negative psychotic malaise."

Perhaps it was the Taos Indians who set the mood for politeness and courtesy. Hundreds lived together virtually in the same house—the Pueblo—with practically no theft and no murder. Perhaps too, it was the wisdom of those who came to escape the rudeness of the 20th century. For whatever reason, the spirit of Taos was actually making the village a mecca for creativity.

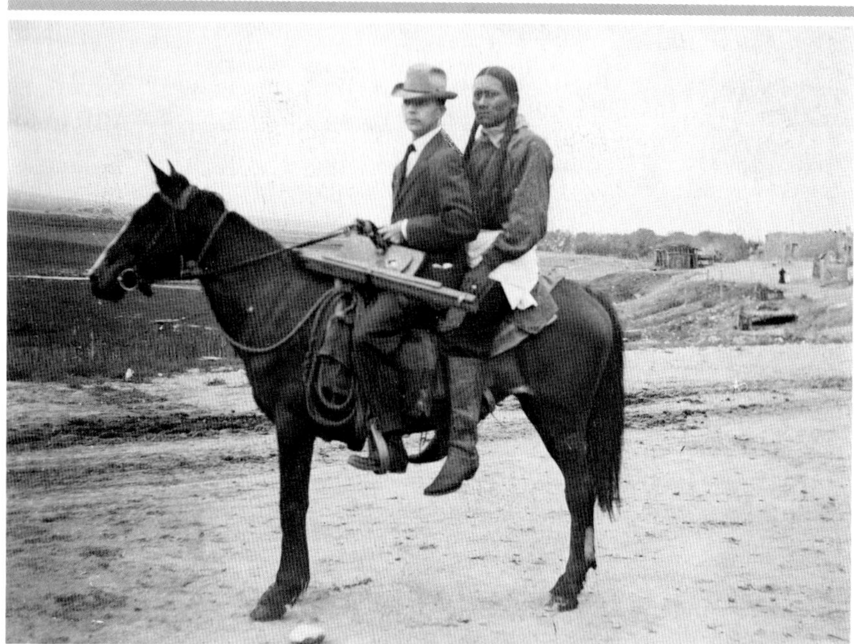

O.E. Berninghaus and Albert "Looking Elk" Martinez, c. 1919.

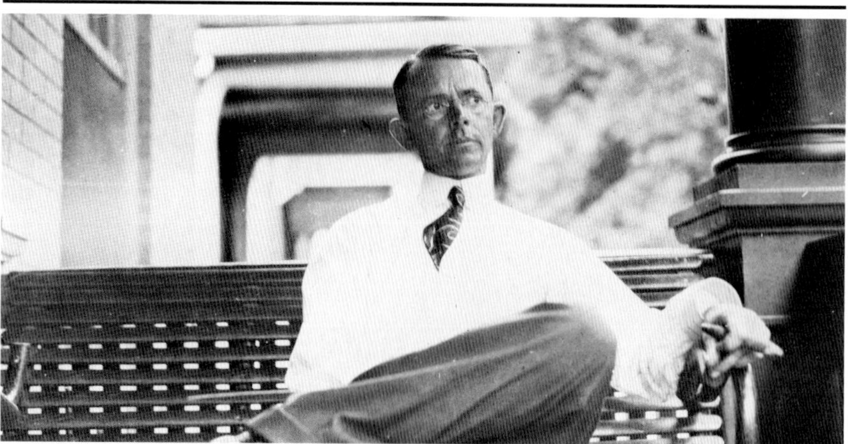

O.E. Berninghaus, 1914.

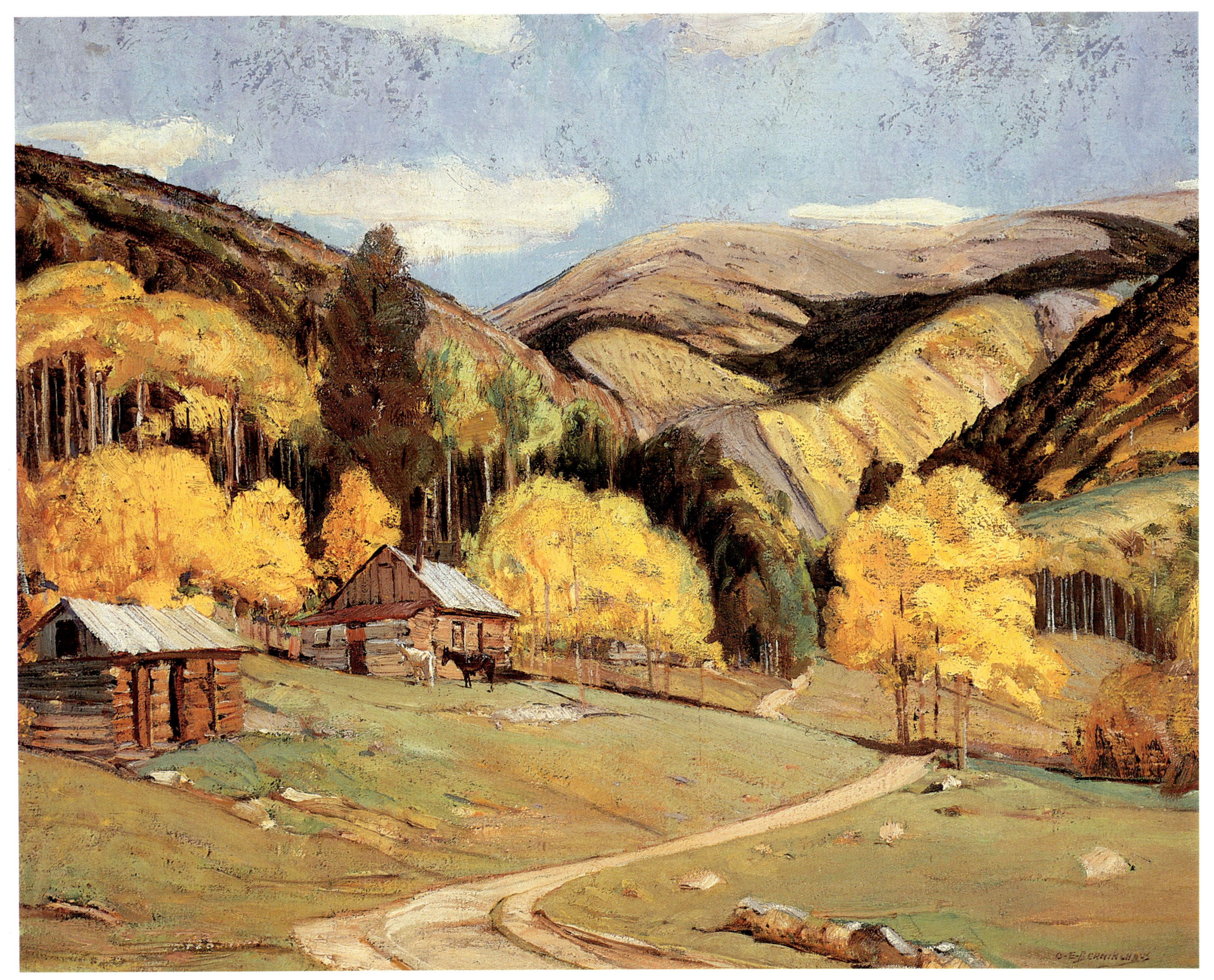

AMIZETTE, c. 1918. 25×30 inches, oil on canvas. Courtesy of the Bent Gallery, Taos, New Mexico.

During the years of World War I, Oscar Berninghaus continued his busy routine. He was too old for the draft, now 43, but made regular appearances to assist in the sale of Liberty Bonds. He also lent his poster-painting talent to the U.S. Army by painting huge range-finder canvases for target practice. This was a contribution made by many artists to the war effort, and the government provided them with first rate canvas for the project. He did not let this interfere with his independent work, and in 1915 the St. Louis Artists' Guild awarded him the Bascom Prize; in 1917 the much coveted Brown Prize for *The Sagebrush Trail* and in 1918, the year the war ended, Berninghaus won the St. Louis Chamber of Commerce Prize for his paintings, *Thirteenth and Locust Streets* and *Levee, Winter of 1917-18*.

By this time, he was spending six months of each year in Taos, and had decided to make it his permanent home as soon as possible. He was becoming known more as a New Mexican, and in 1917 three of his paintings were a part of the opening exhibition at the Museum of New Mexico in Santa Fe.

The Taos Society of Artists was now a household word in the world of art. The annual exhibition tours included not only the Noonan-Kocian Gallery in St. Louis, but the prestigious Babcock and Milch Galleries in New York City. In Chicago, Young's Gallery did a one-man show of Berninghaus paintings and also printed a catalogue, "The Works of Oscar E. Berninghaus." The *Los Angeles Times* ran a black-and-white reproduction of his *A Mountain Trail* on January 20, 1918. All over the country the Taos painters were receiving enormous publicity, and their paintings were selling like hot cakes. Replacements for sold pictures were being crated up and shipped out of Taos every week.

The year 1918 also brought Oscar Berninghaus a distinct honor. He was appointed to the Advisory Board of the School

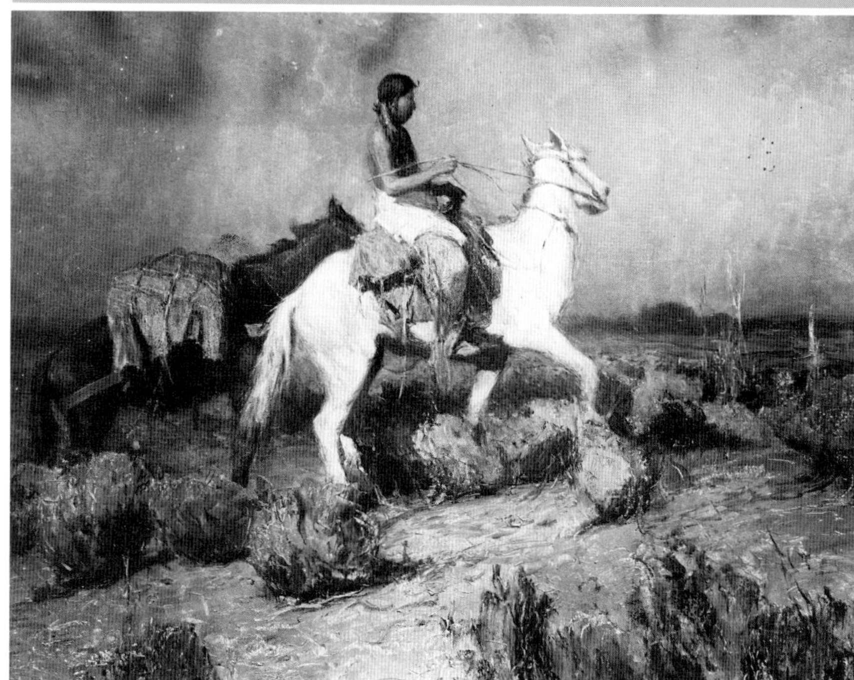

THE SAGEBRUSH TRAIL. 24x30 inches, oil.
Brown Prize, St. Louis Artists' Guild, 1917.

of Fine Arts of Washington University in St. Louis, the same school where he had taken night courses some 25 years before. During winter months, he was teaching illustration at the University. His appointment to the Board was a great honor, considering he had not finished high school. He was now an accomplished artist who had made it on his own, and he wanted to share his experience with young people seeking a career in art. He told his pupils that first you must learn to "draw . . . draw . . . draw" and that "the painter must first see his picture as paint . . . as color . . . as form . . . and not as a landscape or a figure. Paint with feeling . . . not with seeing." This thought process is certainly evident in his *Taos Idyll*, a veritable symphony of color and form.

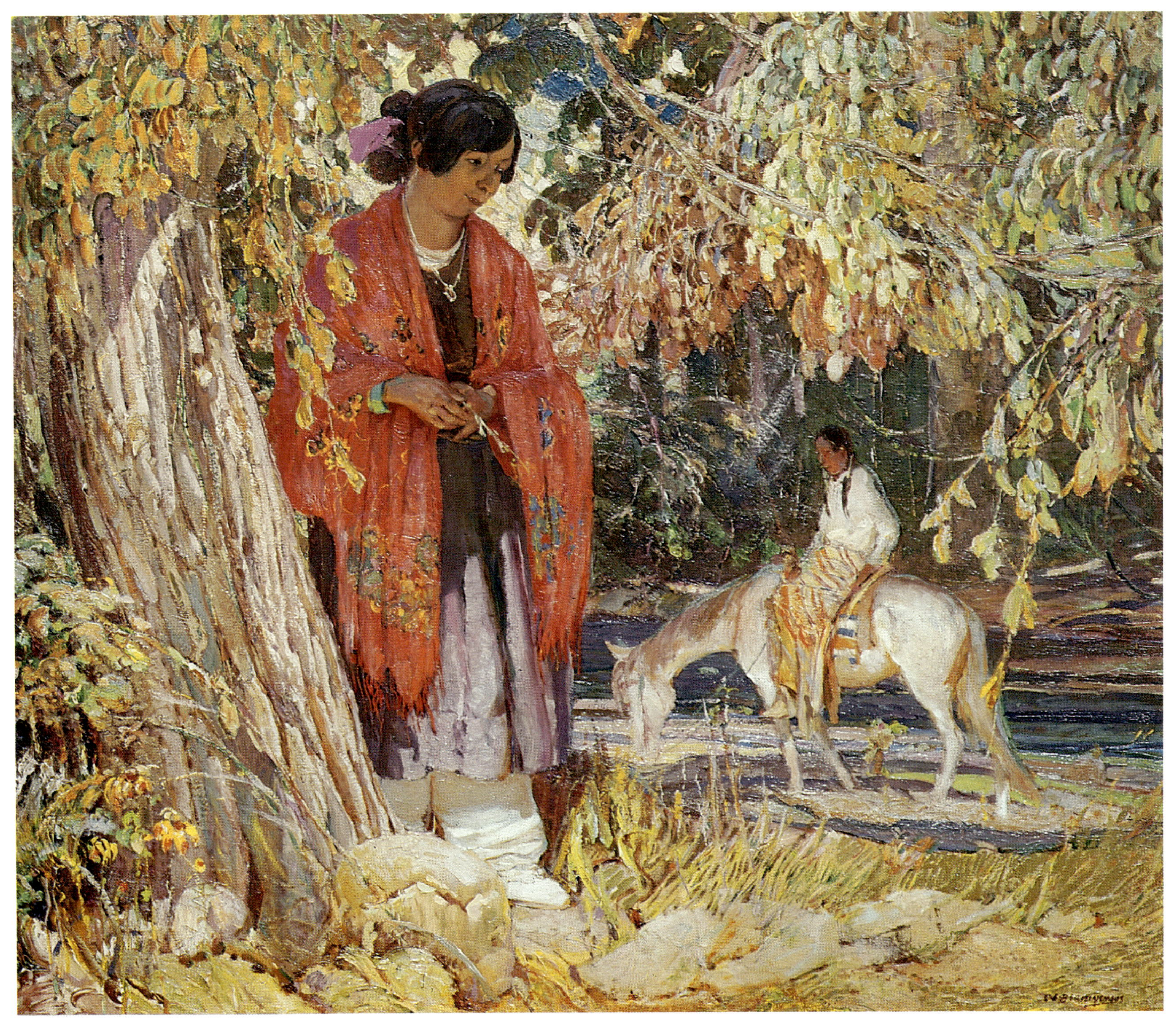

TAOS IDYLL. 36×40 inches, oil on canvas. Collection of Eugene B. Adkins, Tulsa, Oklahoma.

GROWTH, RECOGNITION AND FAME

The Taos Society of Artists in 1919 was a full-fledged, overwhelming success. Art critics were pointing to Taos as a leader in the concept of real American art, and the Taos painters were creating their own American style. One critic, Emily Hutchings, in praising the Taos Ten said, "We need artists with unhyphenated eyes. It has been pitiful to find American painters full of the delusion that their dexterity was too talented for anything less than Italian coloring or Parisian picturesque. It was pitiful to find other clever young artists, after their return from abroad, painting 'American' things overcast and dulled with reminiscences that belonged, not to America, but to France." Of Oscar Berninghaus, she said, "Oscar E. Berninghaus in his paintings gives us a work that is all-American. The very ponies that give their own peculiar tangue to the pictures, are in their essence, American. The desert is American . . . etc." The other members of the Society were also receiving rave reviews across the country.

Berninghaus won a number of important prizes in 1919— two from the St. Louis Artists' Guild, the Popular Vote Prize and the Carl Wimer Prize. He also won the Missouri State Fair Art Exhibit Prize at Sedalia. Another "prize" for Oscar in this year was that he bought a home in Taos, and according to Dorothy, who was then 17, he bought their very first automobile, a model T Ford! She says that when the paint would begin to peel, "Papa" would use black shoe polish to touch it up. She also recalls that the Berninghaus studio was one of great order and neatness—nothing out of place— everything catalogued mentally.

In the Taos community, Berninghaus was a favorite, often being called upon to do posters, greeting cards, signs, lettering—anything that required his talents—for various civic affairs. He seldom, if ever, said "no," and approached each task with skill, care and love.

It seems Oscar was very happy, and now that he owned his own home in Taos, he could stay longer than the summer months—long enough to paint the sacred mountain covered with early snow and the tall aspens in their full glory. He became a good friend to the Taos Indians, and was one of the few white men allowed into the kivas of the Pueblo. He would learn their rituals and customs, but would paint only what the Indians thought proper. He felt a sense of history and wanted to preserve it accurately for future generations, and at the same time respect that which was sacred to them.

But—for now, in the autumn of 1919, it was back to St. Louis to put the children in school and to work on some new commissions.

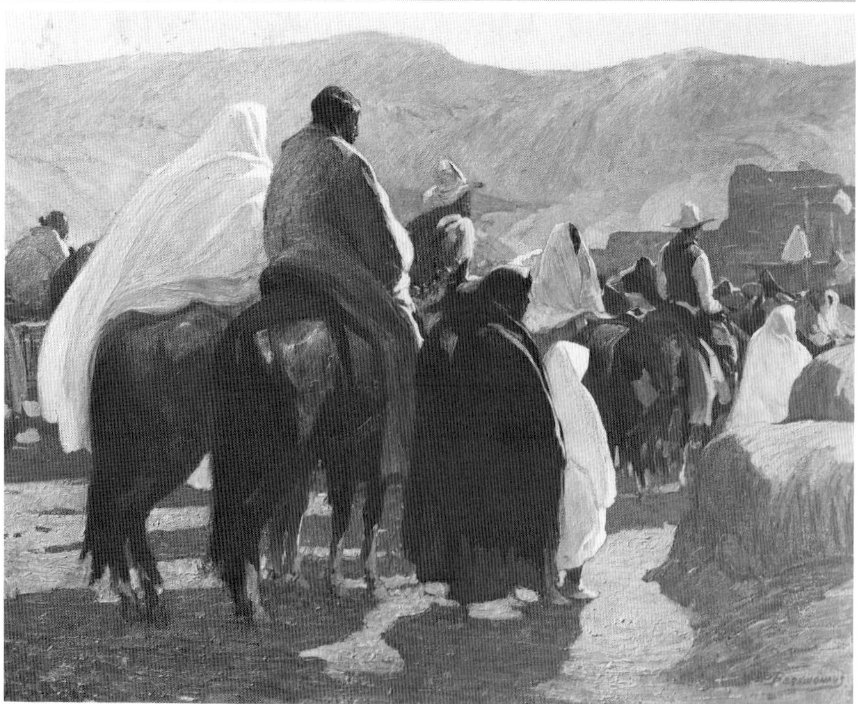

DAY OF THE FIESTA, 1919. Carl Wimar Prize.

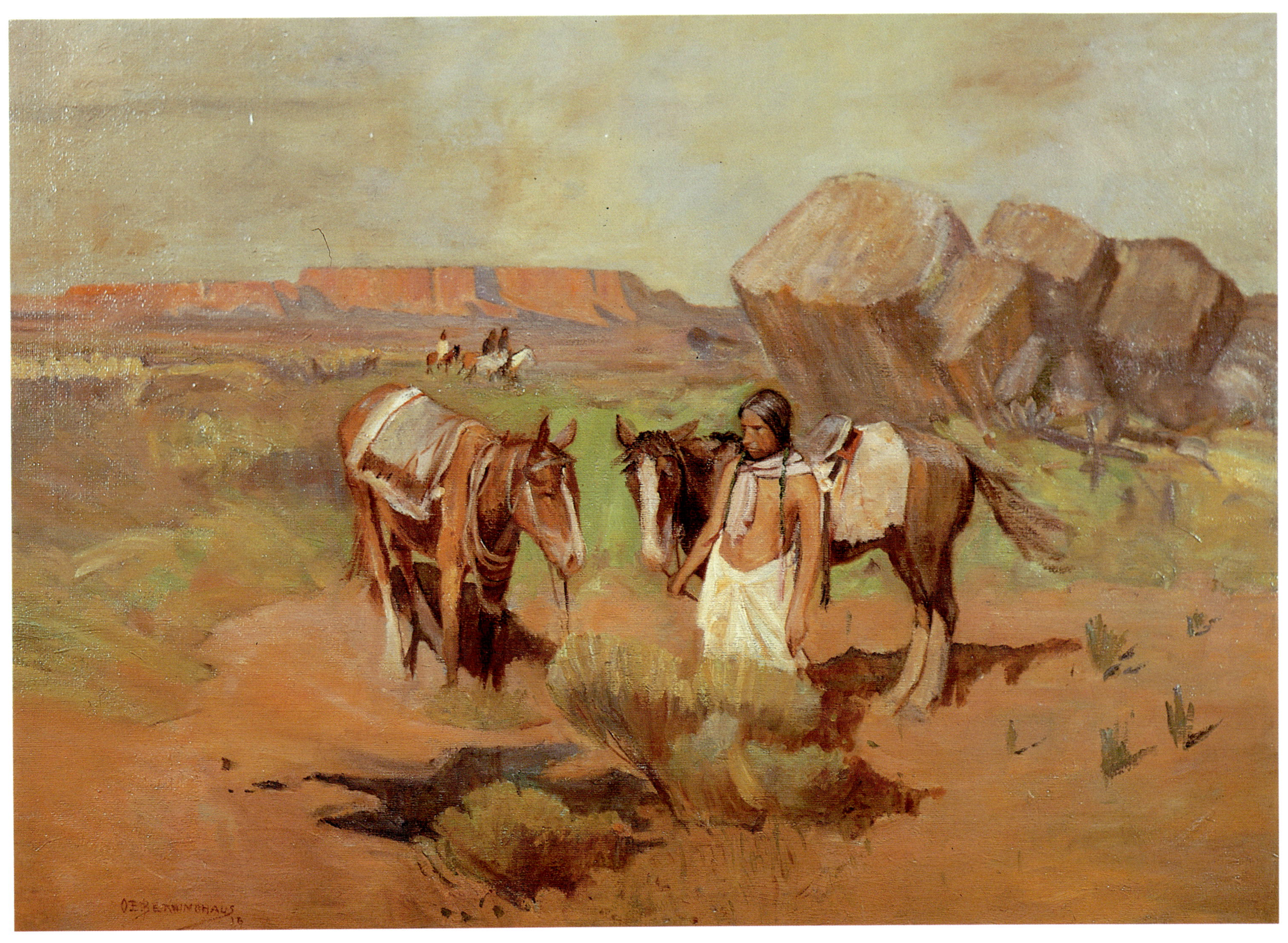

THE WATERHOLE, 1916. 30×40 inches, oil on canvas. Courtesy of the Wiggins Gallery, Roswell, New Mexico.

In 1920, Berninghaus was practically working round the clock. He was doing a series of lunettes for the new Missouri State Capitol in Jefferson City, and a commission for the De Lore Baryta Company. This commission required that he do a sizeable booklet, "The Story of Barytes," which would serve to explain the company's barytes mining operation in the foothills of the Ozark Mountains in Washington County, Missouri. Baryta is an ore that produces barium sulphate, which is widely used in the manufacturing of paints, rubber and scores of other industrial products. In order to research this project thoroughly, Berninghaus traveled to the old town of Mine Au Breton, which was named by the French when they were looking for gold and silver in the area around 1720. Their search was not too successful, and they actually ended up smelting lead until they returned to France in 1742. Now in 1920, the town was called Potosi, was the county seat, and the heart of the barytes fields.

His research on the project was a time-consuming one as he had to know how the ore was taken out of the ground, processed, hauled and stored. He also learned the customs and lifestyles of the mining families. The booklet was published in 1920, and featured four full-color scenes of the miners at work, and a score of pencil drawings. The text was written by Allen W. Clark, a well-known art journalist.

This wasn't his only project this year as those lunettes for the State Capitol were due to be delivered early in 1921!

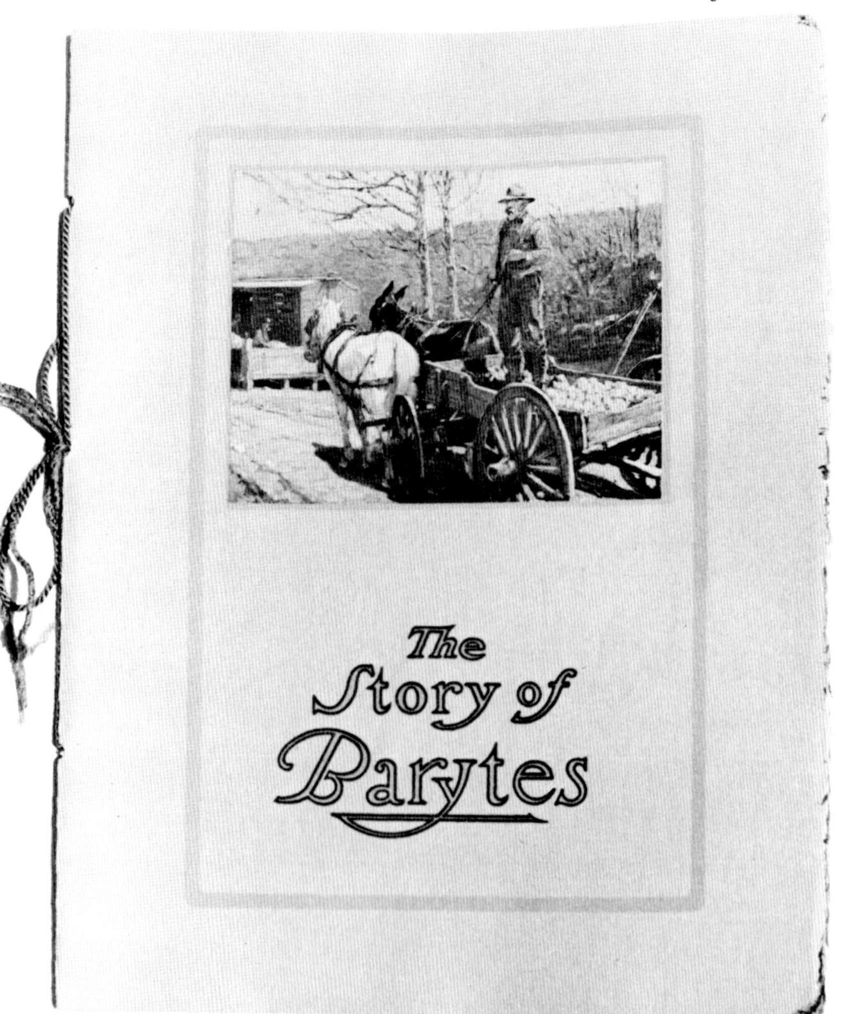

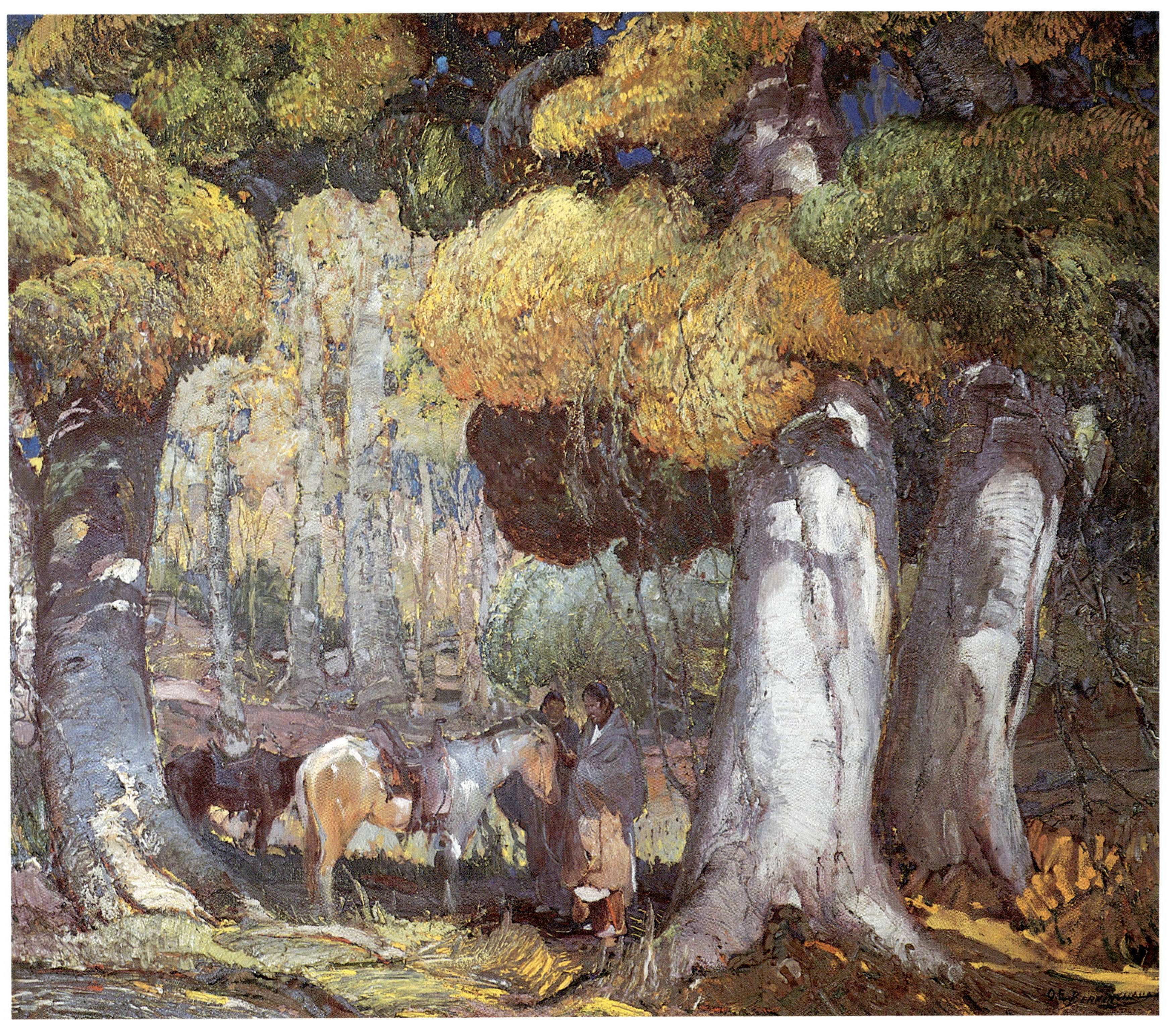

GLORIETA, 1927. 30x34 inches, oil on canvas. Private collection.

The old Missouri State Capitol building burned to the ground in 1911, and a new building was completed in Jefferson City in 1917. In April of that year, Governor Frederick Gardner appointed a Capitol Decoration Commission of five members to consider what type of artwork should appear in the new building. A historical theme was decided upon, and the members, Dr. John Pickard, William Bixby, John F. Downing, Arthur A. Kocian and Mrs. Cora Painter began their search for artists. The Commission chose five artists from Taos: Bert Phillips, Irving Couse, Ernest Blumenschein, Herbert Dunton and Oscar Berninghaus. Berninghaus was the first to be commissioned for the project, and the original agreement stated that he was to paint two murals—each 10 by 18 feet—and that he was to be paid just over $4,000. Later the number of murals was increased to five.

The mural project required an enormous amount of research, which Berninghaus began immediately upon signing the contract. He did a great deal of reading of Missouri history, especially of the period around 1780 when some 1,500 Indians, aided by the British, launched an attack on St. Louis. This reading was followed by considerable physical effort—first there was the sketch on a small canvas, then the squaring and blocking out of the mural on the huge canvas—then, of course, the actual painting. Charles Berninghaus helped his father with this project by blocking and painting in large areas, and his help was much appreciated as the murals took many months to complete.

The actual painting of the murals was done in Taos. When interviewed many years later, his daughter Dorothy spoke of the project: "My father ordered costumes of the 1780s from a company in St. Louis and had them shipped to Taos where his model, Albert "Looking Elk" Martinez, and some of his friends from the Pueblo posed for the scenes depicted in *The Attack on the Village of St. Louis in 1780* and *Surrender of the Miamis to General Dodge in 1814*.

Today the lunettes are as bright and colorful as ever, although their access is somewhat obstructed in certain areas by the installation of air conditioning equipment and other building modifications.

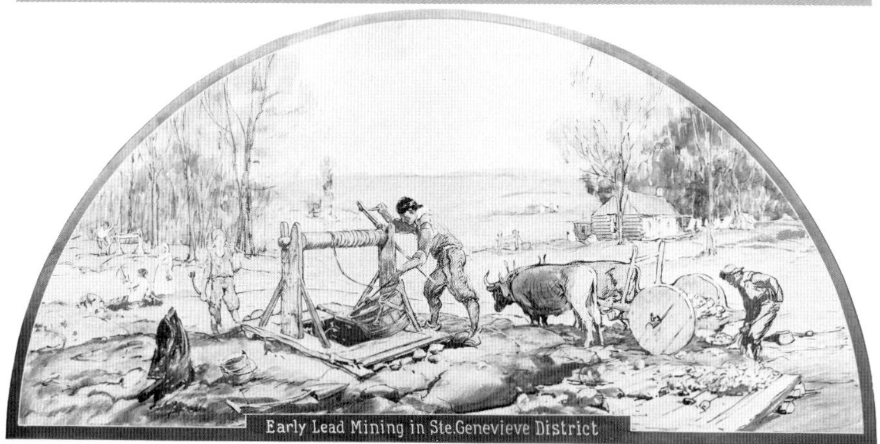

EARLY LEAD MINING IN WASHINGTON COUNTY.
Missouri State Capitol, Jefferson City, Missouri

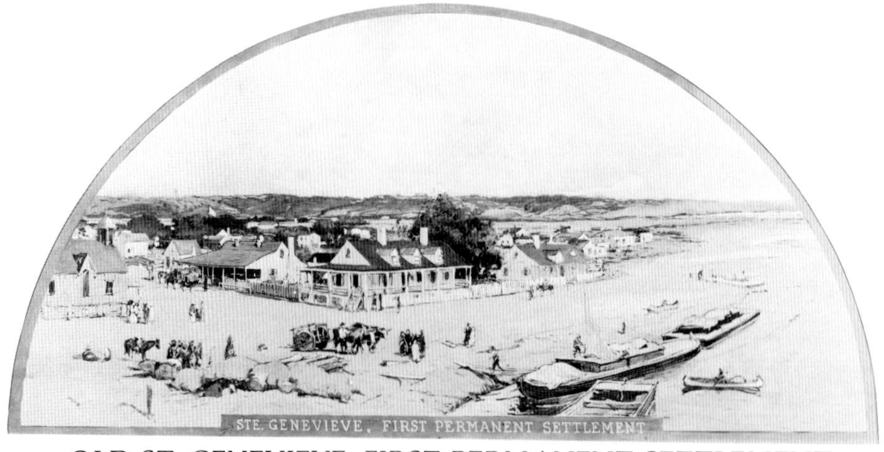

OLD ST. GENEVIEVE-FIRST PERMANENT SETTLEMENT.
Missouri State Capitol, Jefferson City, Missouri.

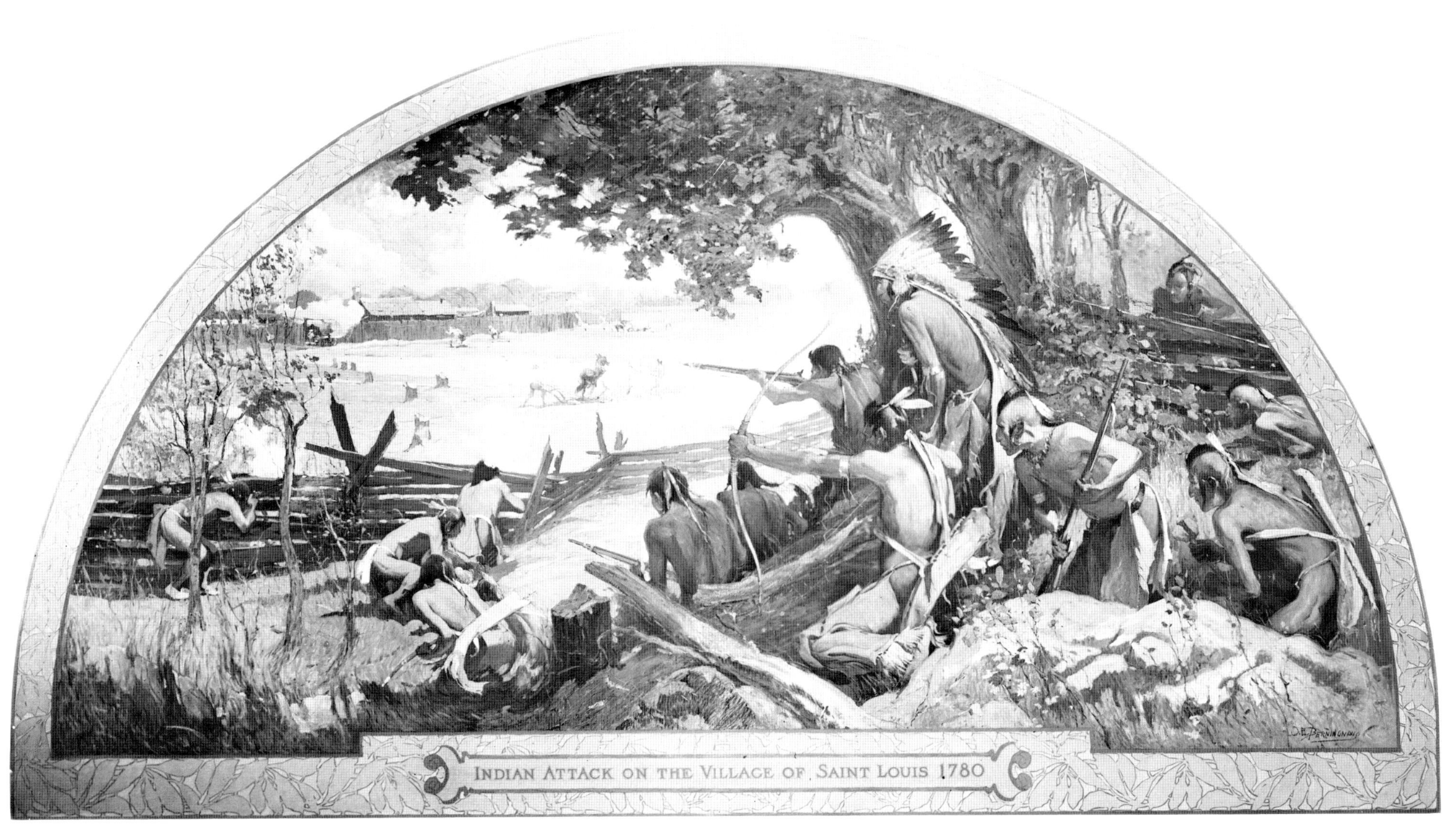

THE ATTACK ON THE VILLAGE OF ST. LOUIS IN 1780. Mural (lunette) in Missouri State Capitol, Jefferson City, Missouri.

In addition to the two large murals, Berninghaus did three smaller lunettes for the Missouri State Capitol building, *Early Lead Mining in Washington County, Old St. Genevieve–First Permanent Settlement* and *Herculaneum–Where Shot Making Was an Industry*. The Decoration Commission obviously chose Berninghaus for this particular task because he was a native of Missouri and had already done considerable research in the area of Washington County while illustrating the booklet for the DeLore Baryta Mining Company.

On January 7, 1921, with the Governor and a joint session of the Missouri State Legislature present, a number of the murals were unveiled. On hand were artists Fred Carpenter, Adolph Blondheim, H.T. Schladermundt, N.C. Wyeth and Oscar Berninghaus. The ceremonies were elaborate to honor the five artists whose works were completed. Dr. John Pickard, chairman of the Decoration Commission, gave a long and glowing speech about the lunettes. His speech evidently did not impress N.C. Wyeth as he later commented that Pickard delivered "quite an elaborate oration in true spread-eagle style, which seems to be the kind of speechmaking that goes in such a place." Wyeth said there was much about Pickard that was unbearable to him, but complimented the good doctor on his organization of the entire project.

How is it that five painters from Taos, New Mexico, managed to do most of the murals in the Missouri State Capitol? The answer appears to center around Oscar Berninghaus, who was a good friend of Commission members William Bixby and Arthur Kocian of the Noonan-Kocian Art Gallery. Berninghaus was introduced by Mr. Kocian to Dr. Pickard, and they jointly journeyed to Taos to meet the other artists. Dr. Pickard was so taken with Taos that later he moved to the tiny village and lived there the remainder of his life.

The entire Capitol decoration project cost slightly over $100,000, and was the pride of Missouri politicians and sightseers visiting the Capitol.

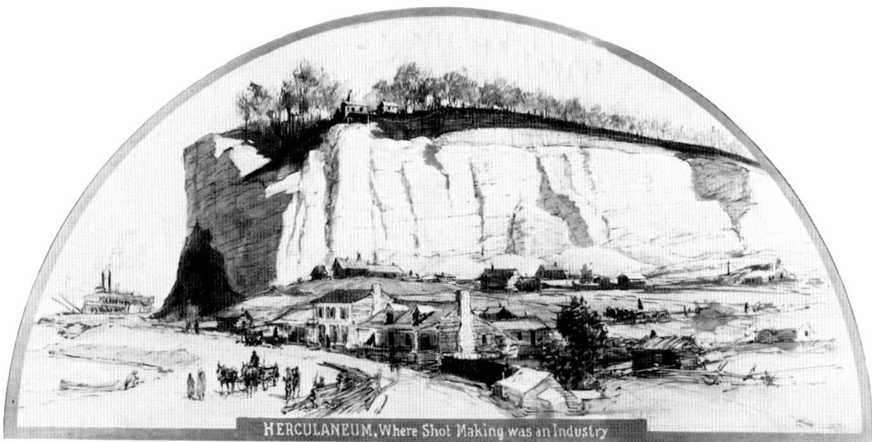

HERCULANEUM–WHERE SHOT MAKING WAS AN INDUSTRY.
Missouri State Capitol, Jefferson City, Missouri.

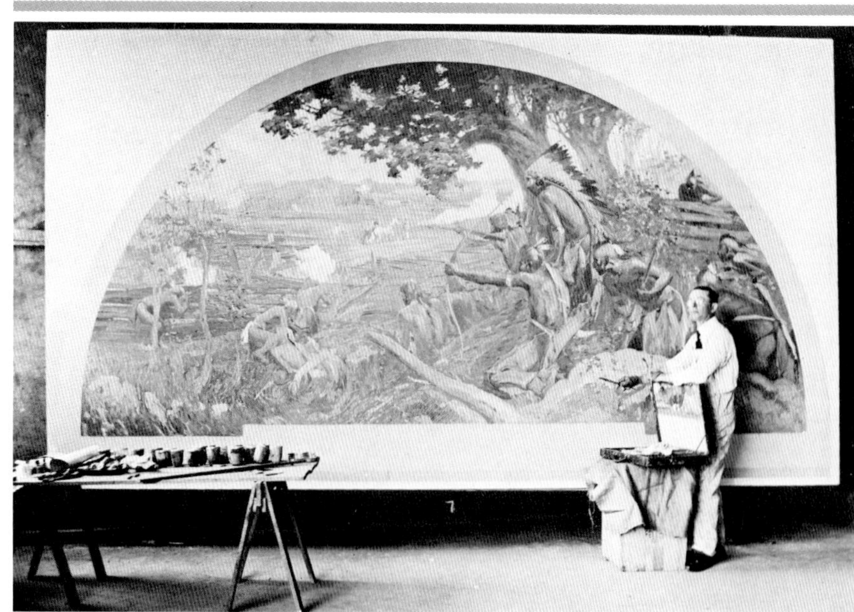

Berninghaus working on mural for Missouri State Capitol.

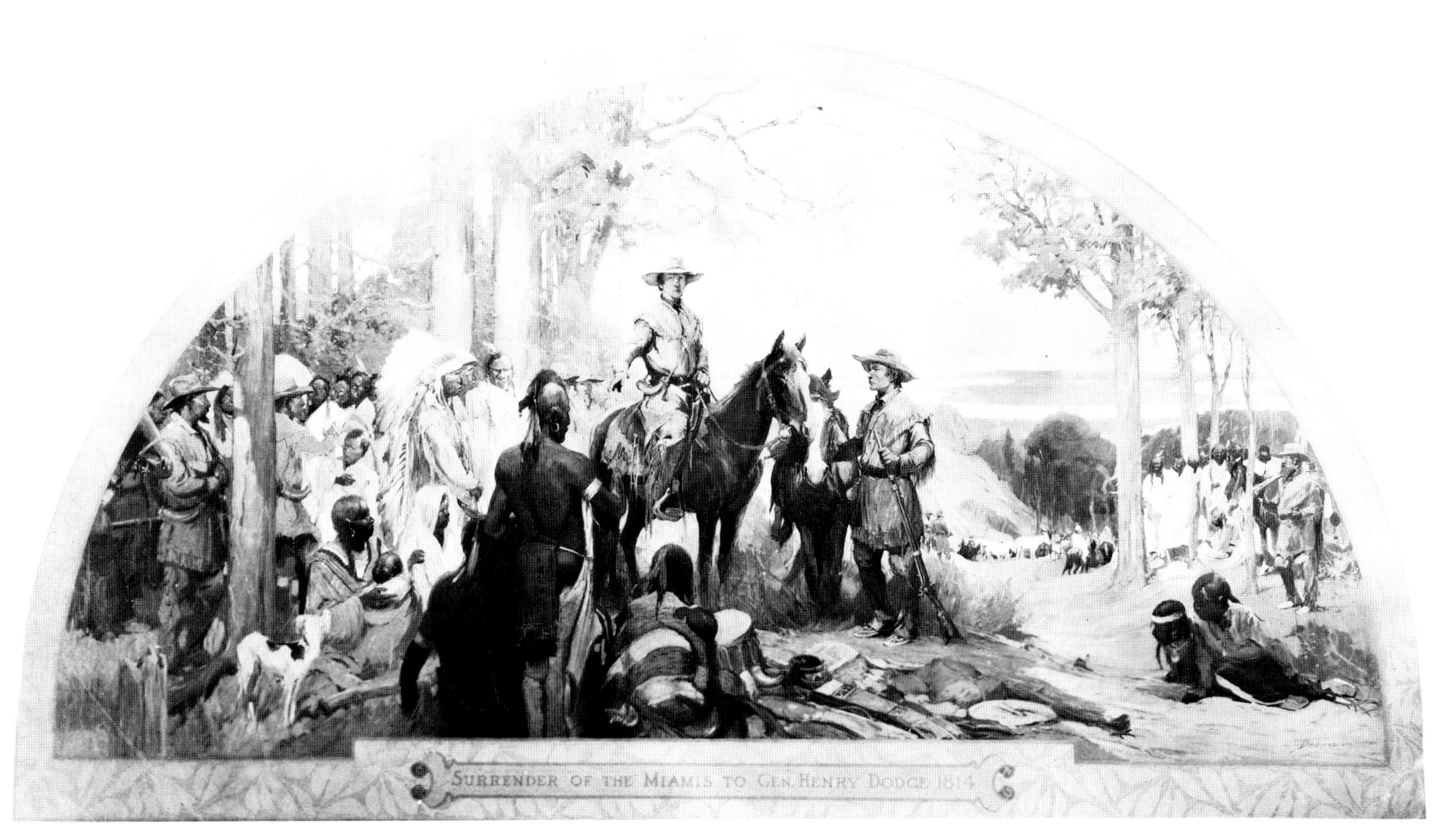

SURRENDER OF THE MIAMIS TO GENERAL DODGE IN 1814. Missouri State Capitol, Jefferson City, Missouri.

All was not smooth sailing in the art life of Oscar Berninghaus, as shortly after the lunettes were installed in the Missouri State Capitol, a large controversy developed. It seems a certain senator decided to become an art critic! Senator Tom Irwin launched an assault on a number of the paintings by the various artists, and especially those by Berninghaus. His main charge was that the Indian attack on St. Louis in May of 1780 was inaccurate. He was also furious with the *St. Louis Globe-Democrat* art writer Emily Hutchings for calling him a "rube" and "hayseed" in her column. The paper denied the charge, saying it was referring to "another" hayseed, not Senator Irwin, but this did not convince him, and the battle continued. Speaking of the Berninghaus work, he said, "The attack took place on the 26th of May, the plowing season was over and there should have been growing corn in the picture." He also complained about the number of Indians (only fifteen) in the picture, as history had it that 1,500 took part in the actual attack. Senator Irwin was critical of the fact that only one side of the Fort was shown, and that the walls were too high. On and on he raved, until finally Lester S. Parker, a renowned art connoisseur, came to the defense of the artist. A joint meeting of the Senate and House was held in the Senate Chamber with the St. Louis Artists' Guild, Senator Irwin, Mr. Parker and Legislators present. Parker praised the artworks as masterpieces, and was very gentle in pointing out that Senator Irwin not only knew nothing about art, but also knew little about farming in Missouri. "Corn," he said, "is often planted in late May and therefore would not be four feet tall; score a point for Berninghaus." Mr. Parker also reminded those present that Mr. Berninghaus was not a cubist and therefore could paint only one wall of the Fort. After this drubbing Senator Irwin disappeared, and was never heard from again—at least as an art critic! Oscar Berninghaus made no public comment and proceeded to pack up his family and head for Taos for another summer of fishing, camping and painting. It was good getting back to the big Taos country and the aspen forests.

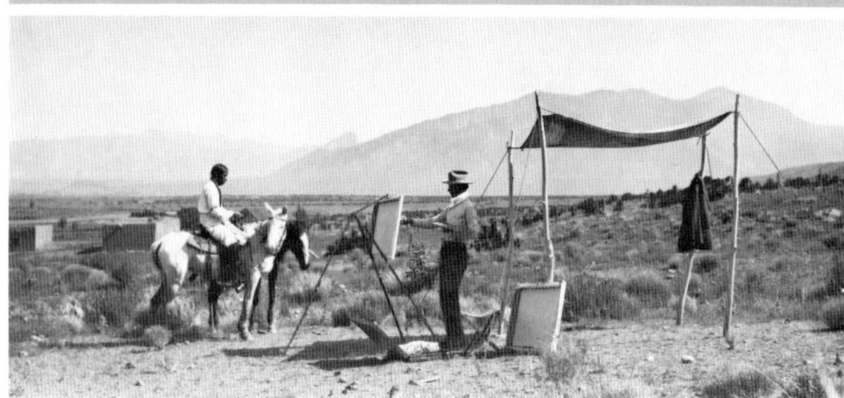

Painting under tent using Albert "Looking Elk" as model.

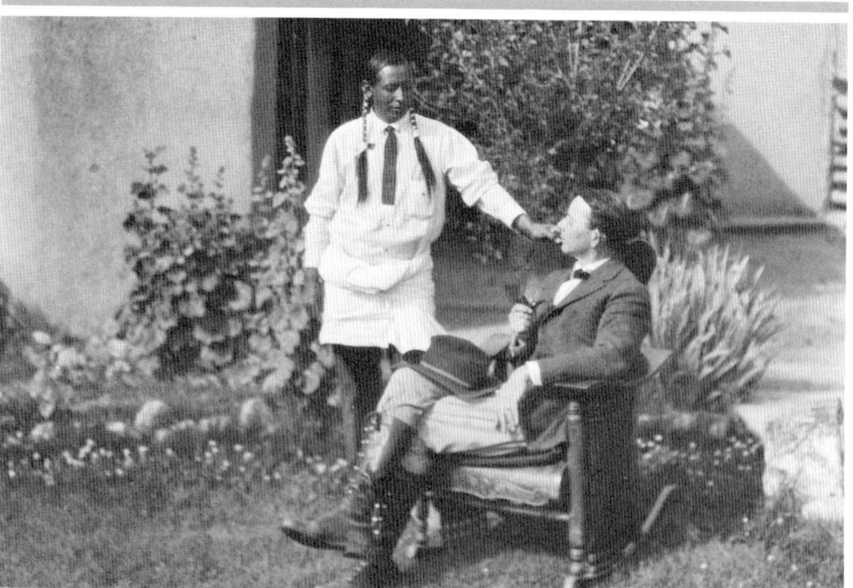

Albert Martinez and O.E. Berninghaus, c. 1925.

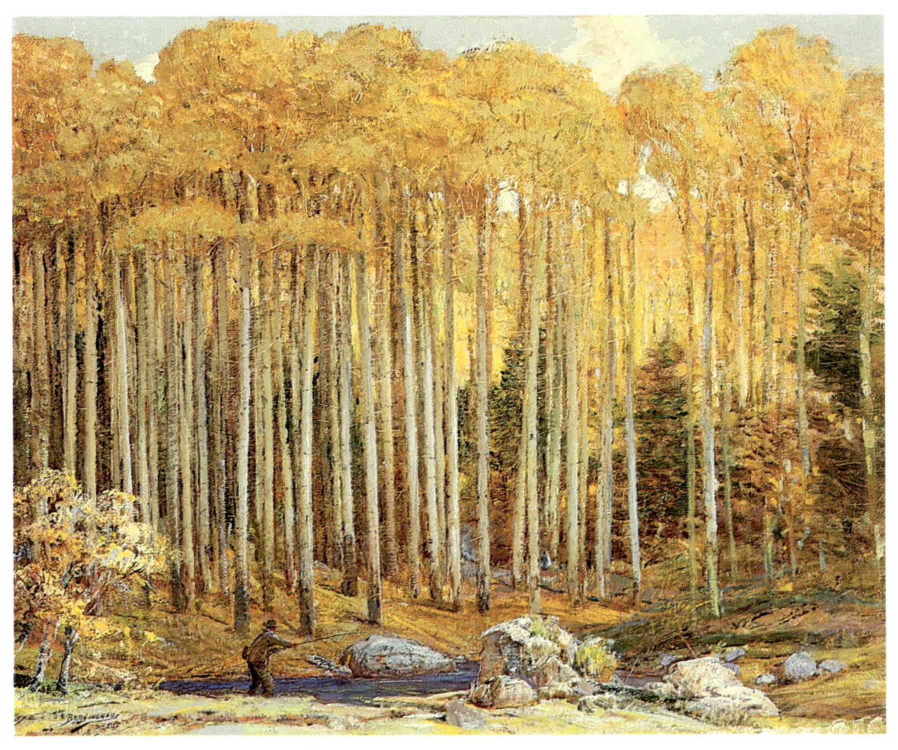

FISHING AMONG THE ASPENS, 1950.
25×30 inches, oil on canvas.
Private collection.

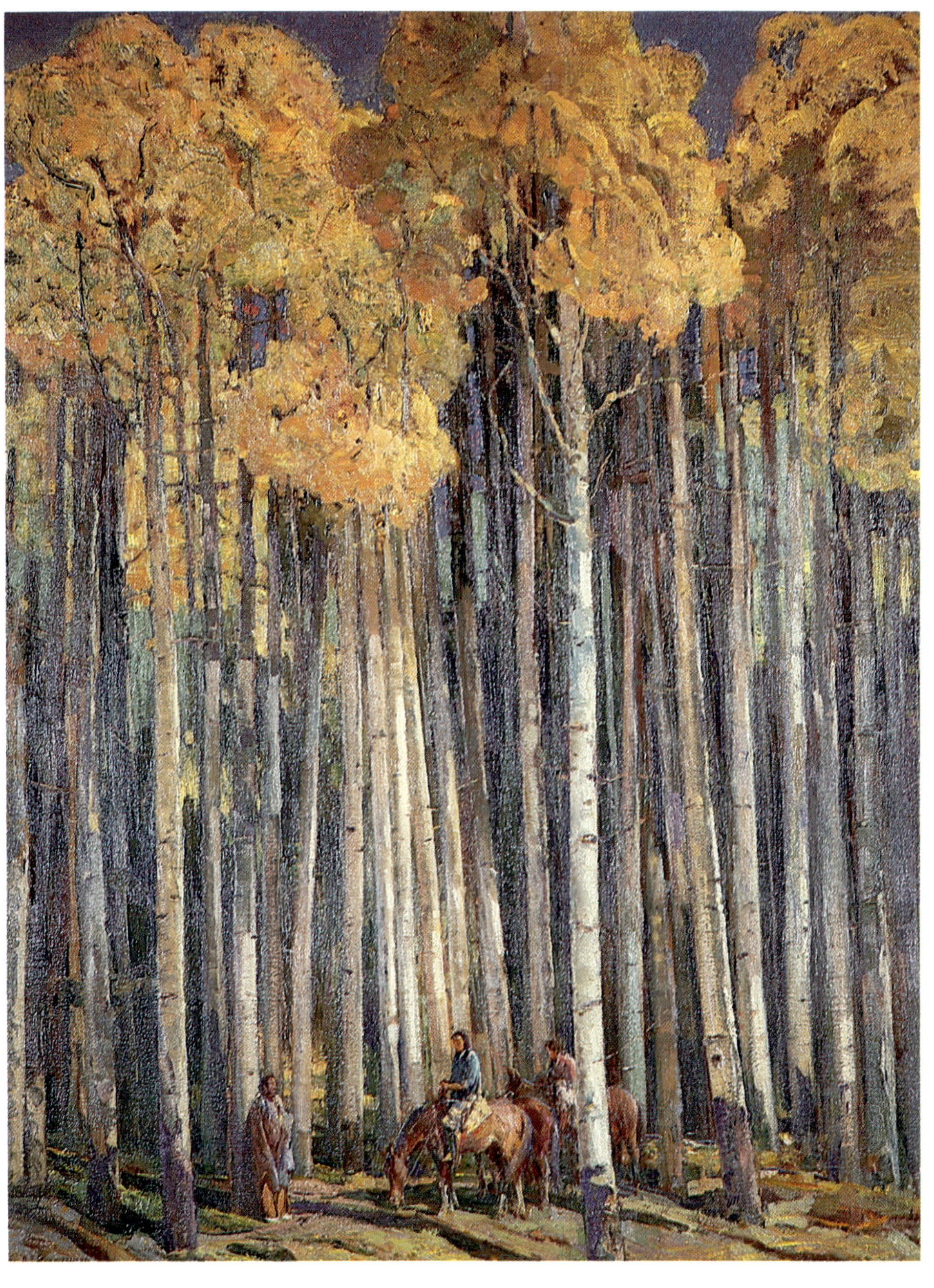

ASPEN FOREST, c. 1940.
40×30 inches, oil on canvas.
Private collection.

It was during the 1920s that Oscar Berninghaus became a major American painter. His canvases were being shown in many important galleries in the United States, and in 1921 he again won the prestigious Carl Wimar Prize from the St. Louis Artists' Guild. He also won, for the second time, the Missouri State Fair Exhibit Prize. In New Mexico, Santa Fe sponsored an artist's "Fiesta" which took place in 1921 and Berninghaus' offering was somewhat of a departure from the artist's usual style. It was a watercolor on canvas entitled *Baseball Game*, and the subject was not the game itself, but rather a crowd of Taos Indians watching the game from horseback. This painting also received critical acclaim in a number of eastern cities.

What was it exactly that gave Berninghaus paintings that special appeal? There was the magic of Taos—the towering Sangre de Cristo mountains, the Taos Pueblo and its Indians, and the village of Taos itself—old, romantic and steeped in history. There was the blue sky, and deep canyons with rivers of sparkling water. In the fall, the aspen trees turned yellow and gold, and to walk under them was like being in a great cathedral of stained-glass windows. When the breezes stirred, the leaves would tumble to the forest floor like diadems of gold. Taos was indeed a painter's paradise, and Oscar Berninghaus loved it all. Perhaps the most appealing aspect of a Berninghaus painting is the portrayal of truth. He saw the great landscapes as a statement of unlimited freedom—a statement of nature, and he painted them that way—simply and freely. He painted the Indians as pure—an ideal, in harmony with nature—but human. He loved horses, and his canvases capture his respect for the animal. Berninghaus was also aware of the changing times and its effect on the primitive wilderness and on the Indians. He wanted to preserve this pristine world truthfully on canvas—and he did.

In the 1920s he devoted more and more of his time to being an independent artist. His fame had spread, and he could afford to turn down commercial commissions, not all of them, but could pretty well take his pick. Financially, he was secure—not rich by any estimation, but "comfortable" as the saying went in those days. His daughter, Dorothy, was attending Washington University in St. Louis and his son, Charles, was rapidly becoming an artist in his own right.

Life was good, and during the summers Berninghaus enjoyed camping and fishing in the high country near Taos. He always took along his painting materials, however—just in case the fish weren't biting!

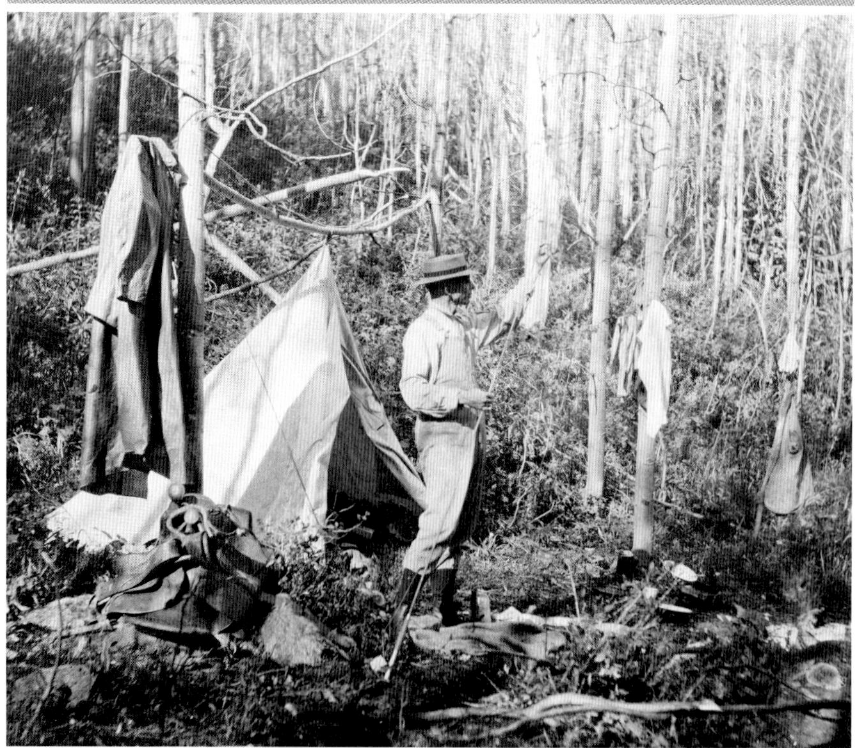

Berninghaus camping, 1920.

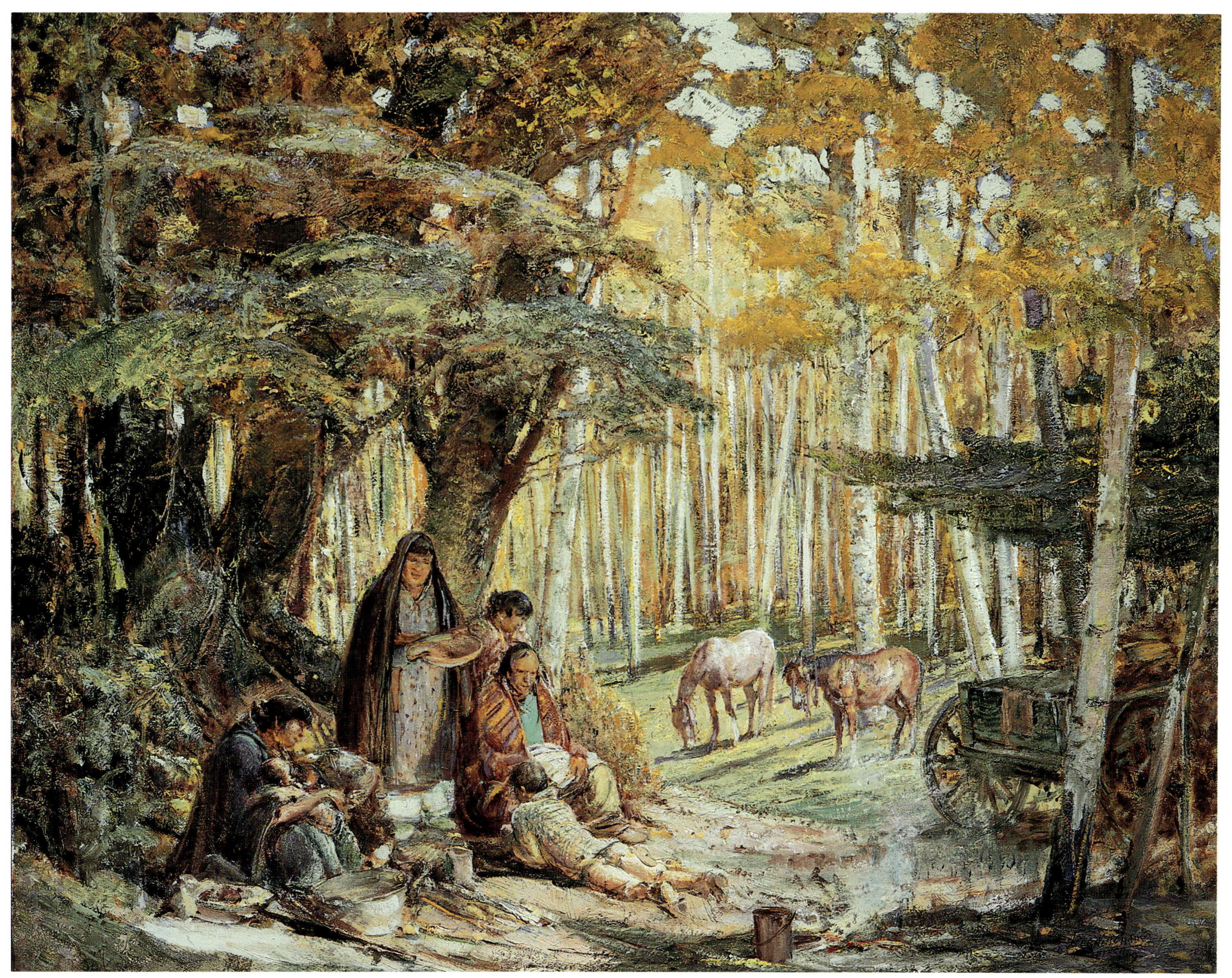

HONDO CANYON, c. 1925. 15½ x 19½ inches, oil on canvas. Photo courtesy of the Gerald Peters Gallery, Santa Fe, New Mexico.

The Taos Indians have been agricultural people for hundreds of years. Farming and hunting were the primary source of food until the turn of the 20th century, and even today they plant and harvest their crops as a part of their livelihood. Berninghaus often captured the Indians at work, and *Threshing Time at Taos Indian Pueblo* is an interesting and colorful example. In a letter from the family files, he describes the activity:

Gathering of the harvest and threshing is a busy activity with the Indians in the late summer. Threshing their wheat is an interesting procedure, as well as entertaining, engaged in by all members of the family and friends of the family from grandparents down to the little ninos.

The method, handed down to them from many generations back, is as picturesque and romantic as it is traditional and primitive.

It consists first of a smooth floor of adobe plaster, circular in form and some 60 feet in diameter. Onto the center of this floor is stacked or piled the harvested wheat and the whole area enclosed by a fence of poles placed horizontally, making a sort of corral. Into this enclosure then are driven some eight or nine horses—these run around in this enclosure dragging down the piled wheat—their trampling feet and hooves soon separate the grain from the chaff. After a reasonable time the horses are removed, the rough chaff pitched away and the remaining finer chaff winnowed, mostly by women, until the grain is completely separated . . . then sacked away for winter's use.

The letter was written in 1945, many years after a similar canvas had won him a prize in St. Louis. That picture was bought by the "Friends of Artists" in 1921 and given to the public school art department. To the letter, Berninghaus added a poignant footnote:

In past years these "arenas" or threshing floors were seen in large numbers in the fields surrounding the village. Gradually they became less and less, and last year, 1944, perhaps witnessed the last of them. Today, the government issue threshing machine does the work more cleanly, economically, rapidly. Such is progress with the Indians, as well as with us.

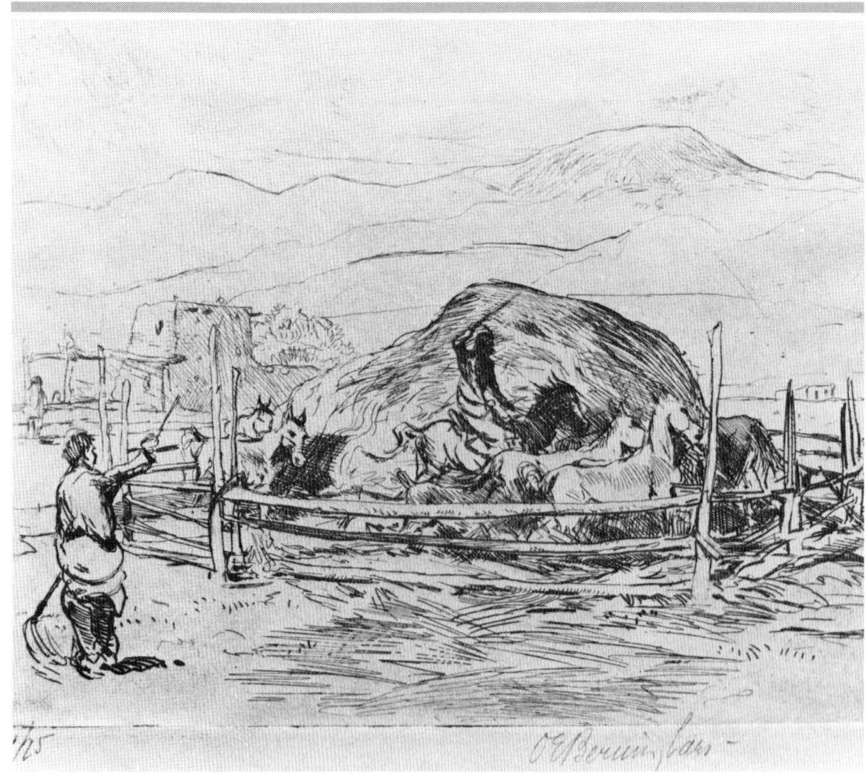

THRESHING AT THE PUEBLO, c. 1930.
6x6 inches, lithograph. Private collection.

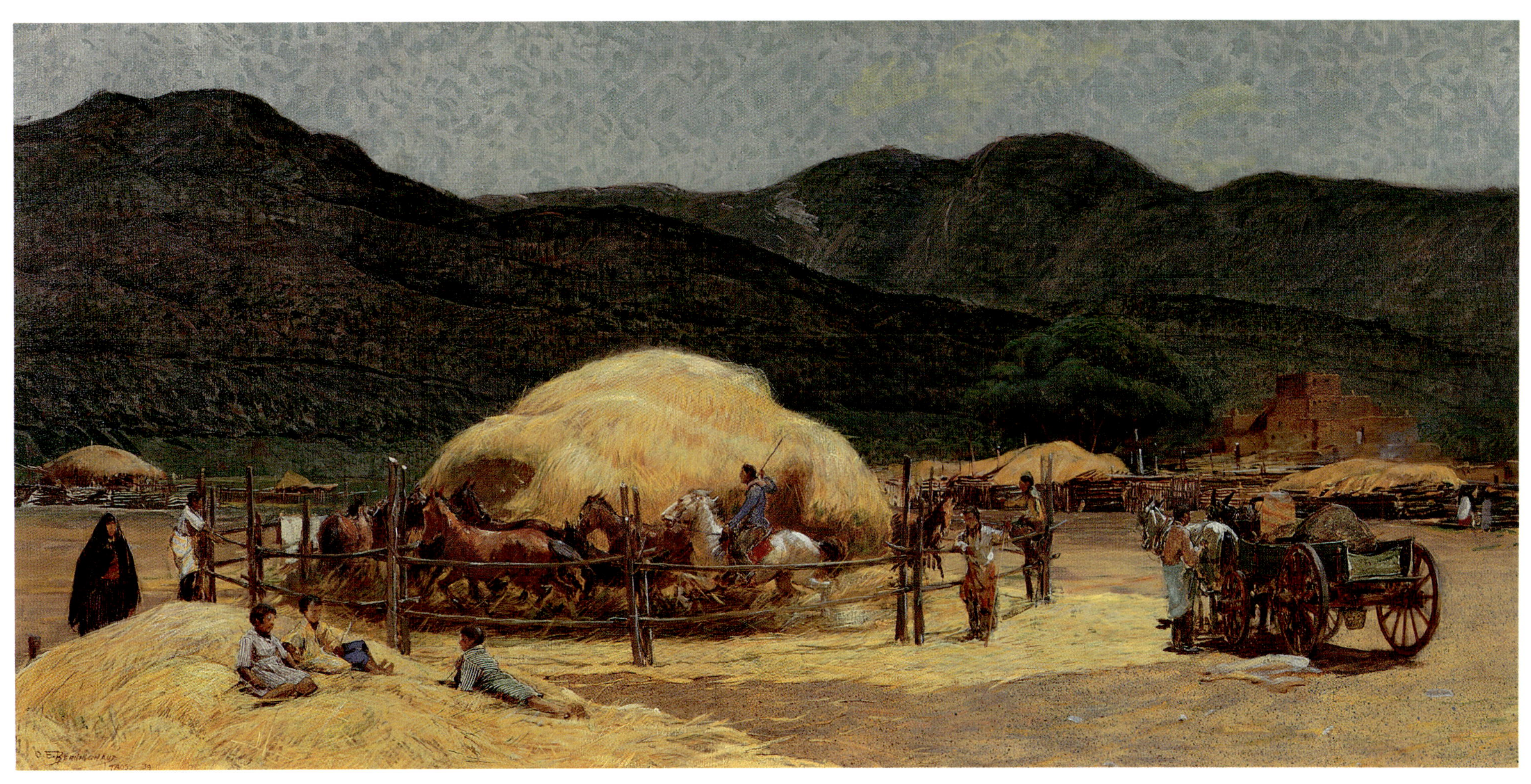

THRESHING TIME AT TAOS PUEBLO, 1939. 24x49 inches, oil on canvas. Courtesy of Woolaroc Museum, Bartlesville, Oklahoma.

Most of the Taos painters used models from the Pueblo, and for many of the Indians it became a lifelong job. Not only did they model, but they helped out with the various needs of the artists such as adobe house repair and general handyman jobs, and looked after their homes and studios while they were away. For many years, Albert "Looking Elk" Martinez was Oscar Berninghaus' favorite model. He had come to work when he was only 12 years old, and Berninghaus took a fatherly interest in him. He was a good model and could sit for hours without moving—a painter's dream! When "Looking Elk" grew up, he married Marina and on many occasions Oscar used the two of them and their children for his canvases. Some of his most beautiful and romantic paintings featured Mr. and Mrs. Martinez. As evidence of their long friendship, the Martinezes named one of their sons "Bernie," and took great delight in showing him off to all of "big Bernie's" friends and family.

Berninghaus not only painted "Looking Elk," but also taught him to paint. One Christmas (at Albert's request), Oscar gave him a complete set of paints, brushes, canvases and easel. Actually, the young man became quite good, and began painting instead of modeling. During the summer months, he would set up his easel near the Pueblo and delight the tourists with his newly acquired skill. Many of the visitors were taken with the idea of owning a canvas painted by a "real" Indian, and would pay Albert five or maybe ten dollars for one of them. This new success ended his modeling career totally!

The friendship between Albert "Looking Elk" and his teacher lasted until his tragic death on December 5, 1940. He fell from the back of a truck on a cold winter night and died from the fall, or perhaps from exposure to the cold. His body was not discovered until the next morning, and Berninghaus had lost a good friend and model.

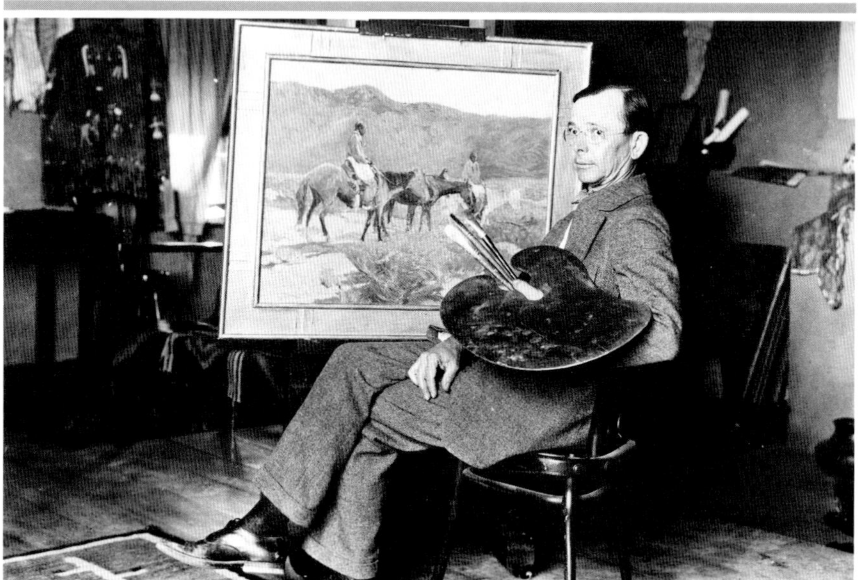

O.E. Berninghaus in his studio, 1920.

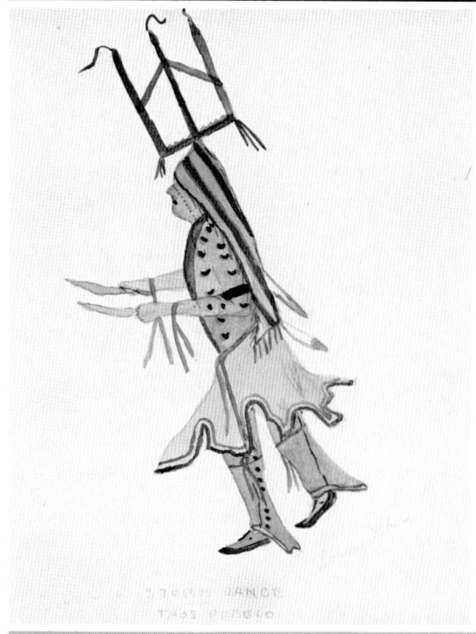

Watercolor by Albert Martinez.

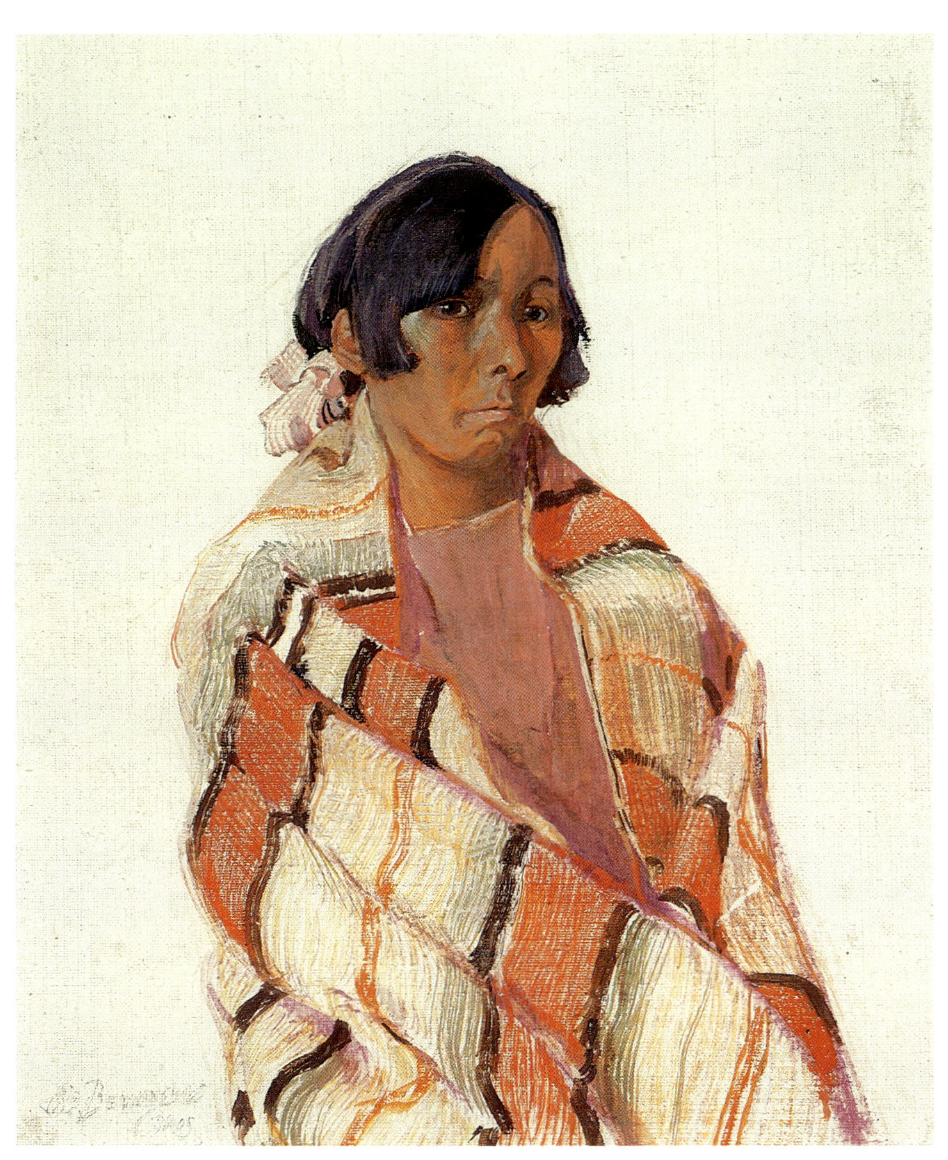

SENORA ALBERT MARTINEZ, 1925.
12×10 inches, watercolor on board.
Private collection.

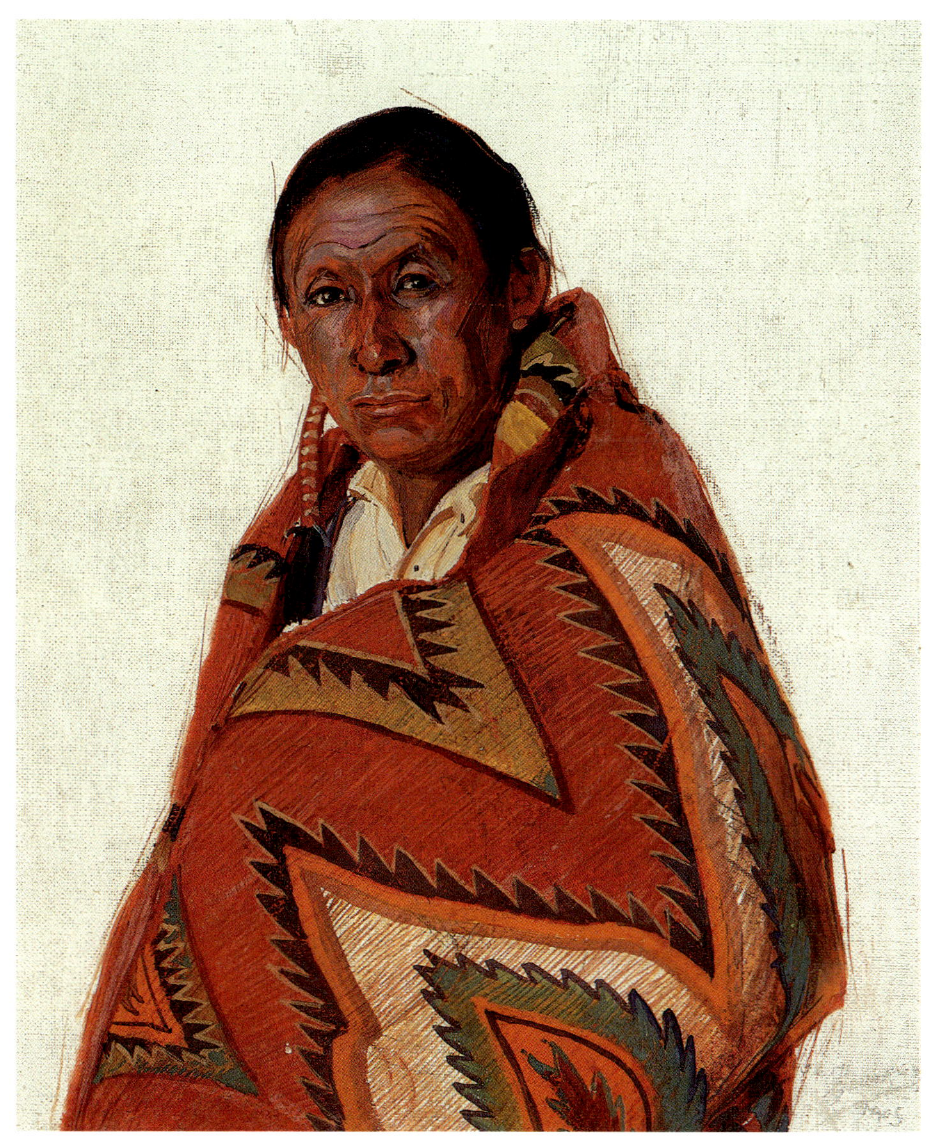

ALBERT, LOOKING ELK, MARTINEZ, 1925.
12×10 inches, watercolor on board.
Private collection.

In December of 1924, Oscar Berninghaus achieved a new height in his career as an independent painter. His painting, *Their Son*, was exhibited at the National Academy of Design in New York City, and was bought by the Ranger Fund—a fund established by Henry Ward Ranger. Ranger himself was a member of the National Academy, and upon his death in 1916 his will specified that the income from his estate was to be spent by the Council of the National Academy for the purchase of paintings by American artists, and these pictures were to be given by the Council to the art institutions of America.

The prize was a big one for Berninghaus, and placed him in an exclusive club of other famous winners like Bruce Crane, Elmer Schofield, Daniel Garber, F.J. Waugh, Gardner Symons and Leon Kroll. Besides the money and prestige, *Their Son* gave Berninghaus national publicity. It was reproduced in the *New York Times, The Chicago Tribune,* the *St. Louis Post-Dispatch, Los Angeles Times* and perhaps a dozen or so papers in other parts of the United States. Under the terms of the Ranger Fund and the Council of the National Academy of Design, *Their Son* was given to the Art Club of Erie, Pennsylvania. It hung there for many years, but is presently in a private collection.

In *Their Son* we see a highly developed Berninghaus style—one of brighter colors, perfect linear perspective and a special handling of space and form. The child is the center of attention, giving impact to the statement of Indian family life. He is obviously proud, sitting his father's horse, even though his feet do not yet quite reach the stirrups. His mother's placement in the foreground is symbolic of her role in the love and care she has given her son. She stares, not at the boy, but to some obscure point in space, freezing her in time as a separate Madonna whose thoughts are as old as the mountains above her head.

The father, too, is a composite of the Indian male, each year carrying out the tribal customs and rituals that serve to introduce the young to adulthood. He is pleased that his son did well in the ceremony today and has rewarded him with a spell in the saddle of the white horse usually ridden only by the Chief.

Their Son is actually a still life—realistic and representative in fact, but idealistic, romantic and even poetic in concept. It demonstrates Berninghaus' deep understanding of the Taos Indians and their harmonious existence. His idealism is also an outgrowth of his concern for the Indian family in the 20th century. Will it survive the intruding Western culture—the automobile, whiskey, the government and modern industry? *Their Son* is perhaps his dream that it will flourish as it has for centuries untold.

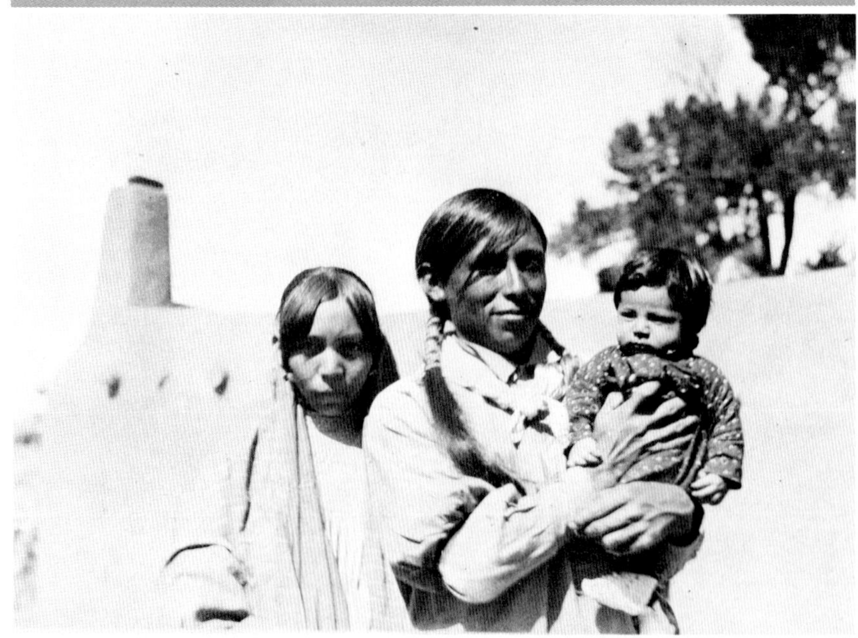

Mr. and Mrs. "Looking Elk" Martinez and "Bernie," 1915.

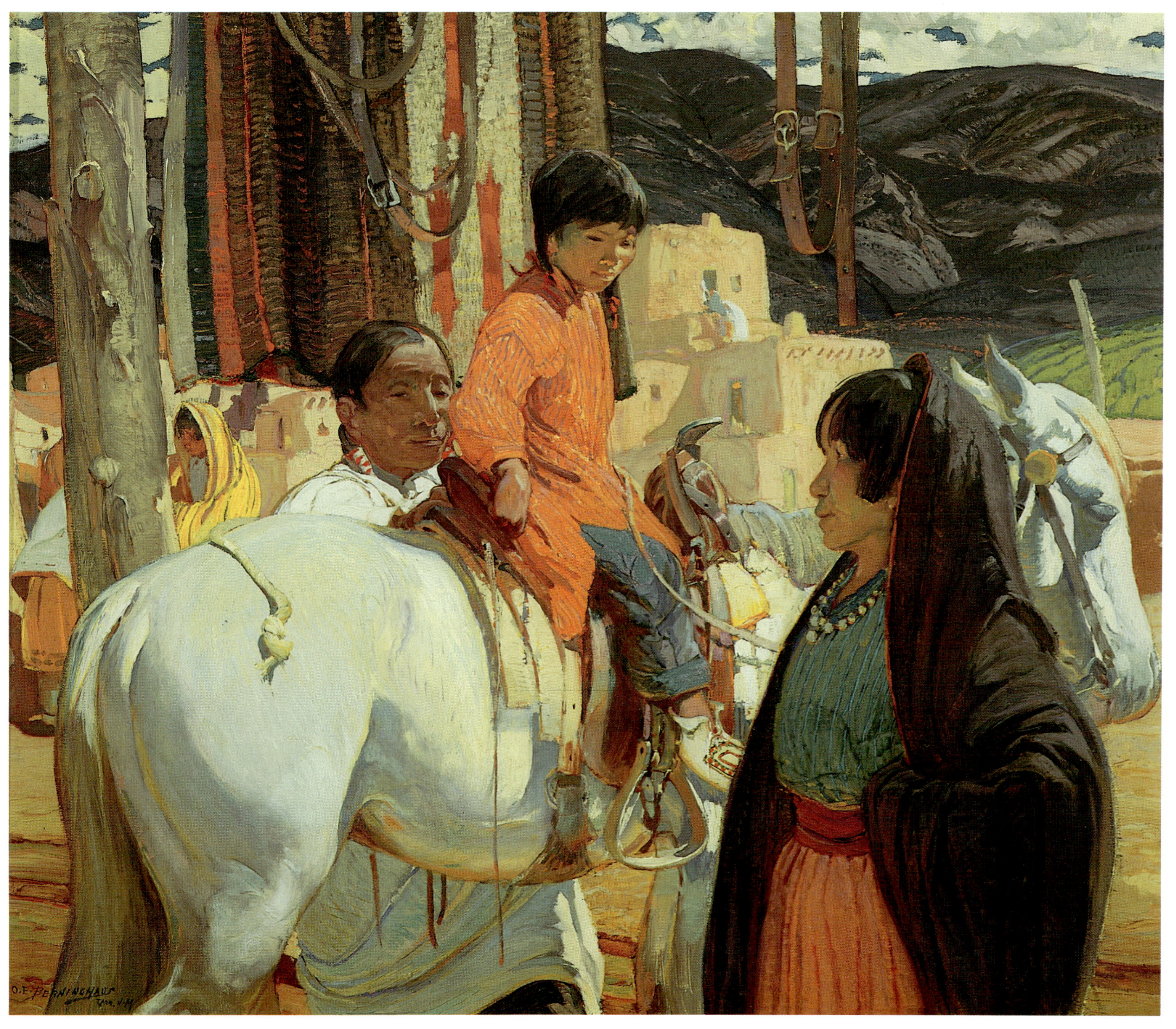

THEIR SON, 1924. 35×40 inches, oil on canvas. Private collection. Ranger Fund Purchase Prize, National Academy of Design, 1925.

The year 1925 was when Oscar Berninghaus moved permanently to New Mexico. For 25 years he had spent summers in Taos and winters in St. Louis, and now at the age of 51, and with a great deal of success and recognition to his credit, it would be good to settle in with time to really study the Taos Indians. He would also be able to experience Taos in the winter and early spring. In no way did he feel the move to Taos was an attempt to slow down or to rest on his past accomplishments. For Berninghaus it was in fact the opportunity he had dreamed of for years—to be a totally independent artist with a ready market for everything he could turn out. He, along with the other members of the Taos Society of Artists, was developing a truly American art.

The Society itself had outlived its usefulness in many respects as all ten men had by now achieved independent fame. During the lifetime of the Society, from 1915 to 1927, the Taos group had produced a great wealth of prize-winning art, i.e.: *My Children*, 1922, by W. Herbert Dunton; *The Plasterer*, 1925, by Ernest Blumenschein; *The Goatherder*, 1925, by E. Martin Hennings; *Girl with Parrot*, 1920, by Victor Higgins; *Hunger*, 1920, by Walter Ufer; *Three Musicians of the Baile*, 1920, by Bert Phillips; *Prayer to the Spirit of the Buffalo*, 1920, by Joseph Sharp and *The Lesson*, 1923, by Eanger Irving Couse. Later Kenneth Adams would contribute *Dry Ditch*, and Berninghaus, in addition to *Their Son*, a number of outstanding canvases.

The artists were competitive with each other, and yet strangely unified in their overall effort. On occasion they would invite criticism which provided a flow of creativeness among members of the group. Life was not totally serious, however—they all had a pretty good sense of humor—and luckily so, it would seem. While Berninghaus was working on *Peace and Plenty*, he took the time to caricature Walter Ufer and his fiery approach to the canvas.

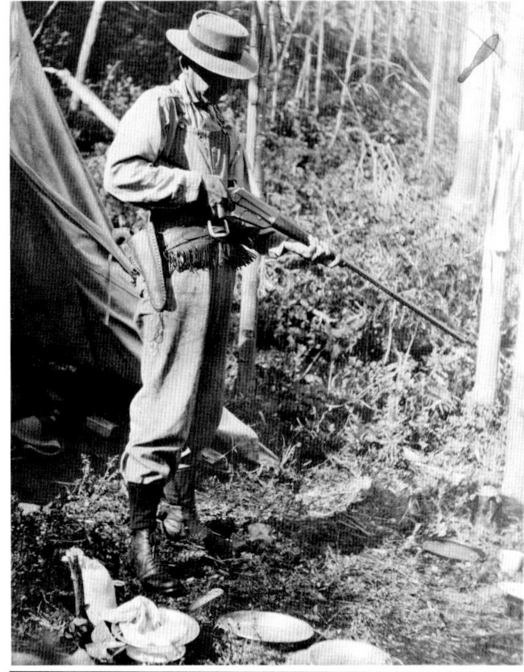

O.E. Berninghaus on camping trip on the Rio Lucero, 1914.

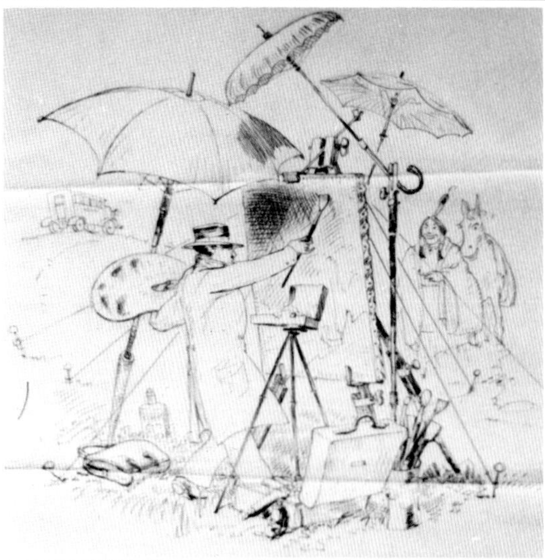

Caricature of Walter Ufer, c. 1925.

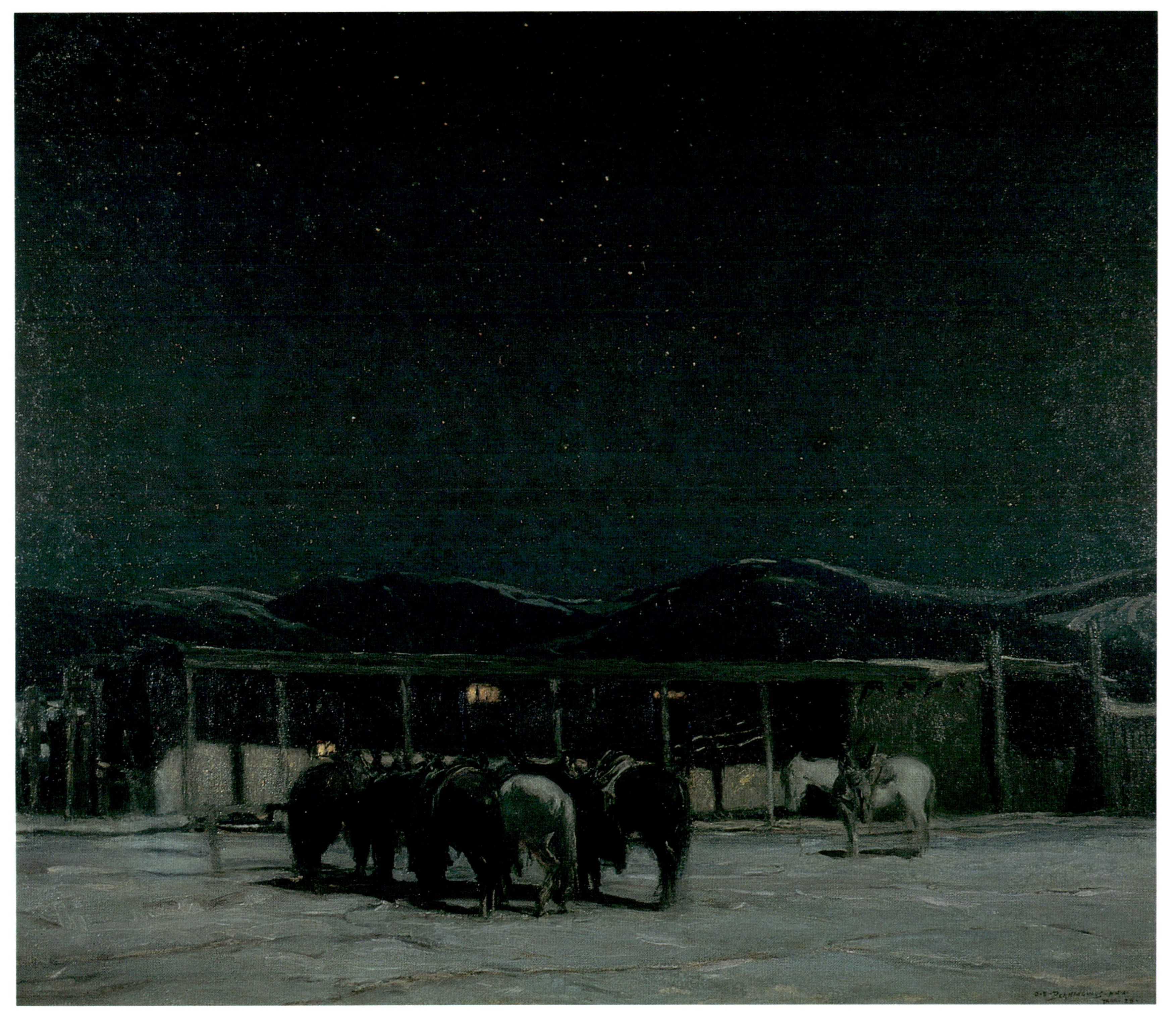

WINTER NIGHT, TAOS, 1928. 34¾ x 40 inches, oil on canvas. Courtesy of Philbrook Art Center, Tulsa, Oklahoma.

Peace and Plenty is a Berninghaus masterpiece. The colors, the concept, structure and balance are all woven into a veritable poem of Indian life. The harvest of corn and pumpkins has been good, and will sustain life through the long, cold winter ahead. The old man shows contentment and wisdom. The feather he still wears is a symbol of his earlier life as a brave, but now with age he is more inclined to the prudence of peace and plenty of this autumn. The young woman, perhaps his daughter, holds a woven cornucopia and sits below the crucifix of Christianity brought to the Taos area in the 1600s by the Spaniards. On the wall, the old man's war bonnet—now only a remembrance of past warlike days when the Pueblo defended itself against raiding tribes from the West, and from the Spanish during the various Pueblo revolts of the 17th and 18th centuries.

Peace and Plenty was painted in 1925, and clearly shows Berninghaus as a mature but still developing artist. The incredible mood of the canvas lends dignity and serenity to the Indian people. His brushwork is almost flawless, and his mastery of the Indian countenance approaches genius. Representative art here is carried to its fullest without sacrificing detail and focus for the more impressionistic emphasis of diffused feeling. The painting is clear—total in its message—yet majestic. It also demonstrates the Berninghaus perception that the American Indian was in fact an equal, not the bloodthirsty savage portrayed by earlier American painters. Fading into the past was Custer's Last Stand, the Battle of Little Big Horn, Crazy Horse, Geronimo and Sitting Bull. The Indian was coming into a different spotlight; scholars were beginning to study the native American, investigating the Pueblos, and writing papers on the customs and rituals of the Pueblo Indians up and down the Rio Grande. Many of the Taos Pueblo Indians held jobs off the reservation, Indian children attended public schools and many modern ways were adopted. Electric lights, the automobile and the white man's medicine were filtering into their lives, but the old men and women of the Pueblo continued to teach the old ways—tried and true wisdom that had sustained their way of life for more than 800 years. Even today, the spring planting and fall harvest are celebrated with colorful ritual. *Peace and Plenty* captures this Indian tribute to the abundance of nature.

This work, purchased by the St. Louis Art Museum, was the front page color cover of the magazine section of the *St. Louis Post-Dispatch* on Sunday, February 13, 1927—quite a printing feat and a fitting compliment to the artist, Oscar Berninghaus.

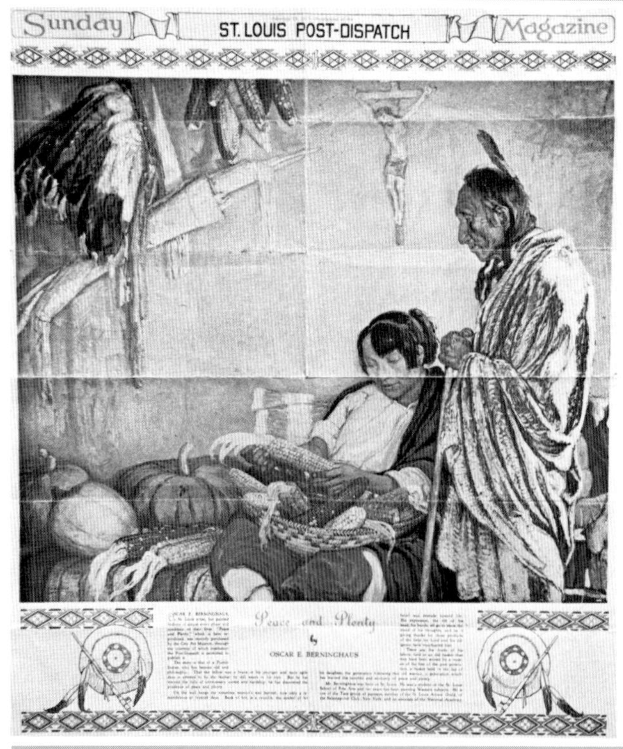

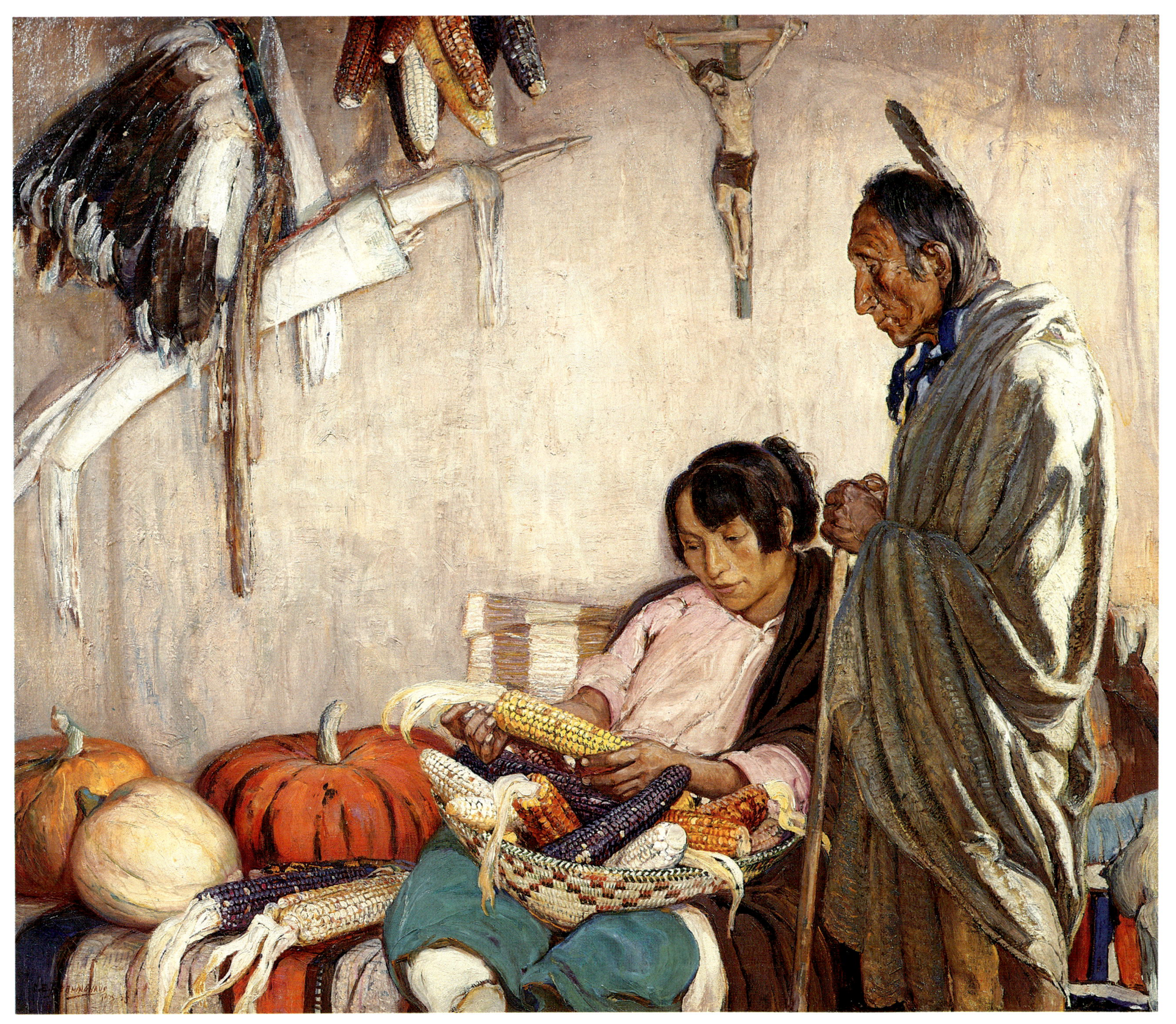

PEACE AND PLENTY, 1925. 35 x 39½ inches, oil on canvas. Courtesy of Saint Louis Art Museum, St. Louis, Missouri.

In 1926 Oscar Berninghaus became an Associate of the National Academy of Design in New York, an honor he received almost in spite of himself. Emily Hutchings, the St. Louis art critic, tells this story about Berninghaus and the award: "It might have been bestowed two years ago if the artist had permitted his friends to pull a few wires. Last year a single word of recommendation would have done the trick. Among the Taos painters, there was the consensus of opinion that this particular A.N.A. was due last year. When William Bixby, Dr. John Pickard and Arthur Kocian were in New York they could have voiced the sentiment not only of Taos, but of Missouri. Such things are commonly done. This is the most legitimate of wire pulling. But those men went East with their hands and tongues tied. Oscar Berninghaus had exacted of them a promise that they would put forth no effort whatever in his behalf." "If I ever get the A.N.A.," Berninghaus declared, "I want it to come spontaneously. It has to come because of my work, not because of my friends."

There is an irony in this story for it appears that years later he was never made a full academician because of some wire pulling by a certain Taos artist. However, we find no printed complaint about the matter from Berninghaus, who was true to his live and let live nature.

The National Academy of Design awarded Berninghaus the second Altman Prize in 1926 for *A Hunter of Taos Pueblo*. This prize carried with it a cash award of $500. The painting is in the collection of the Cranbrook School in Bloomfield Hills, Michigan, and is a great tribute to the style and skill of the artist, and a truthful statement of the American Indian.

Berninghaus painted the Indians in harmonious settings and in real life contemporary scenes. In *A Hunter of Taos Pueblo* we view the subject as he appeared in the past, not the ancient past, as indicated by the presence of horses brought to America by the Spaniards, but the immediate past, a time when game was plentiful and served as the mainstay of the food supply for the Pueblo. The hunter is proud, for he is known as a provider, bringing home deer, turkey, elk, rabbit and bear.

Aside from the perfect balance of form, the picture is a fine example of Berninghaus's draftsmanship and his understanding of not only linear perspective, but also of atmospheric perspective, with the diminution of sharp detail in the background of horses, Indians and foliage. This is a truly American work of art, both in concept and execution.

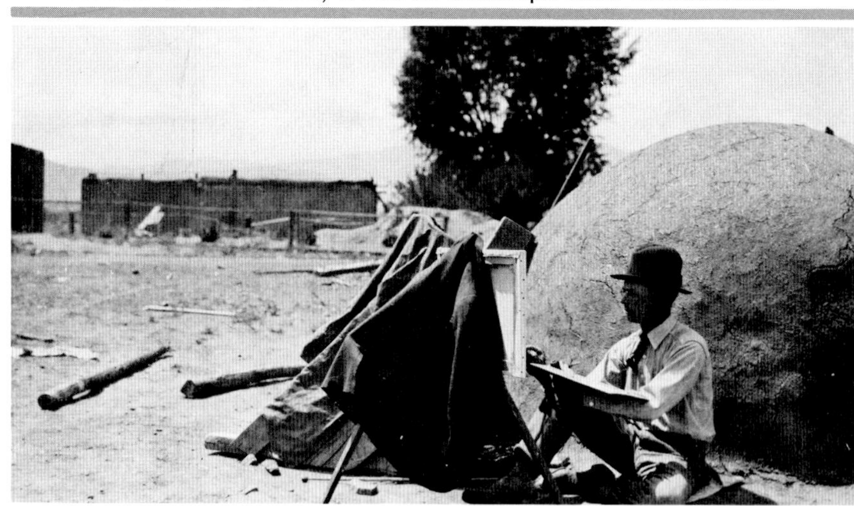

Oscar Berninghaus painting near Indian "horno."

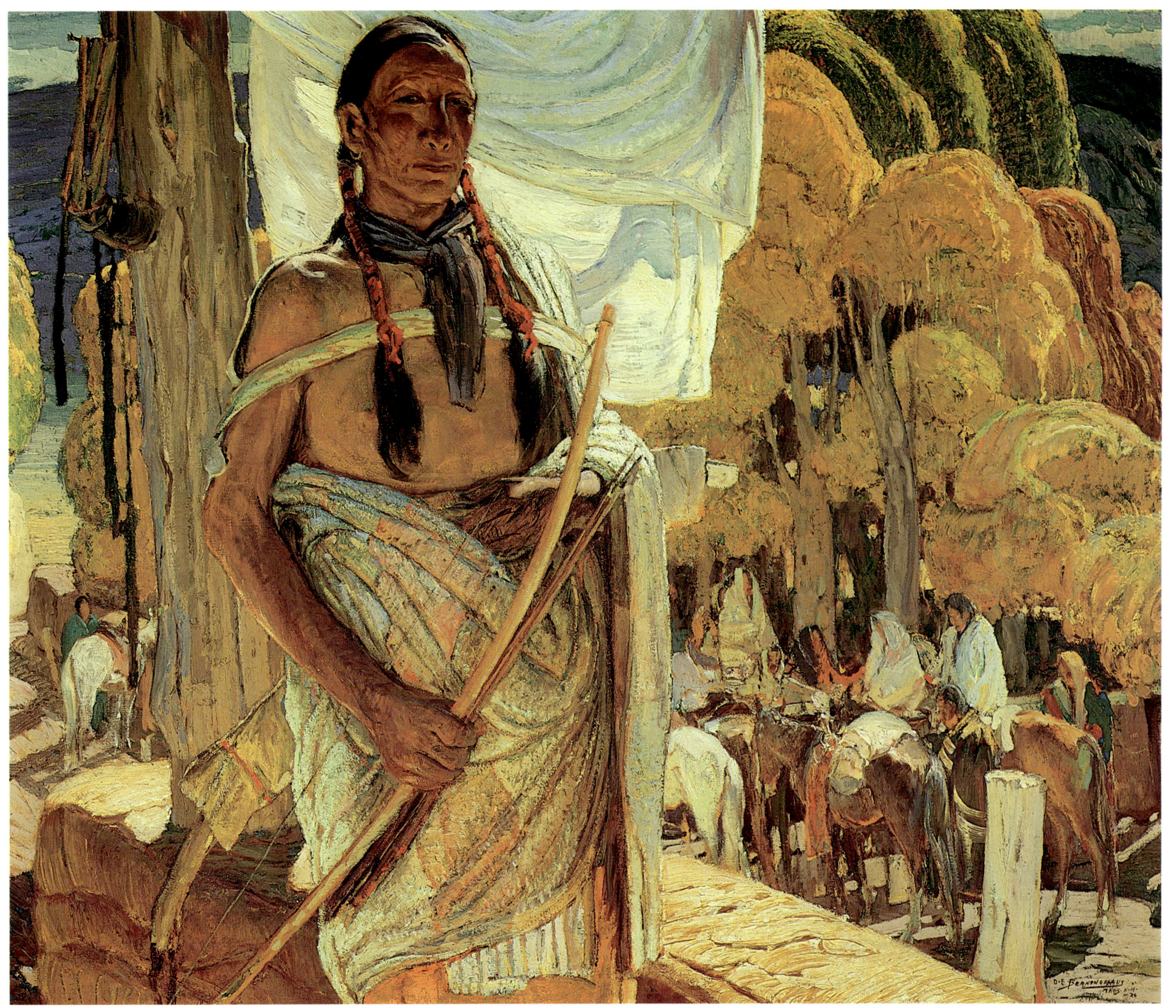

A HUNTER OF TAOS PUEBLO. 35×40 inches, oil on canvas. Altman Prize, National Academy of Design.
Collection of Cranbrook School, Bloomfield Hills, Michigan.

Living in Taos during the late 1920s was a unique experience not found anywhere else in the modern world. For most of the residents, life was primitive by comparison to other American communities. Houses were made of adobe with three-foot-thick walls to keep the heat out in the summer and the warmth in during the sub-zero winter storms. Wood-burning fireplaces, oil lamps, water wells, unpaved streets and outhouses all created an atmosphere of hardship. To the north was the ancient Pueblo and its Indians, a totally separate culture older than time. It was like living in two ages at the same time. In one culture, there were dinner parties and talk of the world situation—economics, art, music and literature—a potpourri of wit and humor. The other culture was a step back in time—a time of hunting with bow and arrow, buffalo and corn dances, and colorful ceremonies offering tribute to the rain and sun and nature's abundance.

It was in this tiny world of contrasts during the 1920s that Oscar Berninghaus did some of his finest work. He would admonish his students to "understand the mystery and learn the secret of paint—paint, the pigment. Too many try for an effect without first learning the underlying principles which produce the effect. The technique of the old masters is lost in their art. They had a deep feeling for and understanding of their craft." *Her Grandfather* demonstrates that Berninghaus not only had a deep and understanding love for his subject, but also his own craft.

Her Grandfather received rave reviews in a number of

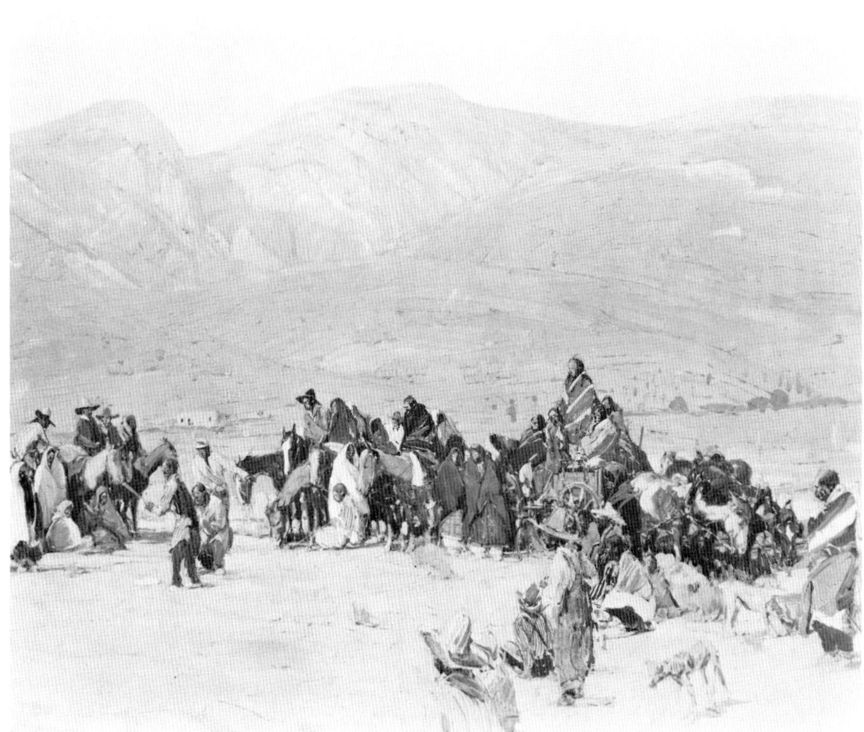

THE BASEBALL GAME, c. 1930. 25×30 inches. Private collection.

leading art publications, including the *San Francisco Chronicle* in 1928 while the picture was on exhibit in the California Palace of the Legion of Honor. On November 11, 1928, that paper had *Her Grandfather* reproduced on the cover of the art section, and a complimentary article about the artist.

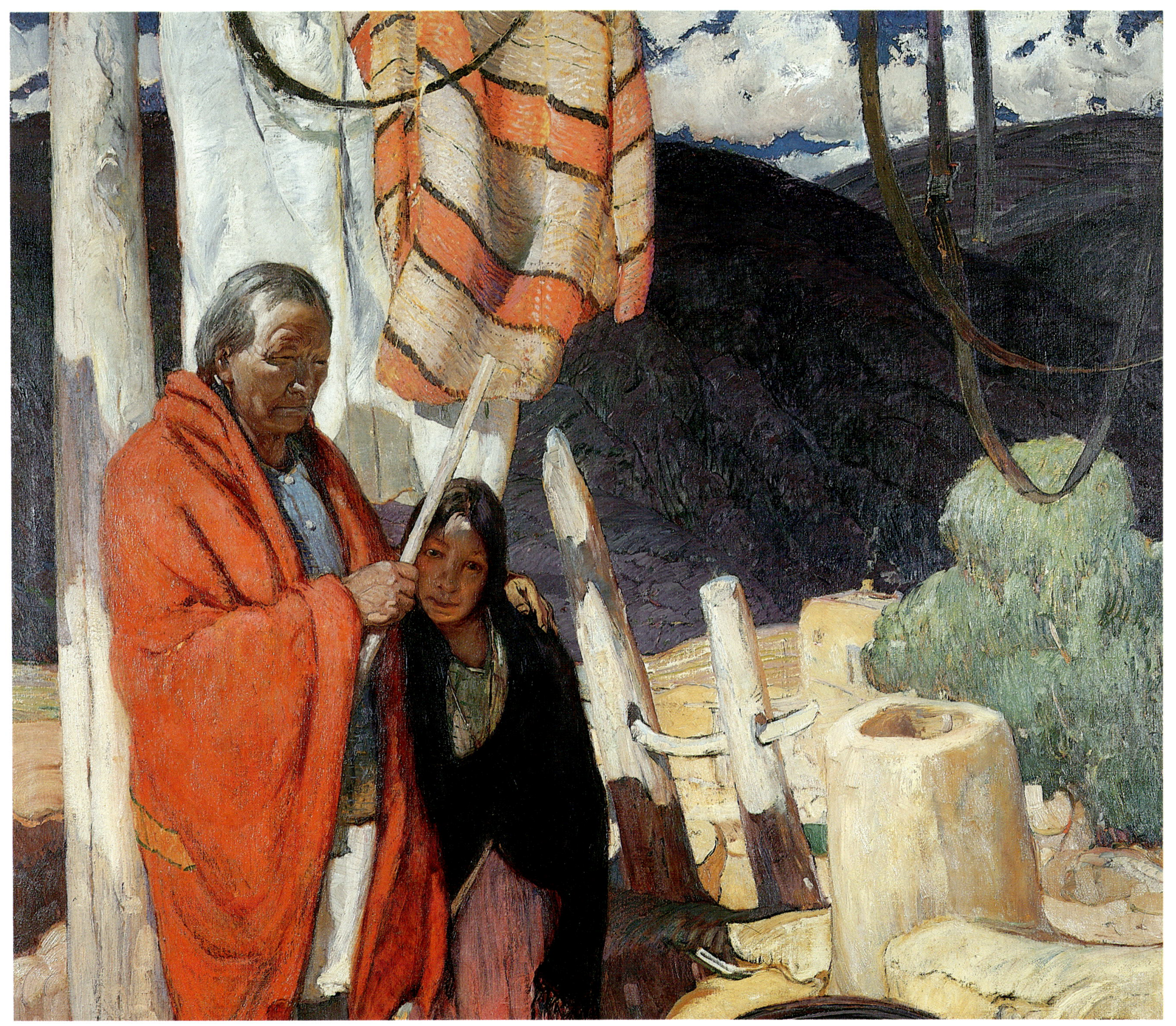

HER GRANDFATHER, c. 1925. 45×50 inches, oil on canvas. Private collection. Photo courtesy of Rosenstock Arts, Denver, Colorado.

Though the Taos artists took their work very seriously, it was not all work and no play during the late 1920s. Among the artists and writers and other assorted professionals, there was time for living, fishing and hunting trips to the mountains, and social gatherings at the brand new Don Fernando Hotel on Taos Plaza.

One of the events of that time affected Berninghaus personally. On August 27, 1927, his daughter, Dorothy, married Oklahoma businessman John Peter Brandenburg. The two had met in the summer of 1925 when Brandenburg and his family were vacationing in Taos. His family had bought a home in Taos in 1923 and came back each summer to escape the hot weather and humidity of the Sooner State. The marriage took place in Santa Fe, and Jack vividly remembers a conversation he had with his future father-in-law. "Jack," Berninghaus said, "are you sure you want to go through with this?" Jack replied that he certainly did, and with that Berninghaus looked over his spectacles, and with a twinkle in his eye said: "Good, but just remember that when you get to the end of that aisle, you're a dead duck!" The wedding went on.

Today, almost 60 years later, Jack is still a "dead duck." He and Dorothy still live in Taos, are still happily married and have a daughter, granddaughters and great-grandchildren living nearby.

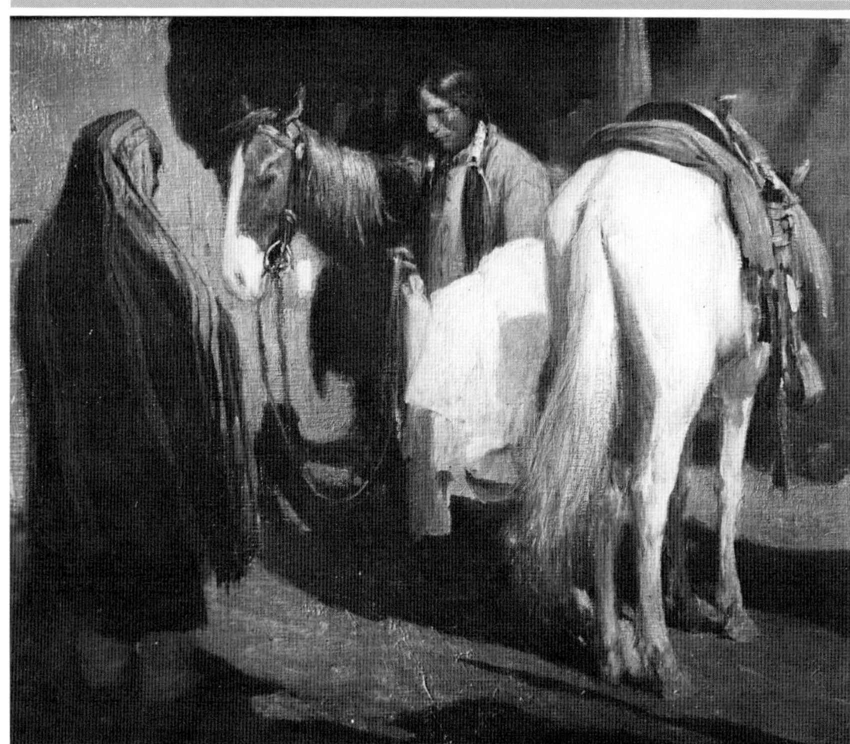

INDIAN COURTSHIP, 1918. Oil. Private collection.

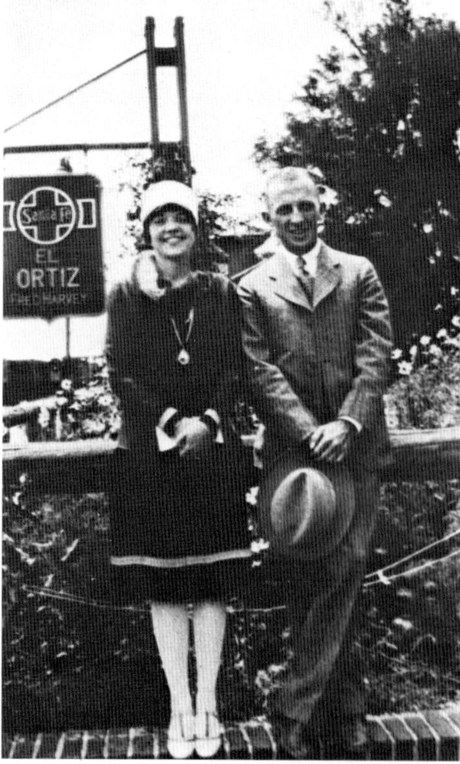

Dorothy and Jack Brandenburg on their wedding day, August 27, 1927.

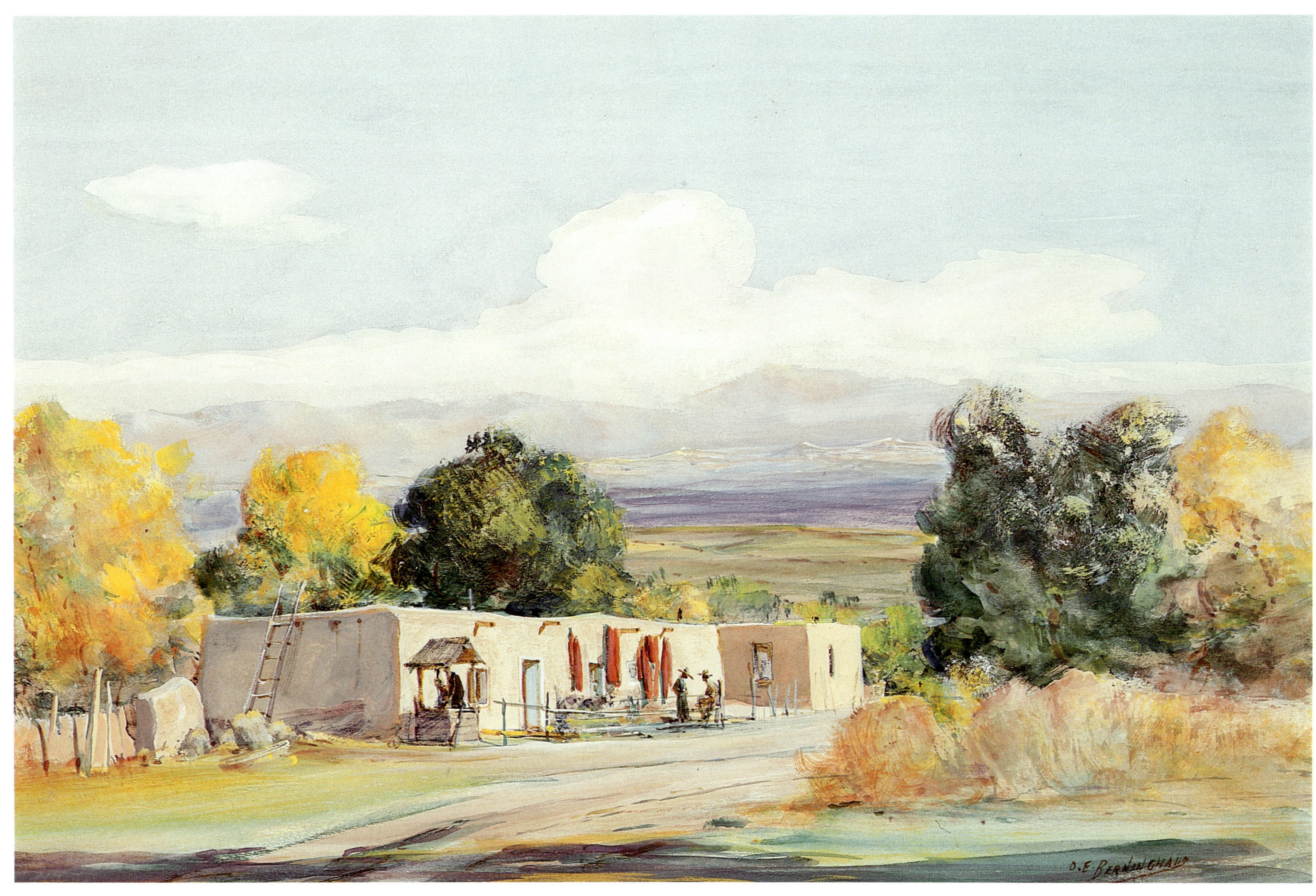

CHILI TIME, NEW MEXICO, c. 1930. 12×18 inches, watercolor. Private collection.

The Taos Society of Artists disbanded in March of 1927, and although there are no records of the meeting, it is believed the main reason was lack of sales, and to some extent lack of interest. The last recorded meeting was July 12, 1926, and the minutes indicate a concern about lagging sales. Present at the meeting were newly elected members Kenneth Adams, Oscar Berninghaus, Irving Couse, Victor Higgins, Joseph Sharp and Walter Ufer. The principal discussion was in regard to placing future exhibitions where there could be a guarantee of at least one sale by each member. They also discussed the fact that some of the member's dues were in arrears as far back as 1924. There had been complaints from art dealers about the price and size of the canvases the society had been shipping. A report made to the society of Joseph Sharp sheds some light on the problems which had started as early as 1923: "If sales are desired, I would advise new pictures, modest in size and price, attractively framed, with a light shadow or protection box of same color as frame. This simplifies packing and handling and saves your frames." In another part of the report he states: "if you want to start from the East again you will have to put up the very strongest exhibition the society is capable of, and of an original character or the critics will turn you down." Sharp concluded his report with this observation: "It is well worth while to go on, even if in the end you must pay something more, for I'm sure you have all felt the indirect value of the immense publicity the society has received. The only trouble is we've got to get out and hustle to make things go."

In spite of all the pep talks, the simple fact was that the Taos Society of Artists had outlived its usefulness. In 1915, it had propelled the tiny New Mexican village into the spotlight of international art. But now, with many of its members getting older and able to sell their art independently, it was quietly disbanded. This is not to say that Taos or its artists

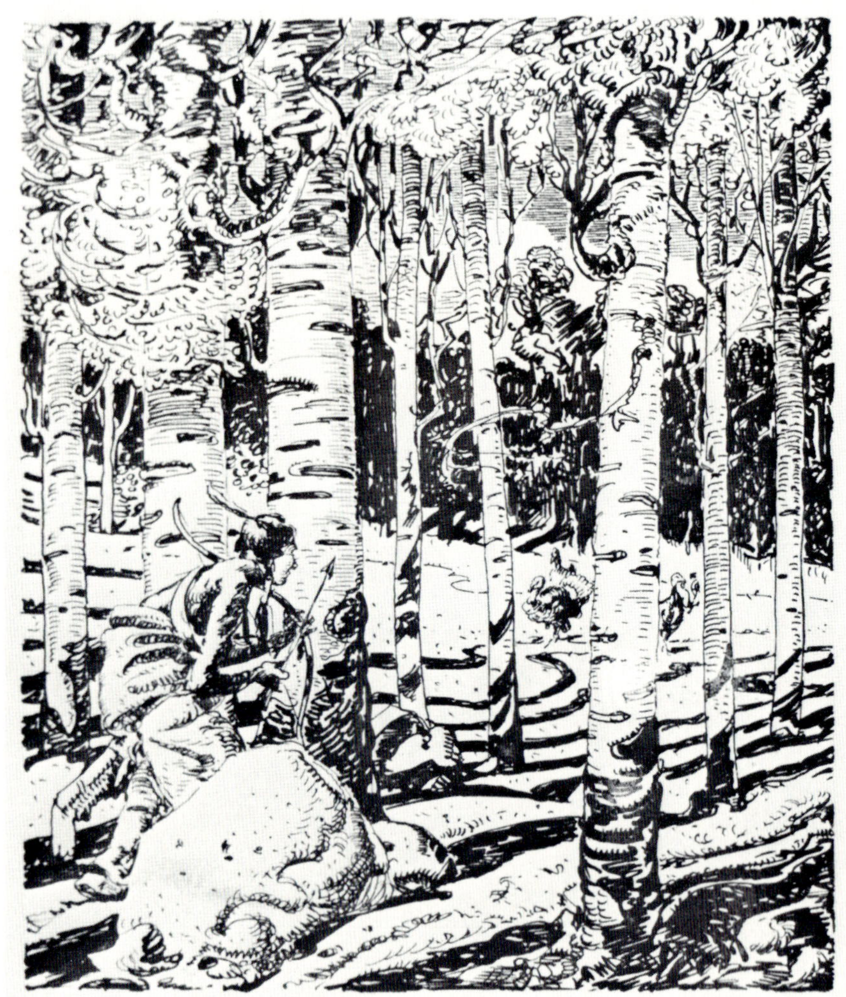

TURKEY HUNT. Pen and ink.

had experienced a decline—quite to the contrary. Taos became an even more renowned art center, as it is today, and all the original members of the society achieved greater fame in the years to come.

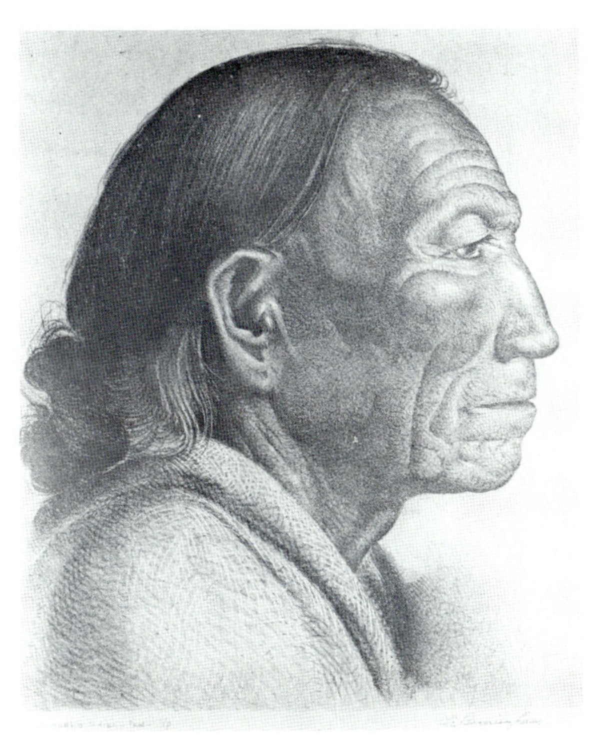

OLD PUEBLO INDIAN–TAOS, c. 1930.
10×8 inches, lithograph.
Private collection.

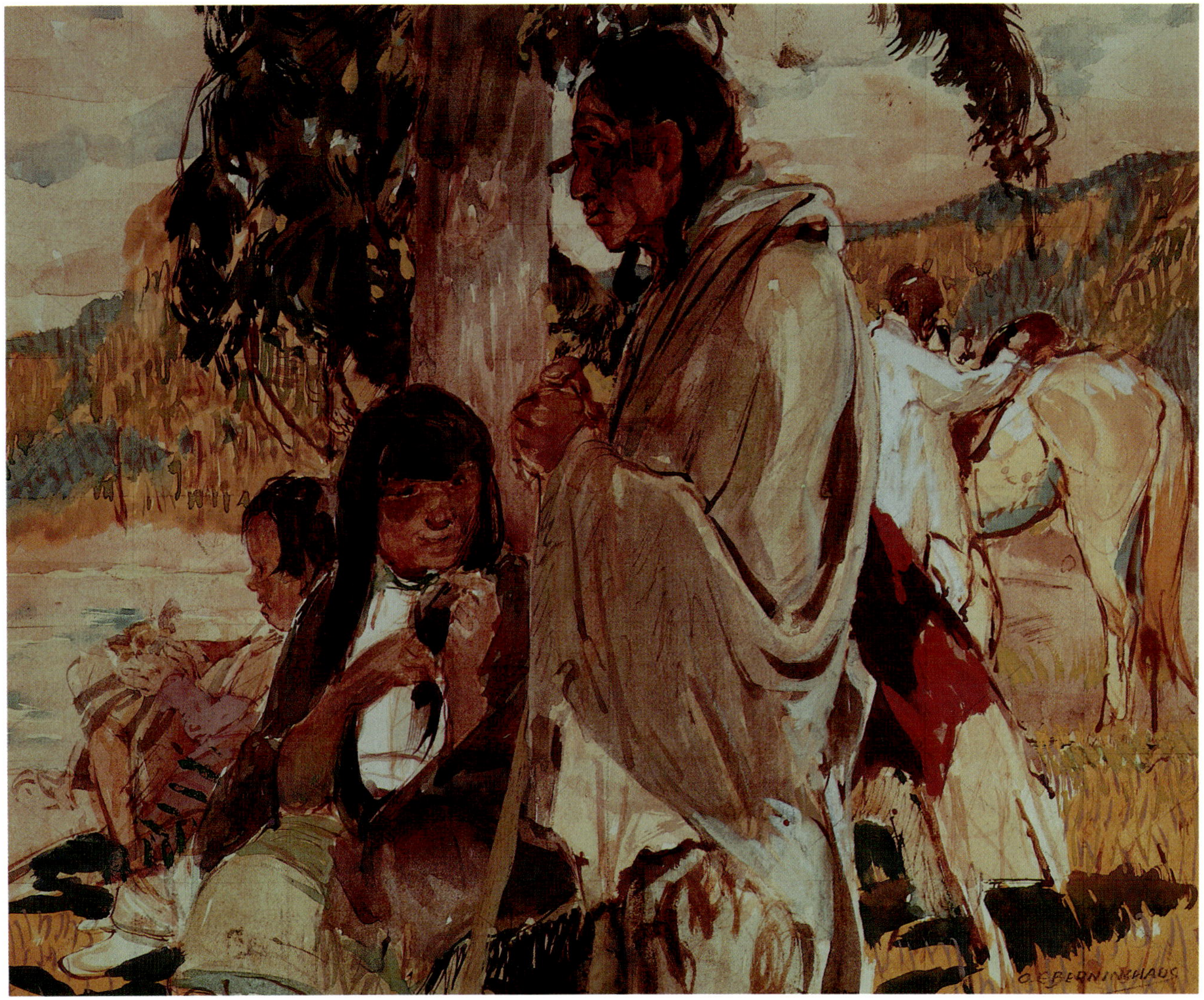

LAZY DAY, 1928.
10×12 inches, watercolor.
Courtesy of Galleries Maurice Sternberg, Chicago, Illinois.

The Taos Pueblo Indians prided themselves on being good hunters—it was a way of life, and it had supported them for centuries. Originally they hunted the great buffalo herds to the east, an area now known as the Texas Panhandle. Forty or fifty braves would make the journey each year and bring back hundreds of pounds of jerky (dried meat) for the residents of the Pueblo. However, by the late 1880s the white man had decimated the herds to provide meat for the railroad camps, and the buffalo hunts were over. It was a shameful slaughter as the hunters kept only the buffalo hump, the hide, and the tongue, leaving the rest of the carcass to rot on the plains. By the turn of the century, the only part the buffalo played in the Indian's life was a symbolic one in the annual "buffalo dance."

By the 1920s and 1930s the Indians hunted deer, turkey, bear and antelope, but the search for wild game was no longer the romantic adventure of days gone by. The "hunt" was still celebrated, however, in the deer and buffalo dances and other colorful rituals. These dances are actually Indian prayers from the days when Indians and animals spoke the same language . . . days long ago when the deer told the Indian how to perform the ceremony to gain power over him so that he might take the deer's flesh for food and his skin for clothing. For many years the Indians would allow no outsiders to view their dances for fear the strangers would destroy the effectiveness of the ceremony. In the 1920s, with government programs and other sources for their food supply now available, they began to welcome others to witness their colorful dances.

The Indians have preserved their hunting skills in the rabbit hunts, which usually take place on the day preceding major ceremonials. These hunts were favorite subjects for Berninghaus, and he has left us a wealth of canvases depicting this Indian custom.

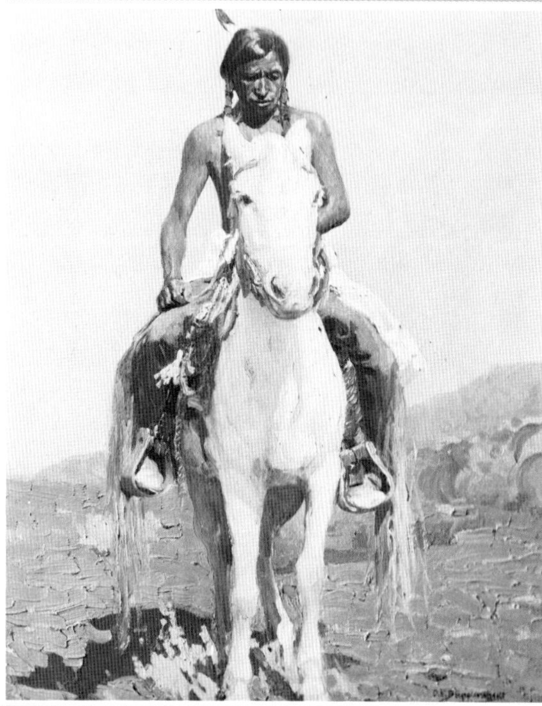

A SON OF THE WAR CHIEF. Unlocated. Photo from artist's file.

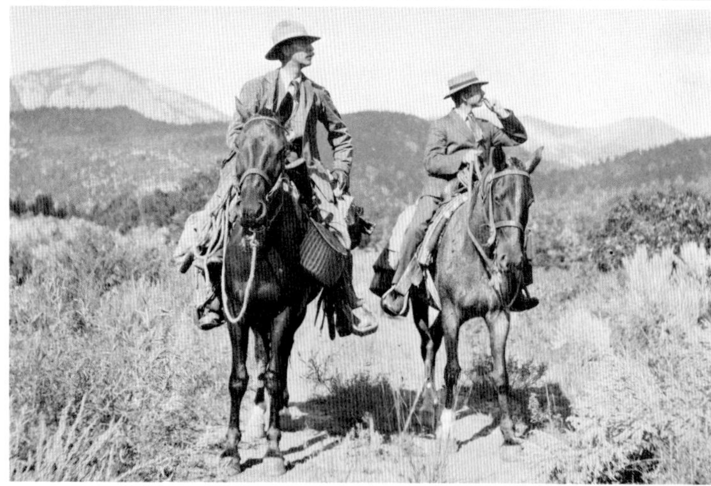

Berninghaus and Dunton.

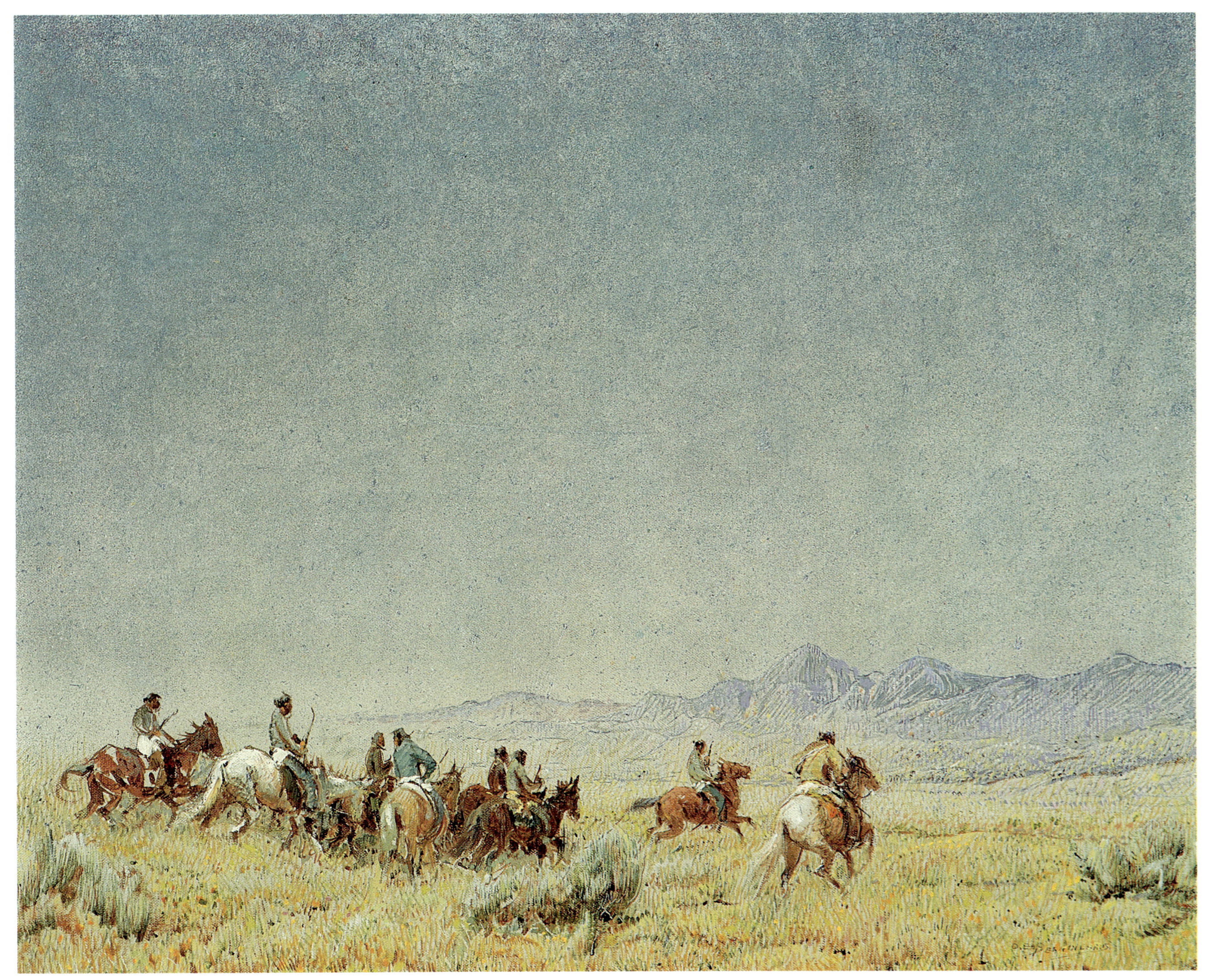

RABBIT HUNT, *TAOS INDIANS*, c. 1945. 20×24 inches, oil on canvas. Private collection.

The rabbit hunt gave Oscar Berninghaus the perfect opportunity to work with his favorite subject: Indians, their ponies and the Taos landscape. In a letter to R.H. Conklin, an art dealer in Aurora, Illinois, Berninghaus gives this colorful description of the hunt: "From my studio window I have a view of some 30 miles across sagebrush, foothills, with the horizon lined with distant mountain ranges. Every now and then I see clouds of dust blown skyward by whirlwinds—this is a common sight these warm and dry days. Looking out now, I see one and it comes nearer and nearer. It is not caused by the wind, but as it approaches I see that it is a band of horsemen, a hunting party of Indians out on the ceremonial rabbit hunt—a hunt which takes place the day before each fiesta dance day. These rabbits are hunted with the aid of bows and arrows, clubs and dogs—no firearms are used, such is their reverence for the days when their forefathers had only such means of procuring their daily food. The band comes on, full speed past my studio, gives a cheerful yell—all mounted on their ponies, some white, some pintos, some buckskins, helping to make the sight colorful, picturesque and animated."

In the same letter, Berninghaus wrote about the actual posing and painting of these scenes: "The Indian models have quickly learned to know the style and character of pose desired. I have but to indicate a desire or wish as to how I want my horses arranged and posed for the composition of the picture, and it is quickly understood. The horses are kept in place and brought back to almost the same pose after each rest. Often I wonder if the ponies themselves do not realize what they are being posed for, and patiently tolerate the blazing hot sun out among the rocks or sage so as to contribute their share to the success of a canvas."

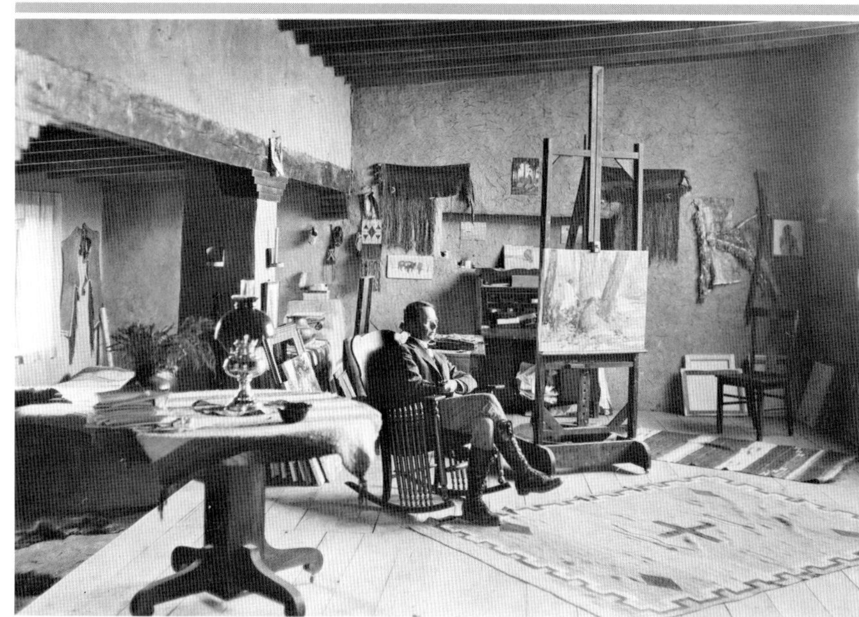
Berninghaus in studio.

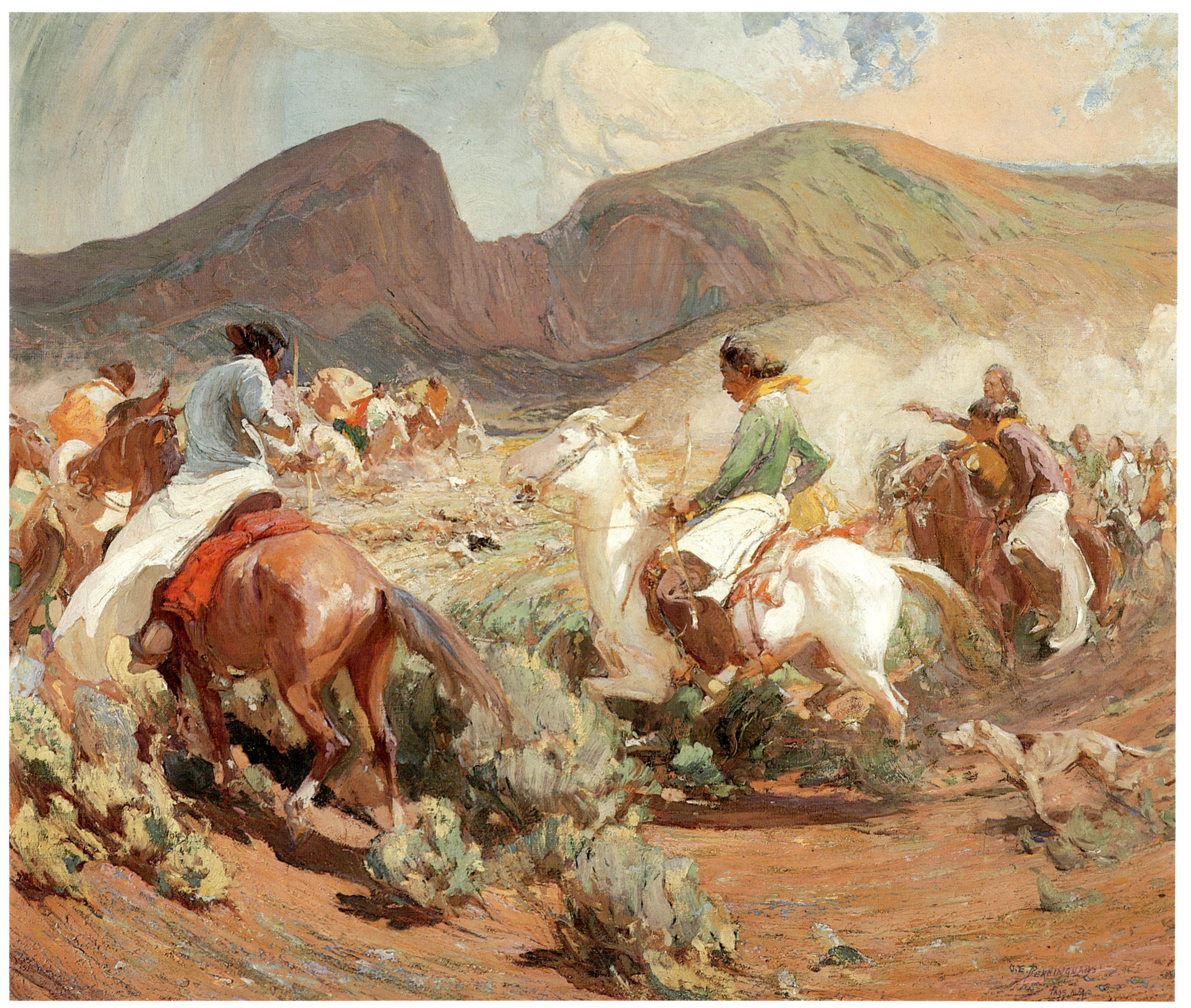

CEREMONY OF THE RABBIT HUNT, 1921. 30×40 inches, oil on canvas. Courtesy of the Museum of Western Art, Denver, Colorado.

Art critics and dealers alike consider *The Rabbit Hunter* to be one of Berninghaus' masterpieces. It is indeed a striking canvas of enormous impact. Here Berninghaus demonstrates his total control of all the elements of a fine painting—color, mass, space and line. He, himself, was evidently happy with the final outcome of the picture as it was used in a class for art students from the University of New Mexico. These students came to Taos during the summer to study with several of the local artists. This program was under the direction of Professor Lez L. Haas, then head of the UNM art department, and was so popular that students from other states were also allowed to attend. Berninghaus and the other Taos painters gave generously of their time and talent, and many young students profited from those classes.

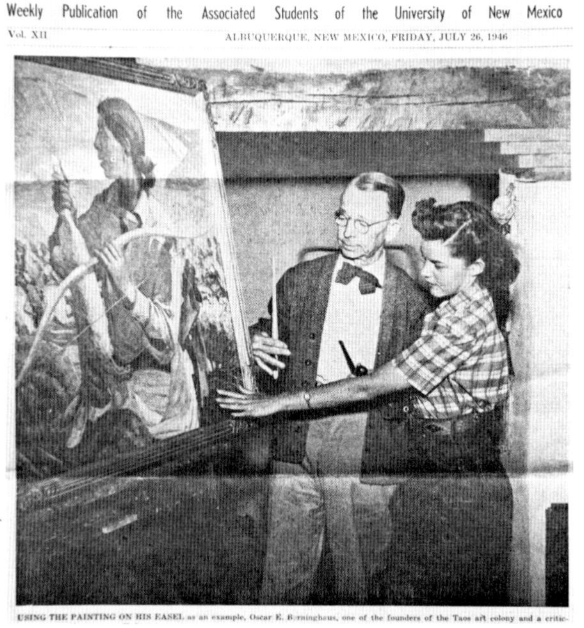

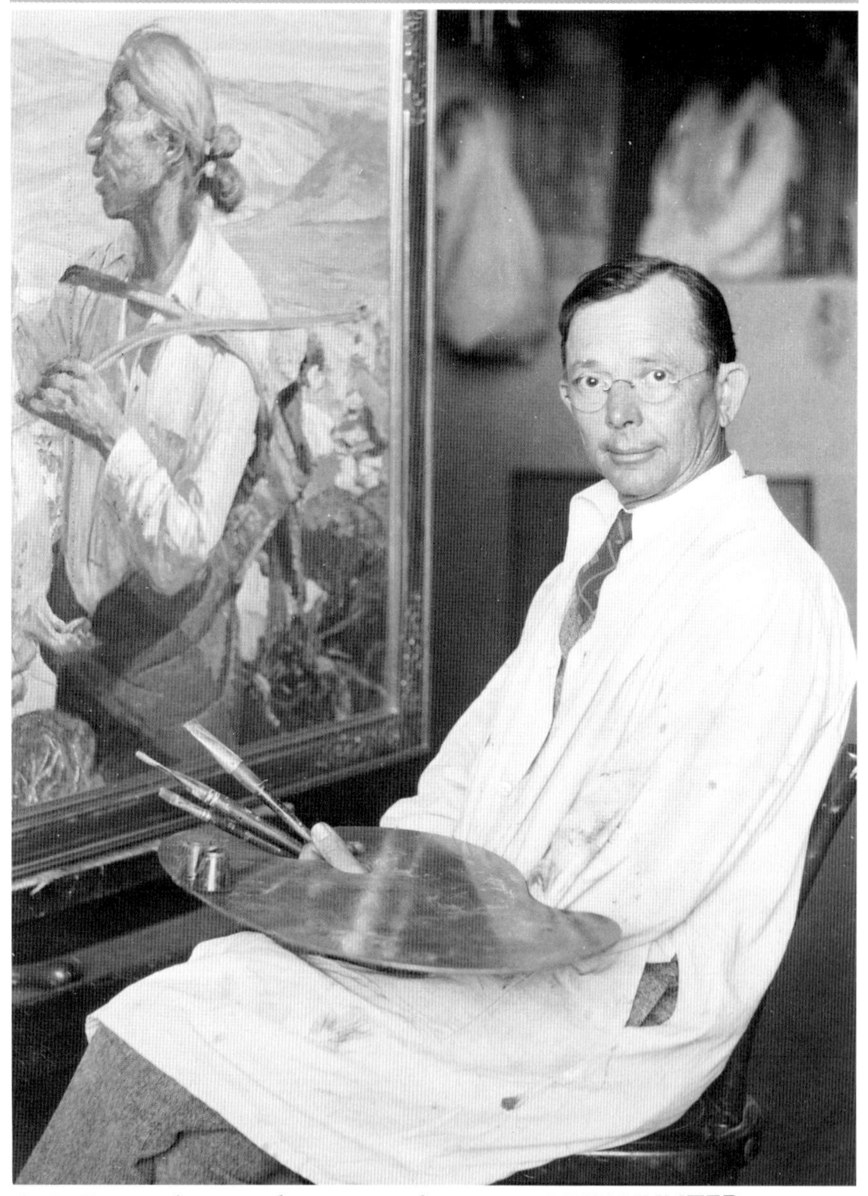
O.E. Berninghaus and painting of *THE RABBIT HUNTER*.

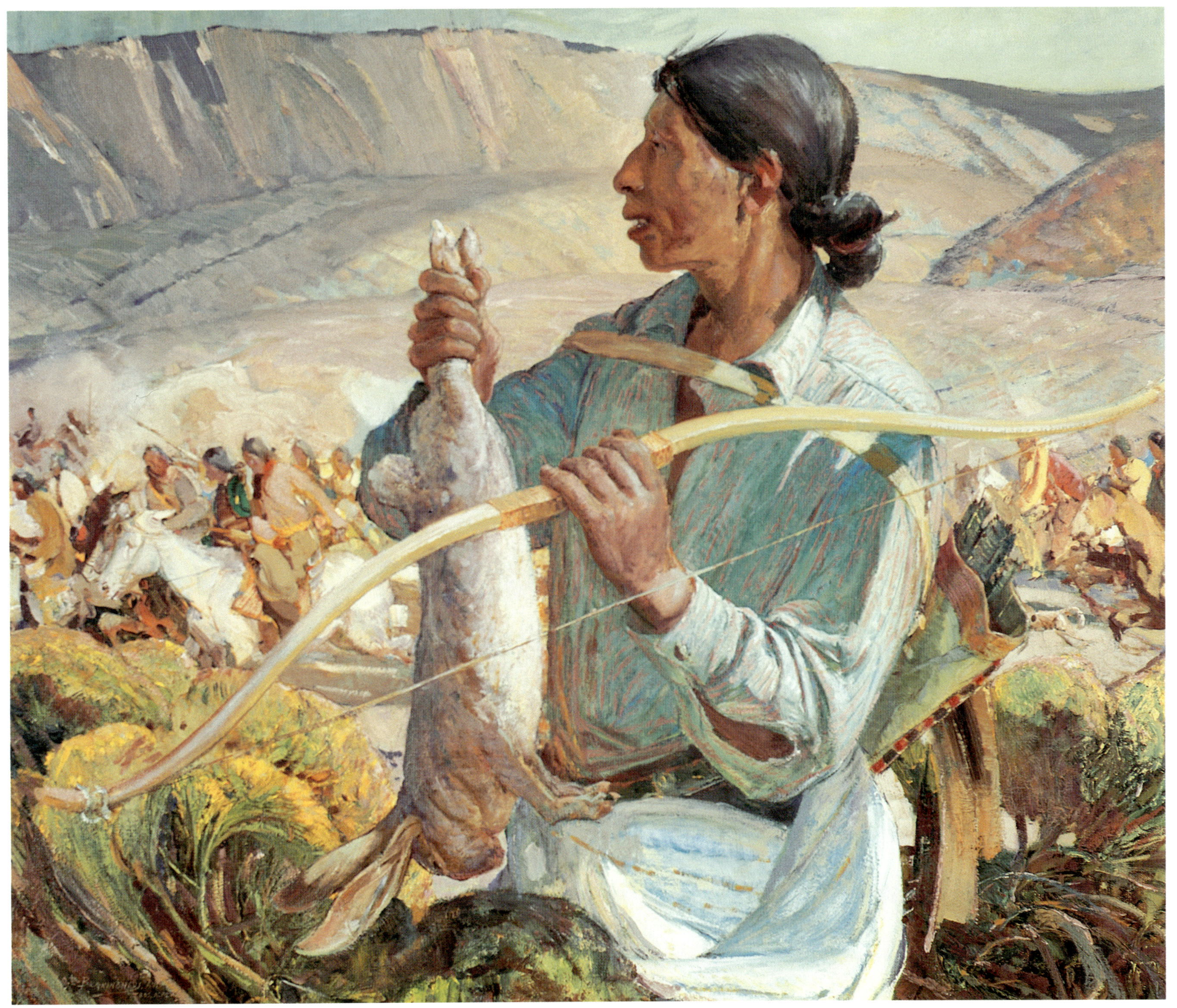

THE RABBIT HUNTER, c. 1945. 34 $^{7}/_{16}$ x 39 $^{1}/_{2}$ inches, oil on canvas. Collection of the Museum of New Mexico, Museum of Fine Arts. Gift of John A. and Margaret Hill.

Some critics expressed the opinion that the Taos painters were too objective in their work, making use of the abundant Taos exteriors, landscapes, Indians, cowboys and Hispanics, and the unbelievably colorful trees and skies, and yet ignoring the subjective element. This charge was not, for the most part, true, as they all loved Taos and had a very emotional attachment to the place and its people. The outside art world was going through a period of belief that artists should direct their thoughts more inward, and certain critics apparently thought that the Taos artists were not following the "trend." One could not possibly find this true of Oscar Berninghaus when viewing a canvas like *Too Old for the Rabbit Hunt*. Here we see the deepest possible love and compassion for his subject, the Indian. The painting cries out with pity and sadness for one left behind during a glorious event. The old man, now bent with age, seems to be saying: "Go my young braves, the lightning and thunder will protect you and bring you luck for the hunt. Now I am too old to ride with you, and would only get in the way. My body is weak, and I must stay to help the women and children with the chores. Go and ride the wind, feel the bite of the crisp mountain air against your faces. Make the kill, and tonight we will sit by the fire and taste the sweet fruit of your hunt, and tell stories of how it was in the old days—the old days when I was young and rode my white pony in the hunt next to the chief. It is good to see you clinging to the old ways—they have sustained us since the time of the great Montezuma, and they will sustain us when the great earthquake comes, and the white man shall vanish and the plains will be dark with the buffalo herds again. Do not weep for me, for even though I am old and the north wind cuts my body, I have my memories. Though my days are numbered, it still gives me pleasure just to see you ride in the hunt. But—it would also give me pleasure to ride with you just once more."

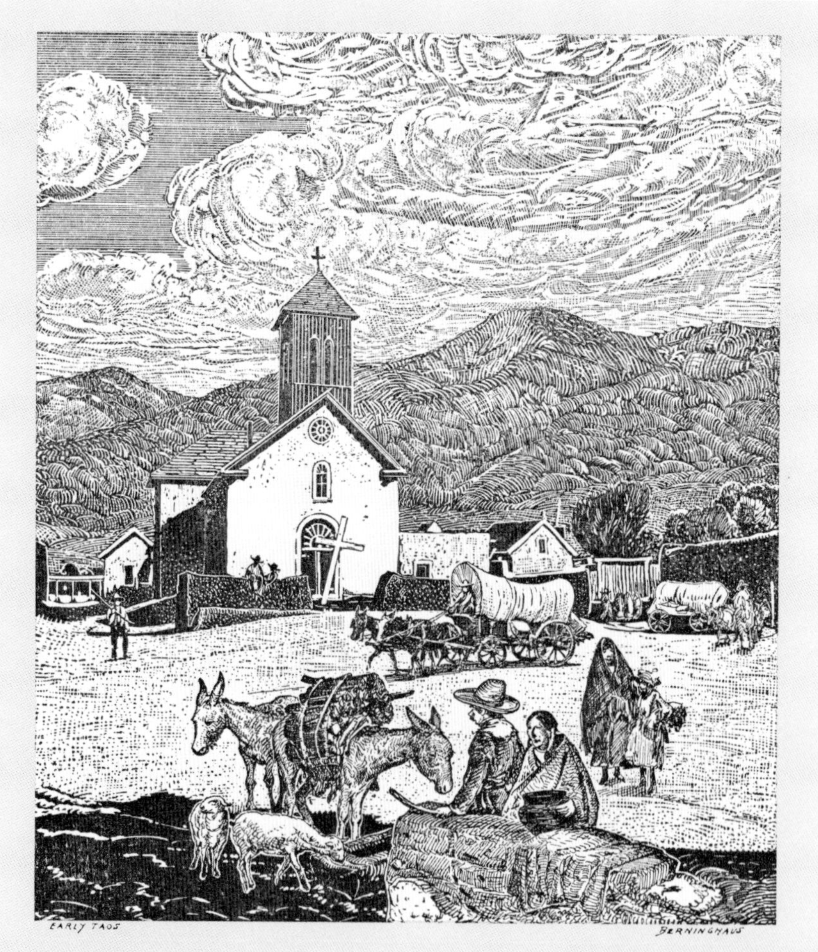

EARLY TAOS. 18×15 inches, scratchboard. Private collection.

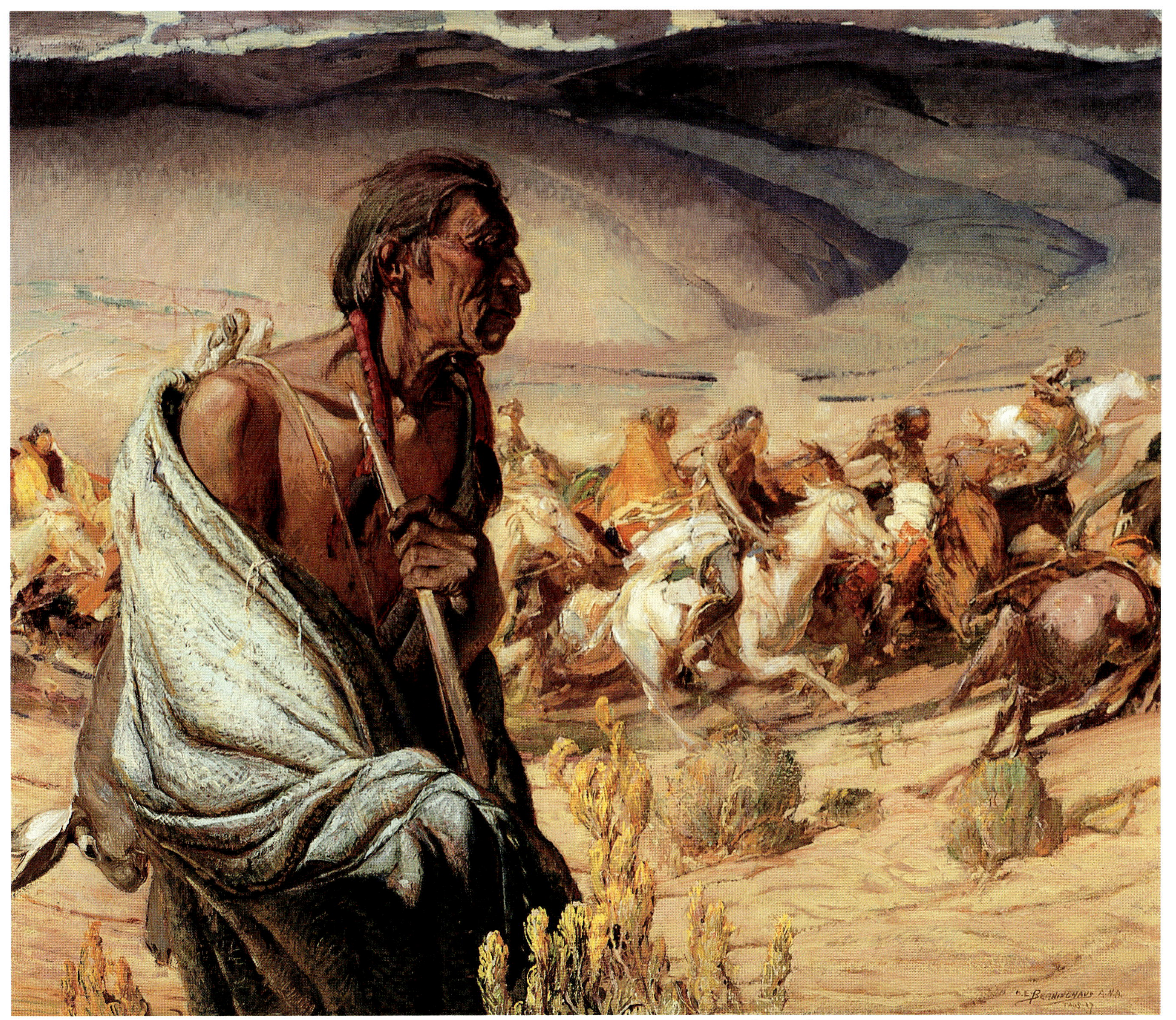

TOO OLD FOR THE RABBIT HUNT, c. 1947. 35×40 inches, oil on canvas.
Courtesy of the Thomas Gilcrease Institute of American History and Art, Tulsa, Oklahoma.

When the stock market crashed in 1929, Oscar Berninghaus was in better shape than most—he owned no stock. He also lived in Taos, where the crash and ensuing Great Depression had little effect on that primitive community. In an interview during the early 1930s, he made a reasonable observation about the hard times in Taos. "Since the native Hispanics and Indians of Taos have always lived a primitive, self-sustaining life, without knowing anything about prosperity, they are at least lucky enough not to know anything about the Depression either."

Though the outside world was in a general state of confusion, the late twenties brought some moments of personal satisfaction to Oscar Berninghaus. At the age of 55, he became a grandfather when Jack and Dorothy Brandenburg became parents of a daughter, Barbara, in August of 1929. It was also comforting to know that his son, Charles, was now making it on his own as a landscape painter. He had received a warm reception at the Noonan-Kocian Gallery in St. Louis on a number of occasions, and during his first one-man show, the *St. Louis Globe-Democrat* art critic, Emily Hutchings, had some encouraging words for Charles in her column: "Charles Berninghaus exhibited some thirty paintings and sketches, which he did this past summer and fall in Taos, New Mexico. The contrast between the work of father and son is striking and vital. No hint of imitation or parental dominance, no slavish following in the footsteps of any master. We fully expect to see Charles Berninghaus at the head of American landscape painters by the time he is 30. When success comes to him, it will be due in large measure to the wisdom of a highly successful father who permitted him to develop his own distinct lines."

A sense of humor was important during the 1930s, and it was no less important to the citizenry of Taos. The artists loved poking fun at each other, and Berninghaus created some entertaining caricatures of his contemporaries for Spud Johnson's "Horse Fly" articles in the local newspaper.

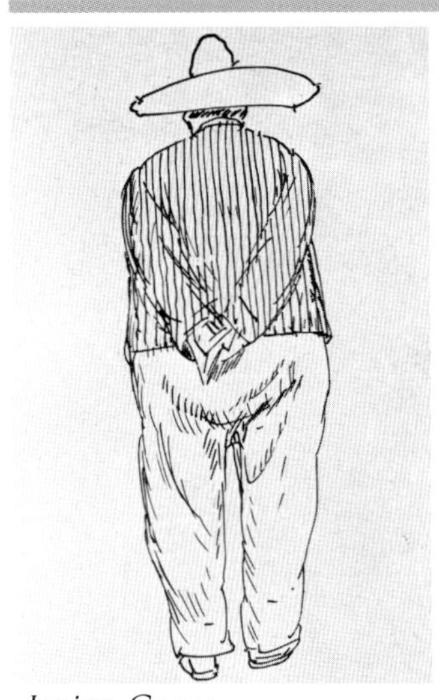

Irving Couse

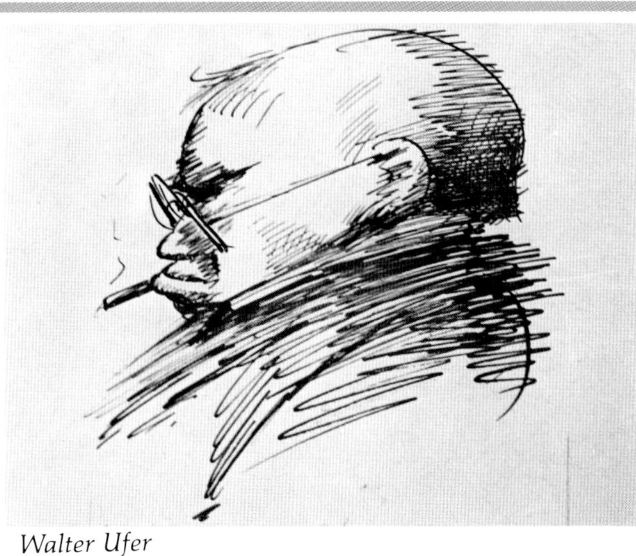

Walter Ufer

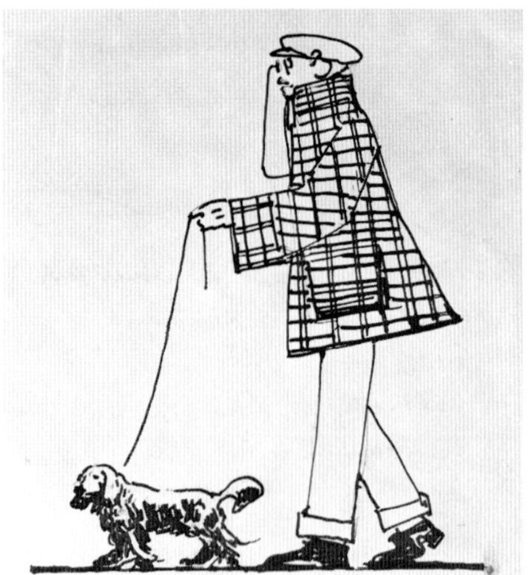

Ernest Blumenschein

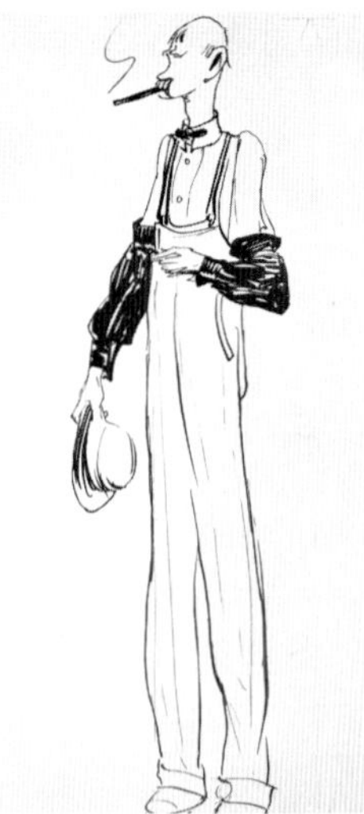

John Dunn

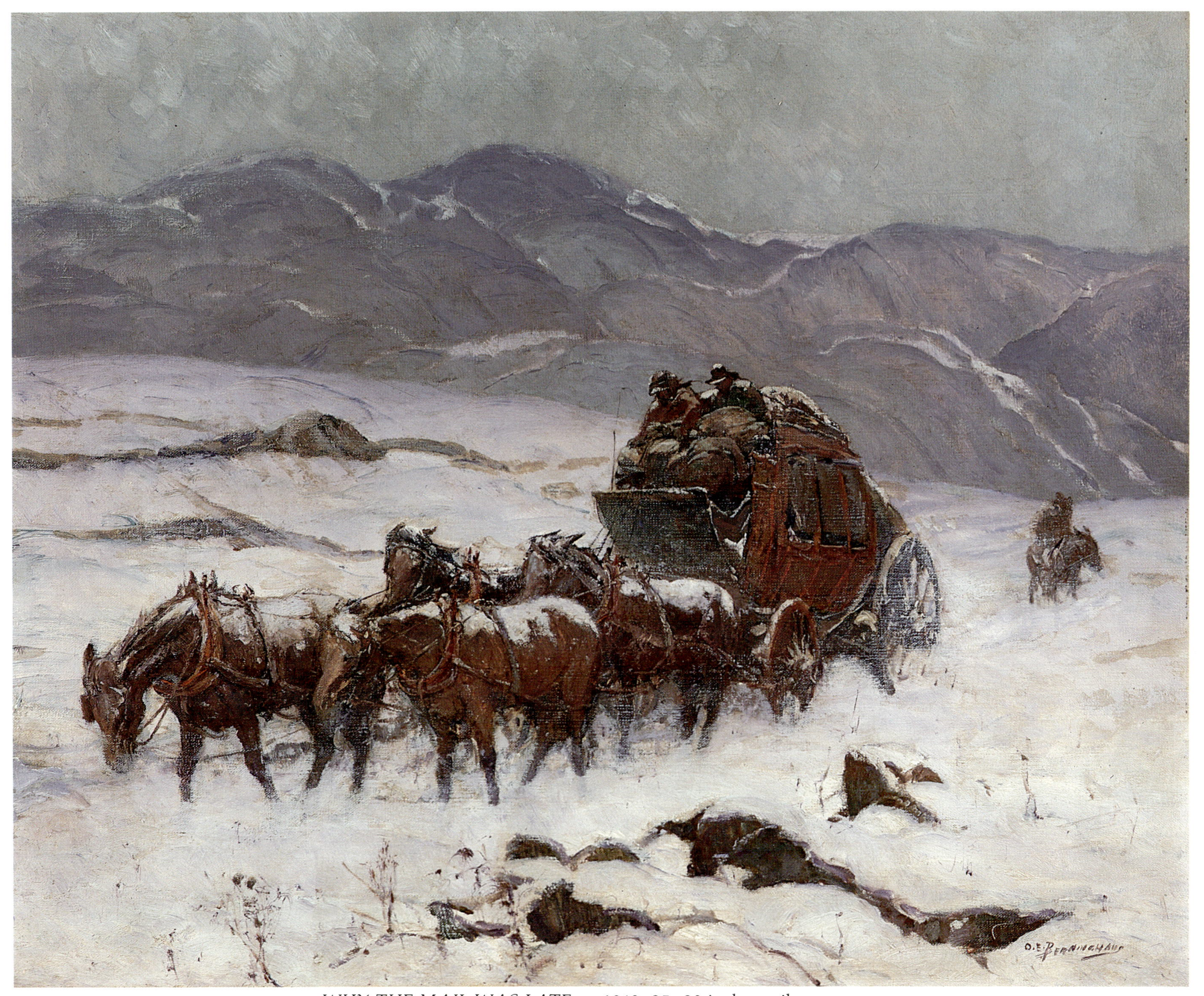

WHY THE MAIL WAS LATE, c. 1940. 25x30 inches, oil on canvas.
Courtesy of the Thomas Gilcrease Institute of American History and Art, Tulsa, Oklahoma.

For a period of more than 16 years, Oscar Berninghaus was the principal designer of the floats and costumes for the annual parade of the Veiled Prophet in St. Louis, Missouri. The organization, The Mysterious Order of the Veiled Prophet, was founded in 1878 by a grain broker, Charles E. Slayback, and a group of St. Louis business leaders who wanted to create a kind of Mardi Gras for the St. Louis harvest festival. Their idea was taken from "Lalla Roohk," an epic poem by Thomas Moore, which was published in 1817. In the poem, the Veiled Prophet of Khorassan was a warlike trickster, but the St. Louis group changed his nature somewhat to a benevolent, civic-minded individual cloaked in fantasy.

The legend of the Veiled Prophet is indeed a beautiful fantasy: "Once upon a time, in the faraway land of Khorassan, there was a wise and kindly ruler known as the Veiled Prophet. This ruler, beloved by his people, gained his title from the veil which covered his face. The veil, it is said, shielded from ordinary mortals the dazzling brilliance of his brow. On the day our story begins, the Prophet and his loyal subjects were holding their yearly celebration in gratitude for the bounty which nature has bestowed upon them." The legend continues with this comment by the ruler: "'The thought comes to me that such happiness should be shared with at least a part of the rest of the world which is sorely troubled. We must find a distant land worthy of such a blessing. I will travel the length and breadth of the globe in search of this land.'

"It was not until the Prophet came to St. Louis that he breathed a sigh of fulfillment. This was the land for which he had been searching. Summoning the officials of the city to him, the Prophet unfolded the idea which he had brought from the faraway land of Khorassan. 'One year hence, I shall return to St. Louis,' the Prophet declared. 'Days before I ar-rive, my heralds will proclaim the date of my visit. With them, you will work making ready for my brief stay, which will be marked by pomp and pageantry. Each year there-after, at the time when the leaves begin to yellow and fall, I shall journey again to my adopted city. Together we will bring to the people of St. Louis a few hours of release from their daily labors.'

"And so the Prophet returned year after year, and his fond-ness for St. Louis grew deeper and deeper. And it came to pass that the Prophet selected the fairest maiden in the city and crowned her Queen of Love and Beauty, to carry on his reign until his return."

The pageant was a complete success from the very begin-ning, and became more elaborate each year. In addition to the parade, grand masquerade balls, fireworks, concerts and street pageants were added to the annual celebration. To-day, the parade is viewed by more than half a million people each October.

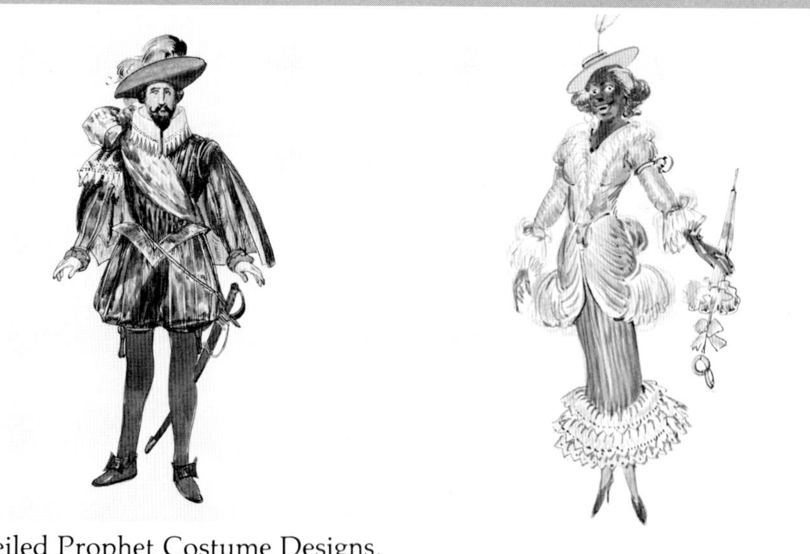

Veiled Prophet Costume Designs.

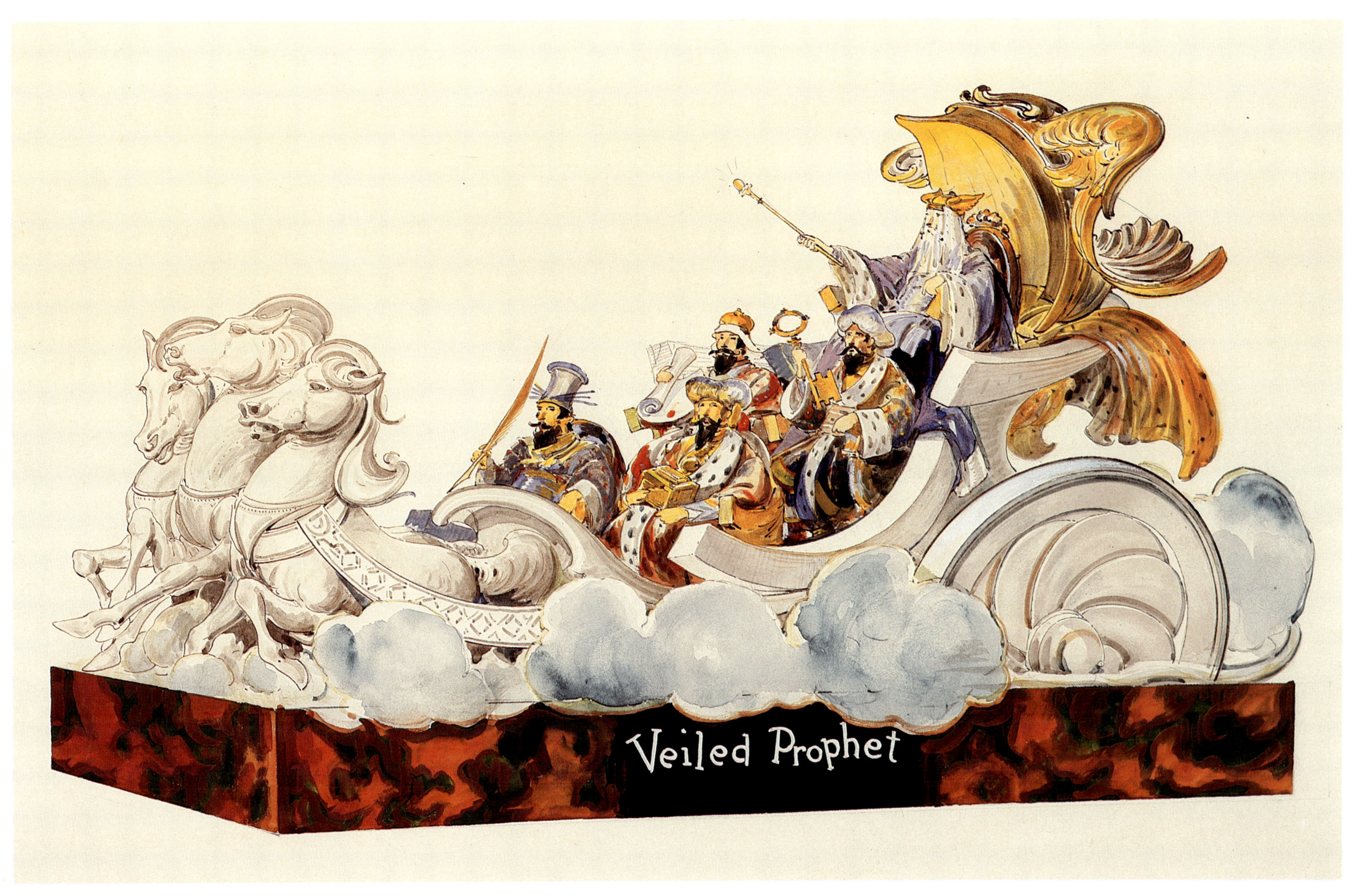

THE VEILED PROPHET, c. 1930s. 15x21 inches, watercolor float design. Private collection.

77

Oscar Berninghaus was first chosen in 1929 to design twenty floats for the Veiled Prophet Pageant. His excellence represented a new phase in the history of the organization. The St. Louis newspapers raved about his creations, and the Veiled Prophet committee was more than delighted with his historical accuracy. In a review of the designs, the *St. Louis Times* wrote: "In his designs, this artist has lifted the street parade out of the carnival classifications and has made it a real pageant of history, and has vividly pictured the various events that have brought the little village of the time of Laclede and Chouteau to the great city of today."

Later Veiled Prophet committees decided that because of the artistic and historical value of the Berninghaus designs, the original paintings from which the floats were designed would be presented to the Missouri Historical Society as the nucleus of a permanent Veiled Prophet exhibit. Today, the collection of some 239 watercolor float designs are housed in the Jefferson Memorial Building in St. Louis, along with photographs, costumes, ball gowns worn by the Queens of Love and Beauty, and other historical information and memorabilia of the Pageant.

During the time that he worked for the Veiled Prophet Pageant, Berninghaus would travel from Taos to St. Louis, usually in January, to meet with the parade committee, decide on a theme and discuss the multitude of details involved in the upcoming event. He not only supplied the designs, but in many cases suggested the overall themes. For his efforts, he was paid an average of $4,000 per year, which, in depression years, was not insignificant. Considering the amount of time required, and the fact that his paintings were commanding a good price even then, it was obvious that much of this work was done out of loyalty and love for the community in which he grew up.

The Pageant was cancelled during the war years (1942-1945), and resumed in 1946. Again, the Parade Committee came to Berninghaus for his float designing talent, but he felt he had to decline. In a letter to the committee chairman, he stated that he thought it would be a good idea to get a St. Louis artist to design the floats. He also suggested a theme for the 1946 event. With his usual dry humor, Berninghaus, now 72, quipped to the committee, "I'm too old for the rabbit hunt!"

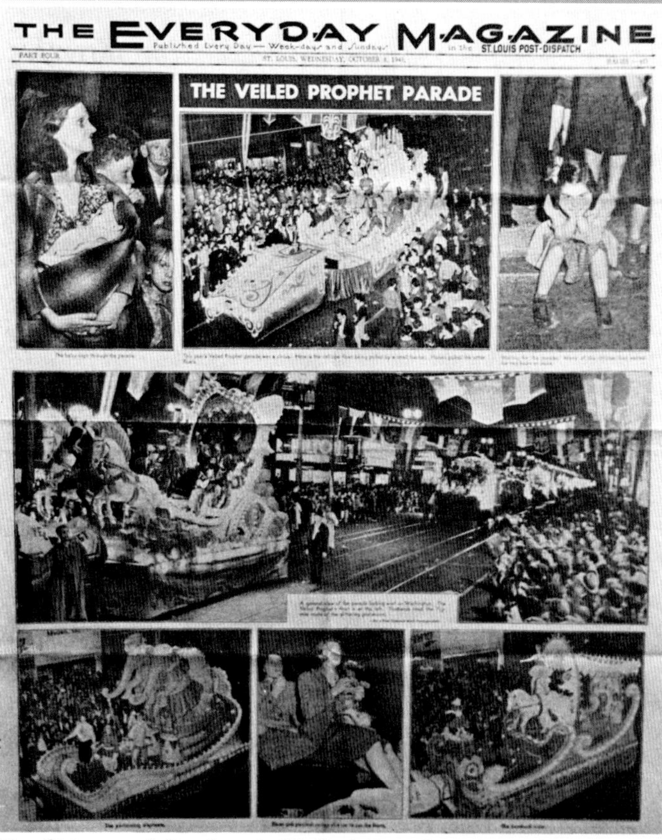

Traditions of St. Louis Veiled Prophet Parade, 1930.

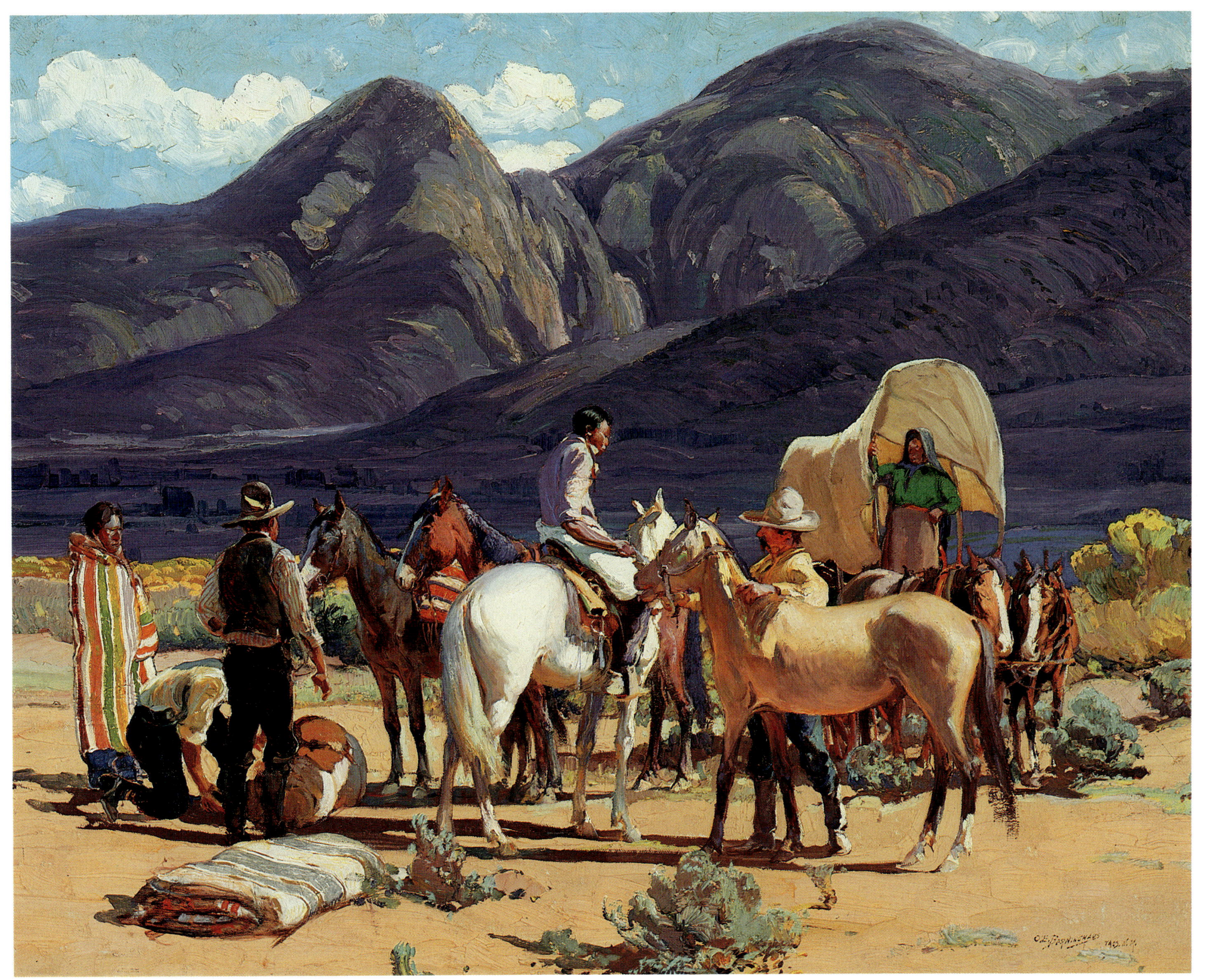

HORSE TRADERS, 1924. 24×30 inches, oil on canvas. Private collection.

OSCAR E. BERNINGHAUS
CITIZEN OF TAOS AND MASTER PAINTER

On January 31, 1931, Oscar Berninghaus married Winnifred Shuler, the daughter of Raton, New Mexico, pioneer doctor, J.J. Shuler. She was a native of New Mexico, well educated and had been active in civic projects for a number of years. Her working years included a stint with the Fred Harvey organization, and she led tours to Taos as part of that employment. The two were married in Raton, and departed a few days later for a one-year honeymoon in Mexico. It was a happy occasion for Oscar, as he had been widowed for almost 20 years.

There was a special reason for his decision to go to Mexico. For years he had heard stories from his colleagues about the beautiful subject matter there. This trip would not only be a holiday, but a working vacation, an opportunity to paint a different culture. Oscar and "Winnie" took the train to El Paso and then to Mexico City. During their stay, the couple lived in a number of towns and villages throughout Mexico. Taxco had a special appeal for them, and there he did several watercolor sketches of the local church which he sent home along with numerous other drawings to convert to oils upon his return to Taos the following year. Oscar was relaxed and delighted to be home, where he immediately went to work to complete the subjects he had started in Mexico.

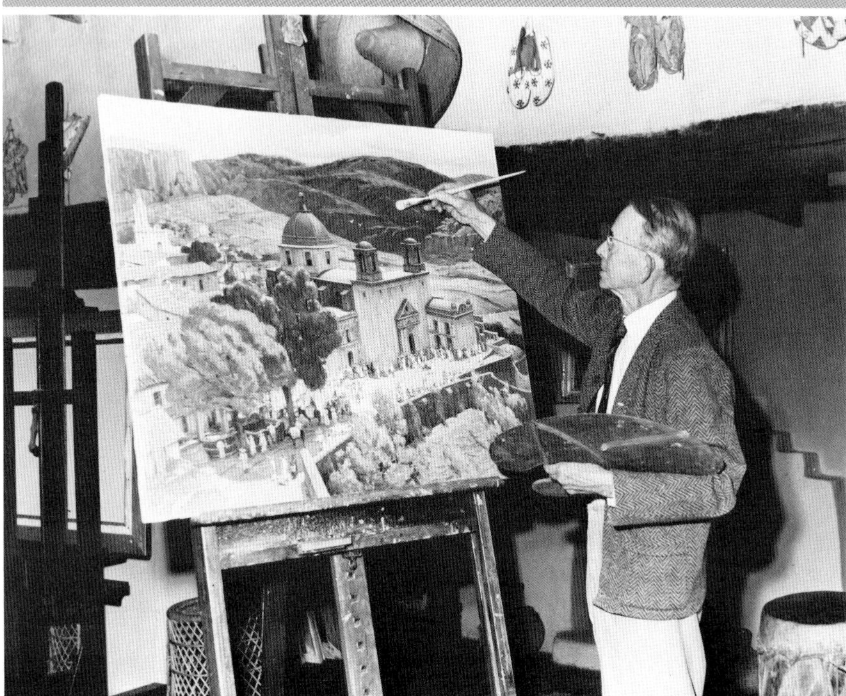

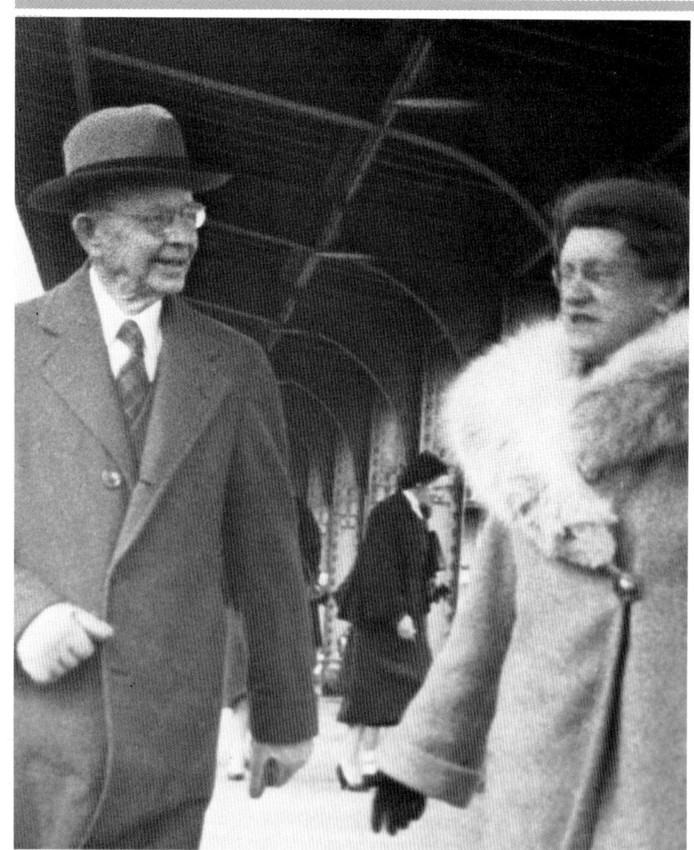

Oscar and Winnifred, March 1952.

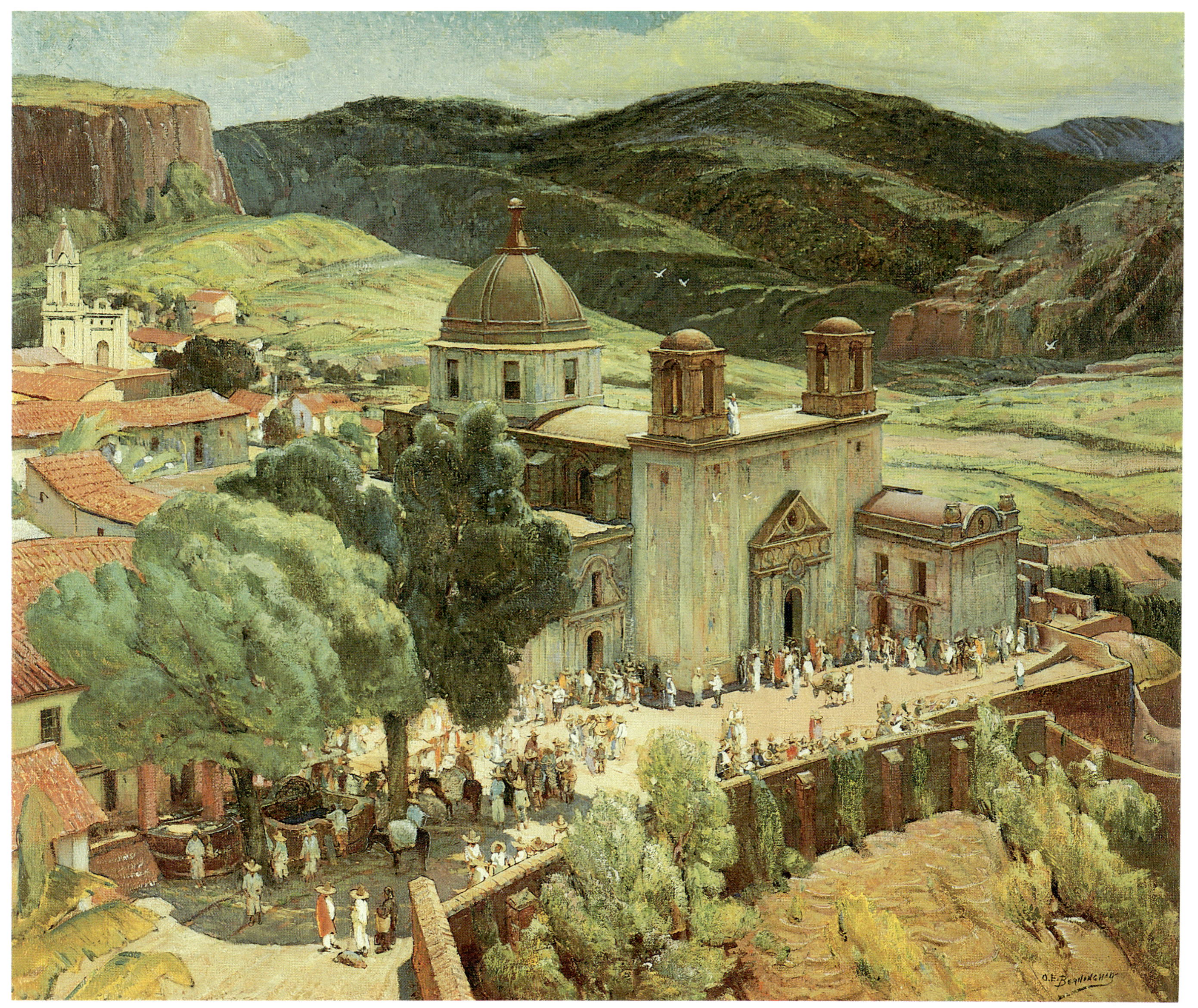

TAXCO, c. 1933. 35×50 inches, oil on canvas. Stark Museum of Art, Orange, Texas.

The Berninghaus home in Taos during the 1930s and 1940s was often the scene of friendly social events. The house itself was charming, with lovely green lawns, Taos delphinium, shasta daisies, poppies and shrubs in front of the property. It was located at the top of a small hill (La Loma) overlooking a green valley below. In the home, Oscar had two studios—one for his prize paintings and canvases in progress—the other a converted garage used for large murals.

Winnifred Berninghaus was a great help to Oscar, as a hostess, homemaker and "secretary." Her typing was much better than his, and together they managed to keep his business affairs in order. At home, her household chores were both helped and hindered by Little Joe Gomez, an Indian who worked for Oscar both as a model and general handyman for many years. Winnie said that through working with Joe, she learned a great deal of patience! In an interview with a visiting reporter from the *Albuquerque Journal* in 1937, she said, "Now Little Joe certainly has a mind of his own. He has worked for Mr. Berninghaus for years, but he never learned to take instructions from me. Indian men don't like to be ordered around by women, you know, and Joe is convinced I know nothing about gardening. He's been everything in Taos—tribal dancer, war chief, artist's model—and now he states he's too old to work. He can't be disproved because he doesn't know how old he is. But he can still dance all night, and often does!"

Oscar Berninghaus just smiled at these minor tiffs in his otherwise serene household.

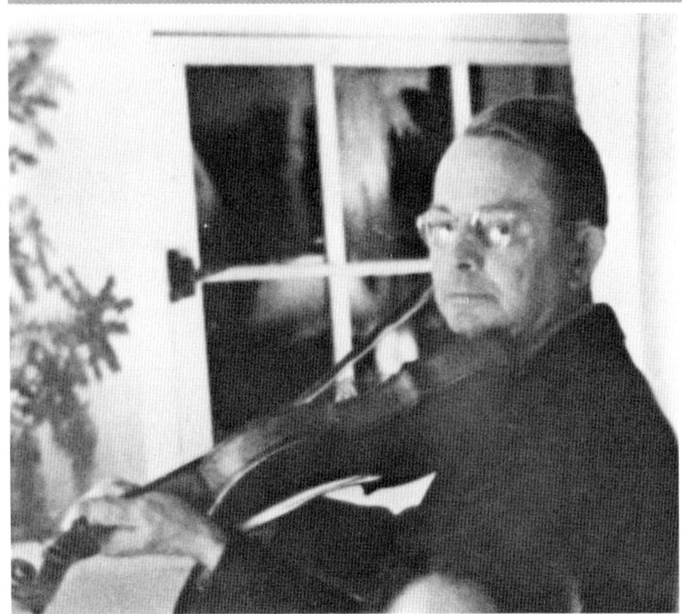

Another art form for Oscar Berninghaus.

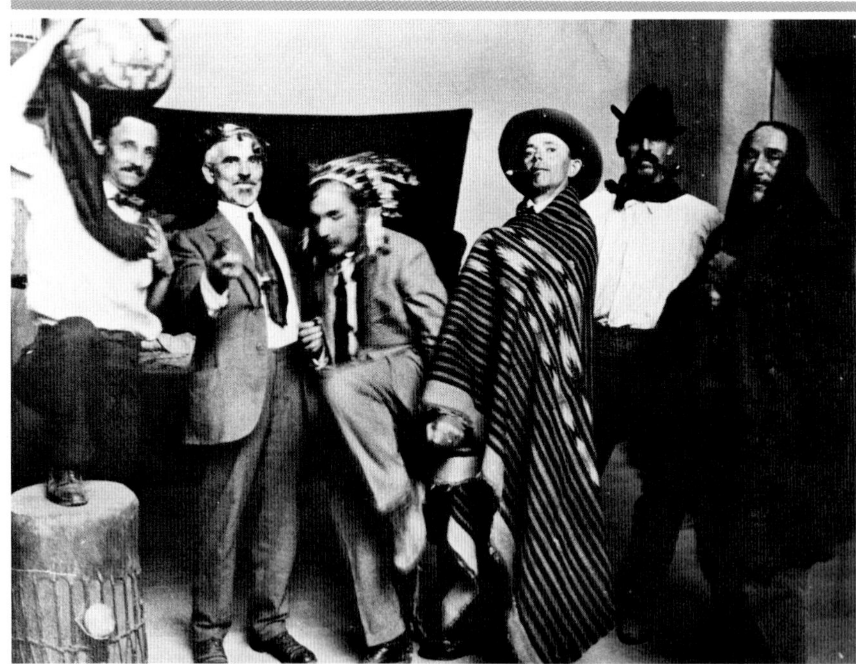

Party. Left to right: Ernest Blumenschein, Joseph Sharp, Bert Phillips, Oscar Berninghaus, "Buck" Dunton, Irving Couse.

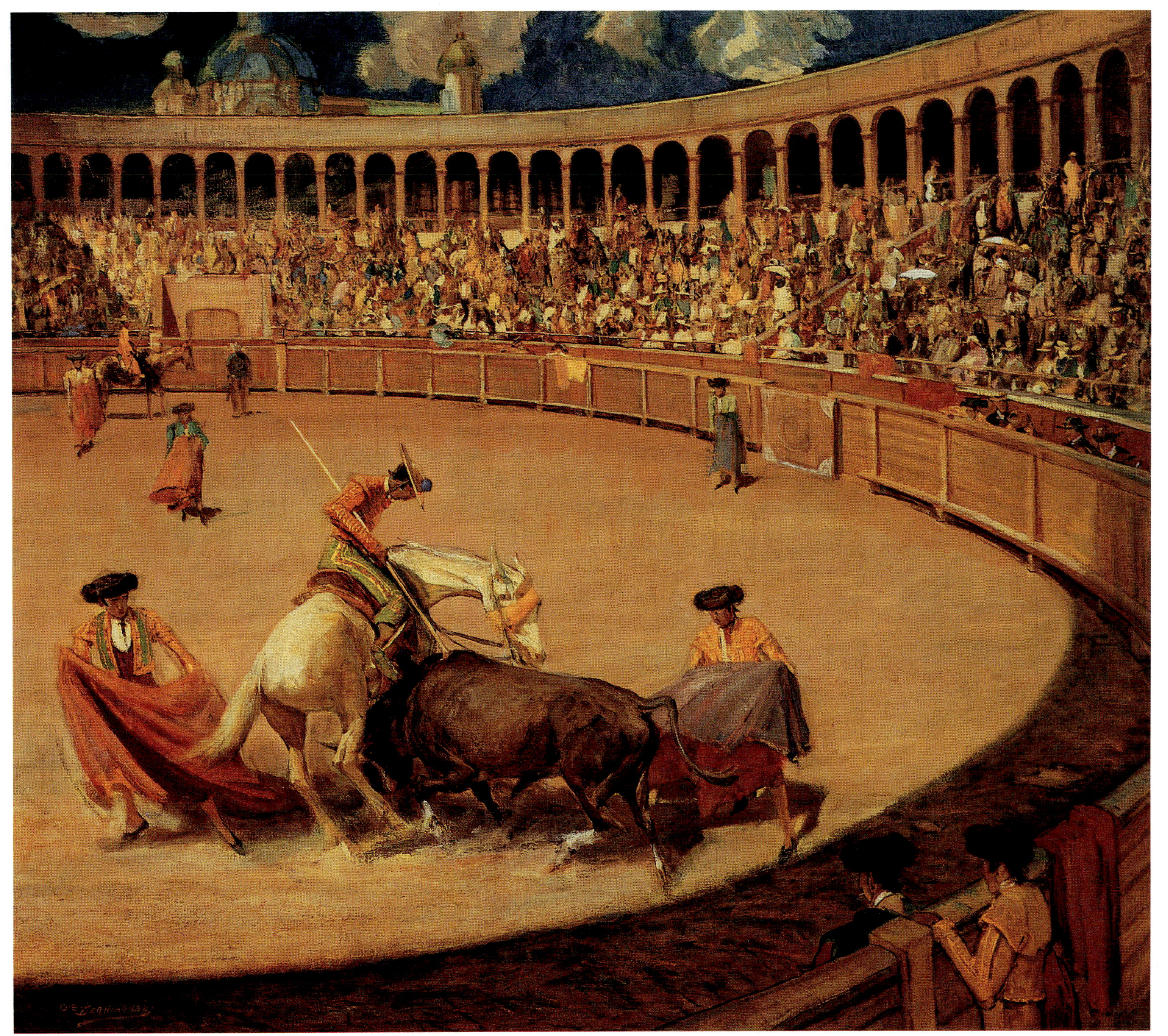

BULLFIGHT, MEXICO, c. 1932. 45×51 inches, oil on canvas. Private collection.

Buying a painting was not the top priority on most shopping lists during the Depression years of the 1930s. Food, clothing and a place to live were the most sought after items for those lucky enough to have a job, and for hundreds of thousands of others it was bumming around, riding the rails and begging a free meal. Times were hard, but there were those who knew and loved art. Such a person was Miss Florence Breece, an instructor of art at the University City Junior High School in St. Louis. She decided that the school should have its own art collection, and encouraged the students to put on bake sales, marionette shows, book sales and parties to raise money to purchase art works. After much effort, the students raised $600 in pennies, dimes and quarters, a feat that so impressed the Board of Education that it donated an additional $500 for a grand total of $1,100. One of the items decided upon by Miss Breece and the children was an Oscar Berninghaus, *The Indian Farmer of Taos*, and for it they paid $400 in 1931.

In 1983 the school decided to sell the painting to raise funds for scholarships in the University City School district. It was assigned to the Selkirk Galleries in St. Louis for public auction on May 18th. The proposed sale of such a major Berninghaus work received much publicity, and an expert on Berninghaus paintings, Martin Kodner, was called in to comment. He told the *St. Louis Globe-Democrat*: "the auction will not bomb because *Indian Farmer of Taos* is such a significant piece that there will be bids galore. There are a lot of people who love Berninghaus as much as I do."

Kodner was right. The auction drew a sizeable crowd, and Bruce B. Selkirk, Jr. opened the bidding at $75,000. Immediately came a bid for $100,000, four individuals jumped the bid to $150,000, quickly followed by another for $175,000. Selkirk paused briefly and said: "I've got 175, do I hear two, I've got 175, do I hear two, I've got 175, do I hear 185—I've got 185, do I hear 190, I've got 190, do I hear two? 190 once, do I hear two, 190 twice, do I hear 195—sold for $190,000!! The hammer came down on the highest price ever paid for a Berninghaus work up to 1983. The buyer was not identified at the time. It is apparent that Miss Breece and her class of 1931 were not only art lovers, but knowledgeable investors!

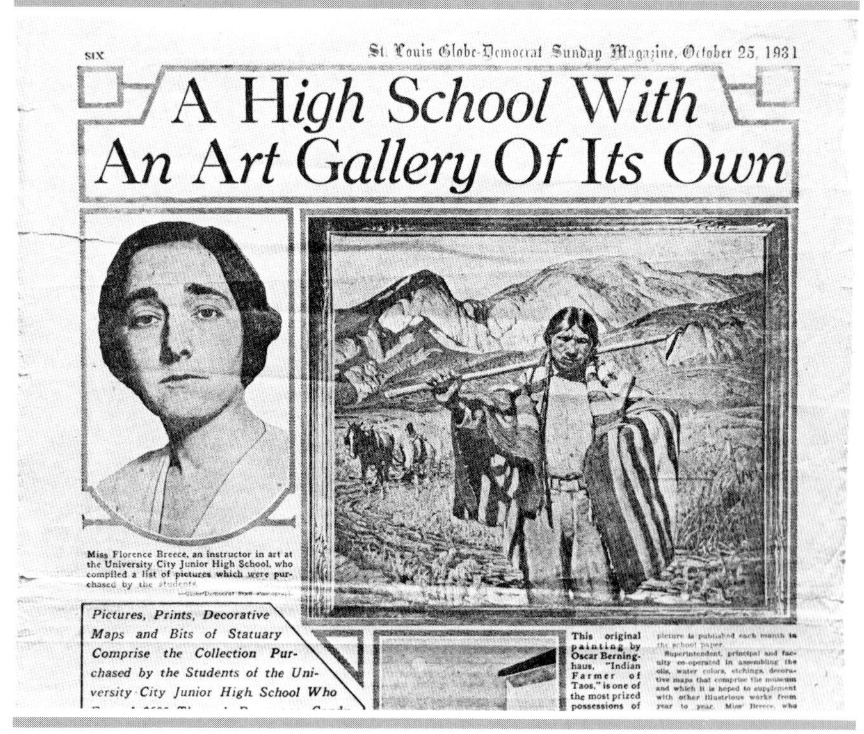

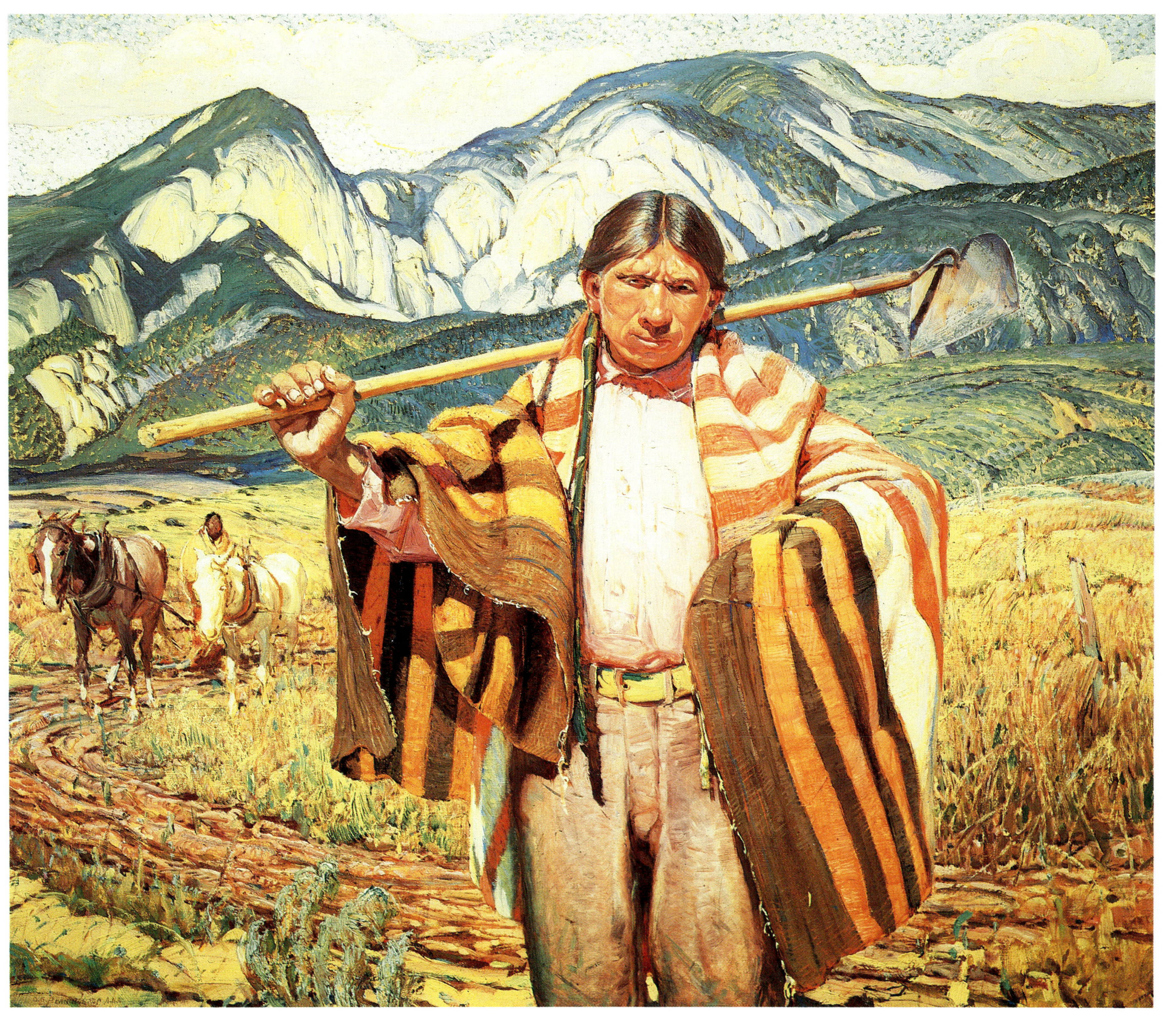

INDIAN FARMER OF TAOS. 35×40 inches, oil on canvas. Photo courtesy of Selkirk Galleries, St. Louis, Missouri.

As a mural painter, Berninghaus did a number of historical works for post offices and other public buildings during the 1930s. The murals were commissioned by the Public Buildings Administration Section of Fine Arts of the Federal Works Agency after a competition open to many artists. The paintings were executed in oil on canvas at his studio in Taos, and upon completion mounted on the walls of the chosen buildings. The subject for one work in a post office was the Weatherford, Oklahoma, railroad station as it appeared at the beginning of the century. Other murals included two for the Phoenix, Arizona, Post Office, and an enormous 8-by 20-foot painting in the federal courtroom in the Post Office Building in Fort Scott, Kansas.

For these murals, Berninghaus was paid an average of $2,000 each, and they are all still very much a part of their respective buildings.

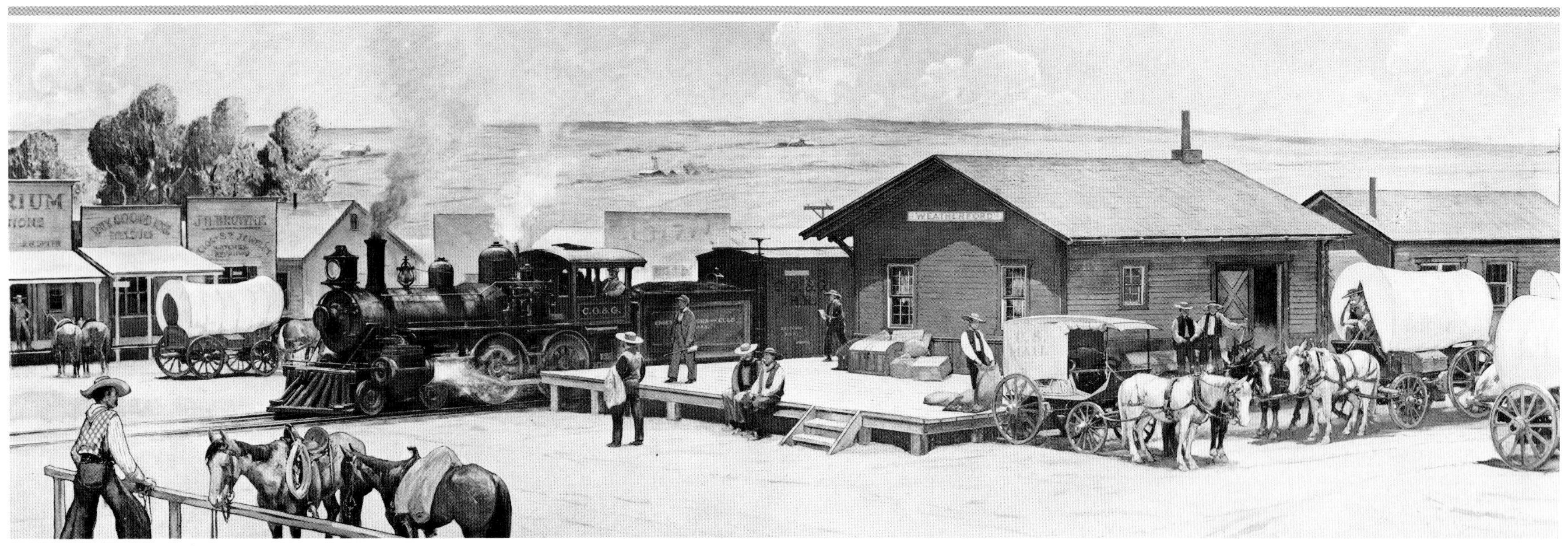

WEATHERFORD, OKLAHOMA RAILROAD STATION, AT THE TURN OF THE CENTURY, 1939.
4 x 12 feet, oil on canvas. Weatherford, Oklahoma Post Office.

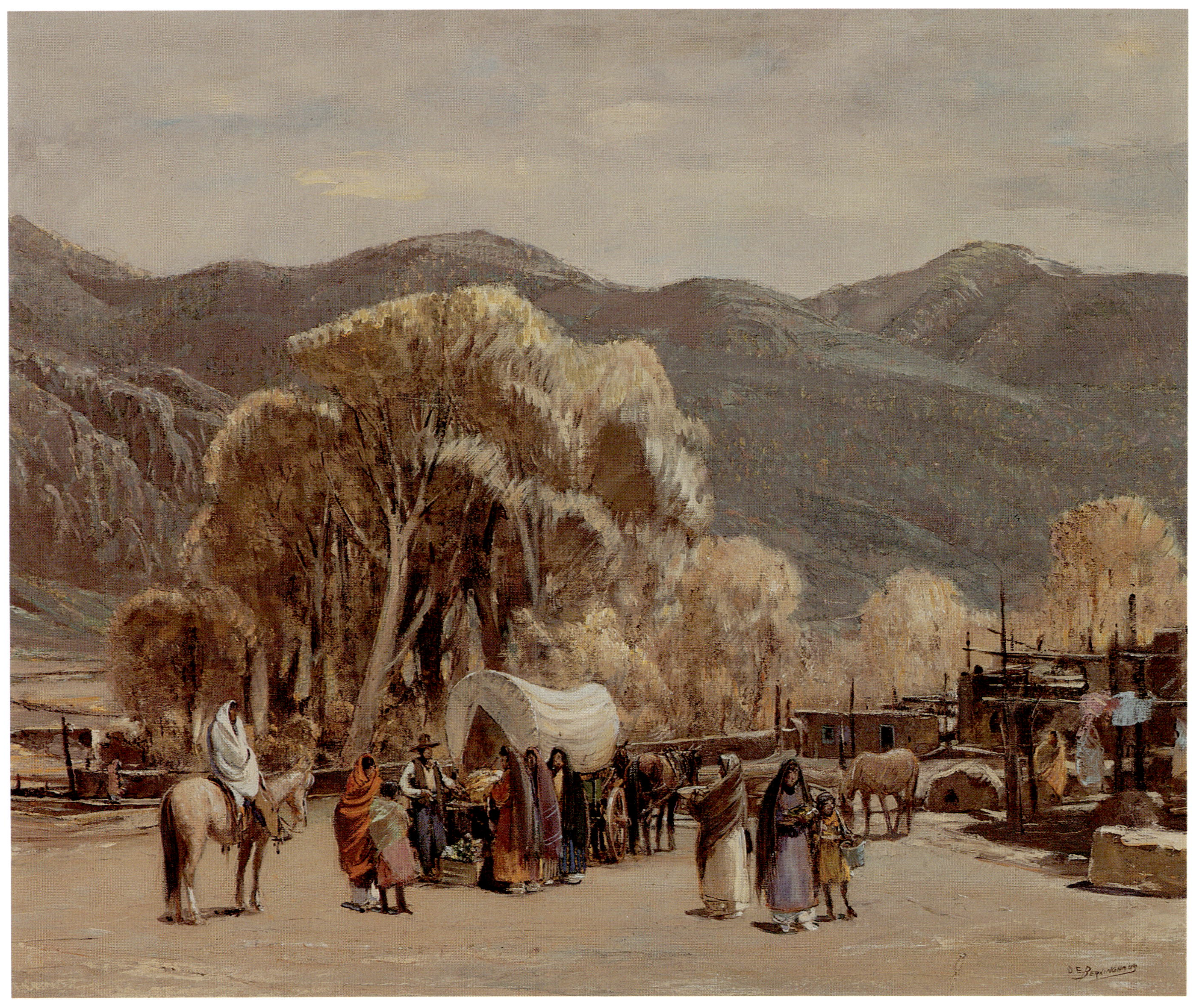

THE FRUIT VENDOR. 25x30 inches, oil on canvas. Courtesy of the Thomas Gilcrease Institute of American History and Art, Tulsa, Oklahoma.

America was beginning to recover from the Great Depression by the late 1930s. More jobs were available, and people had money to spend—even a little left over for things like Benny Goodman records and a Saturday afternoon at the movies. In Taos, going to the movie was often the big social event of the week! Berninghaus' son-in-law, Jack Brandenburg, and his partner, Floyd Beutler, built a new movie theater in Taos in 1939, and it was a great success with the diverse population. It was a common sight to see the theater packed with cowboys, Hispanics and Indians, and the action was often lively both on and off the screen. Westerns were the favorite and the cowboys would whoop it up when the Indians were being chased across the screen. The Indians in the audience remained silent. But—when the Indians in the movie pulled off a successful raid, shot a few pioneers and took a couple of scalps, the shoe was on the other foot, and the Indians cheered and hollered while the cowboys hissed and moaned! Surprisingly, it was all taken in fun, and there were never any serious consequences. Needless to say, *Custer's Last Stand* was always a big hit with the Indians!

Oscar and Winnie Berninghaus enjoyed the movies as much as the rest of the Taos population, so after noticing the audience reaction to these "whoop-it-up" shows, he decided to paint *Movie Night at Taos Theater*, and gave it to his daughter and son-in-law as a gift in 1939.

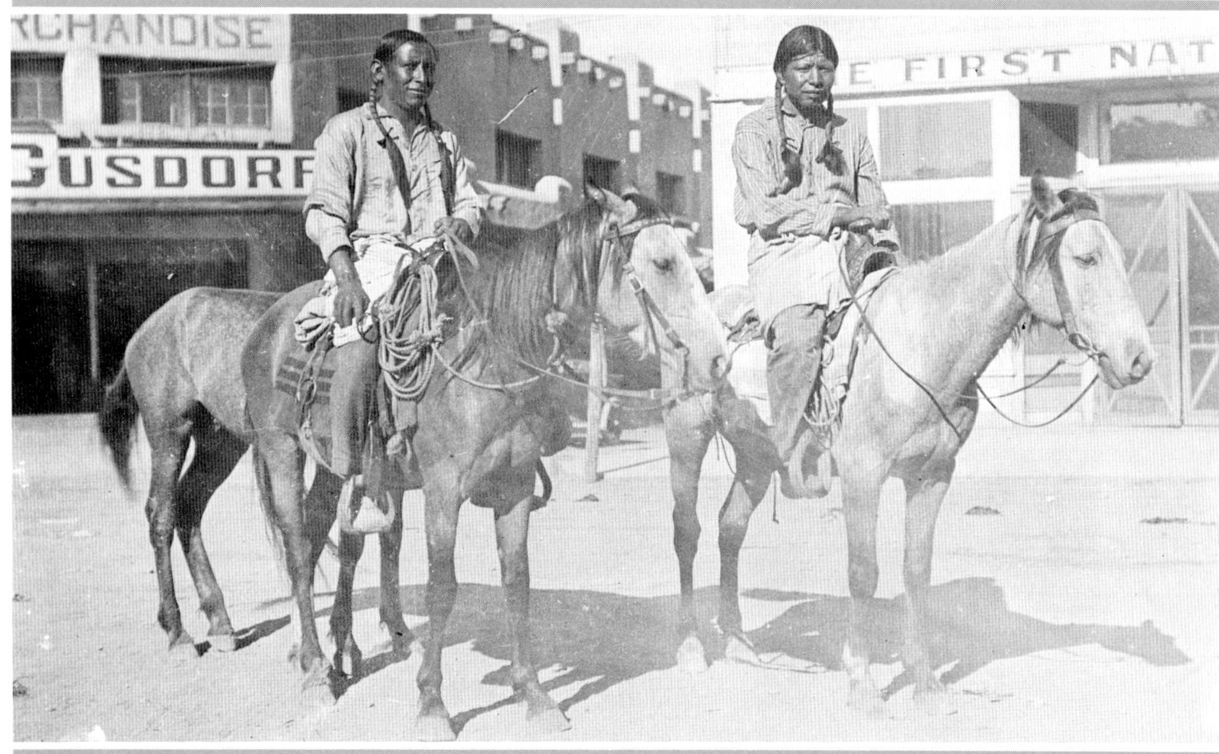

Albert (Looking Elk) Martinez
and friend, c. 1920.

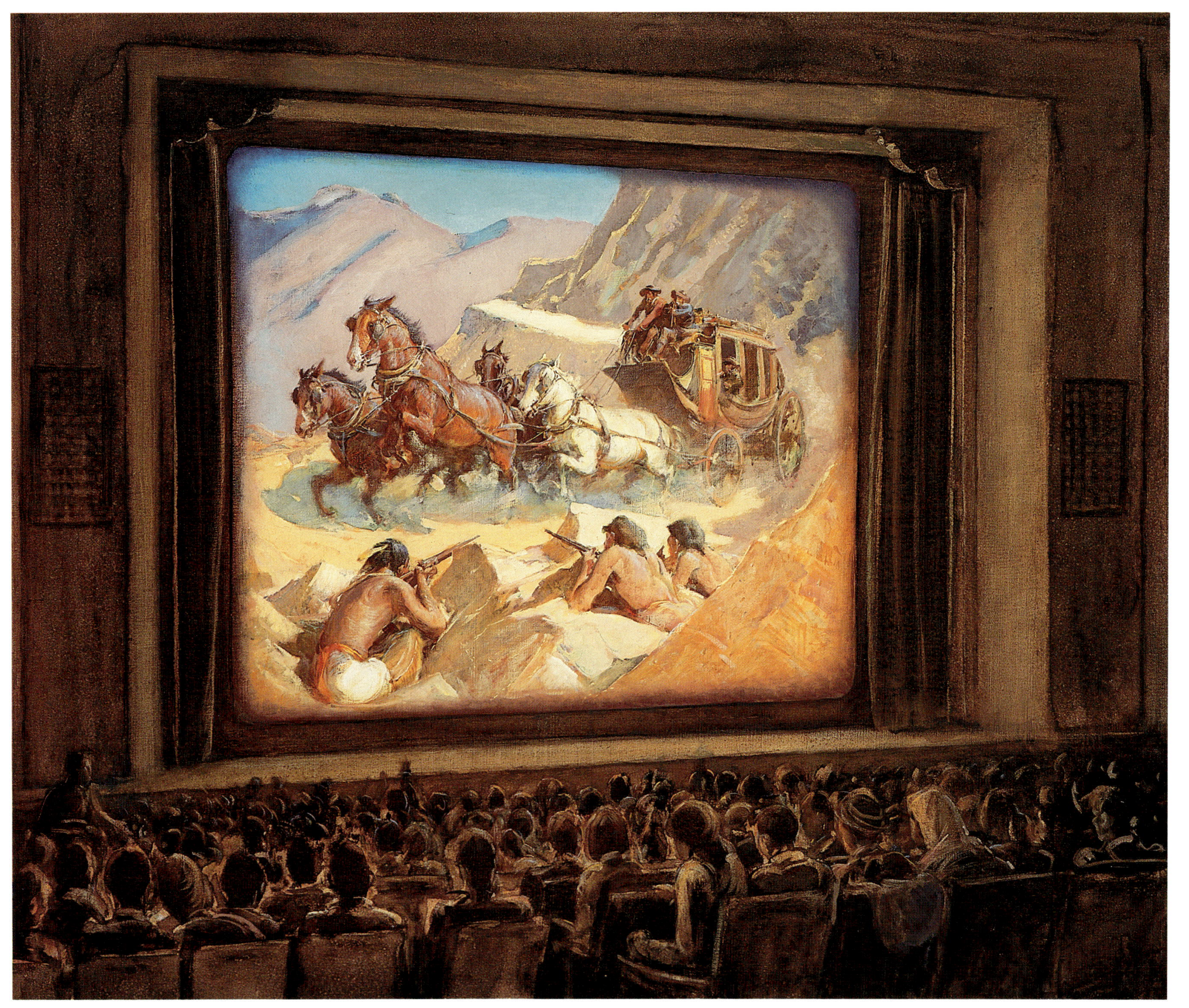

MOVIE NIGHT AT TAOS THEATER, 1939. 30×40 inches, oil on canvas. Private collection.

Although Berninghaus was now a totally independent artist, he could not resist taking an occasional commission from some of the large corporations that he knew so well back in St. Louis. In addition to designing the Veiled Prophet floats each year, he did some work for Anheuser-Busch and the Boatmen's Bank. In 1936 Boatmen's Bank commissioned him to do a series of oils depicting the different modes of transportation during the last quarter of the 19th century.

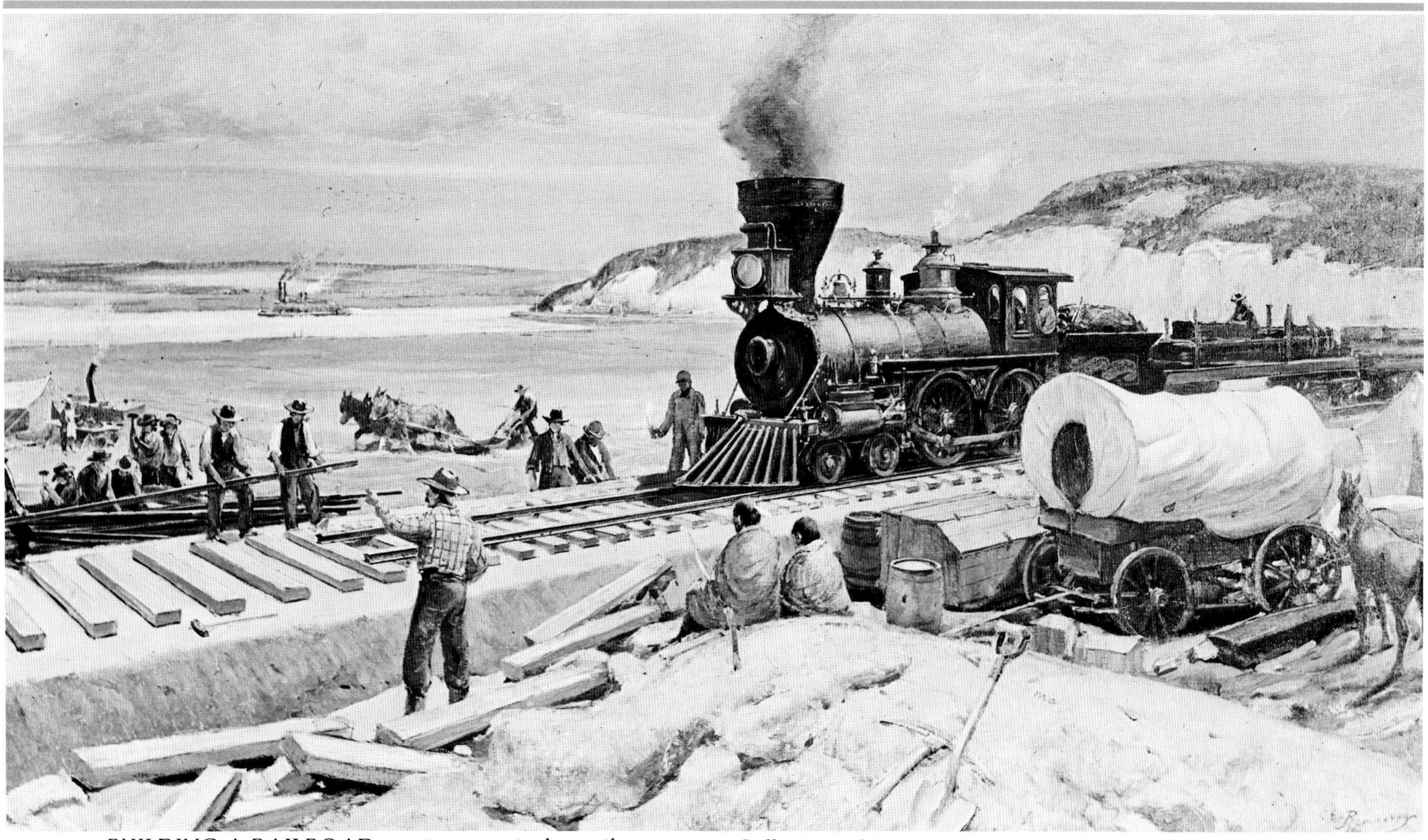

BUILDING A RAILROAD, 1938. 24 x 36 inches, oil on canvas. Collection of Boatmen's National Bank, St. Louis, Missouri.

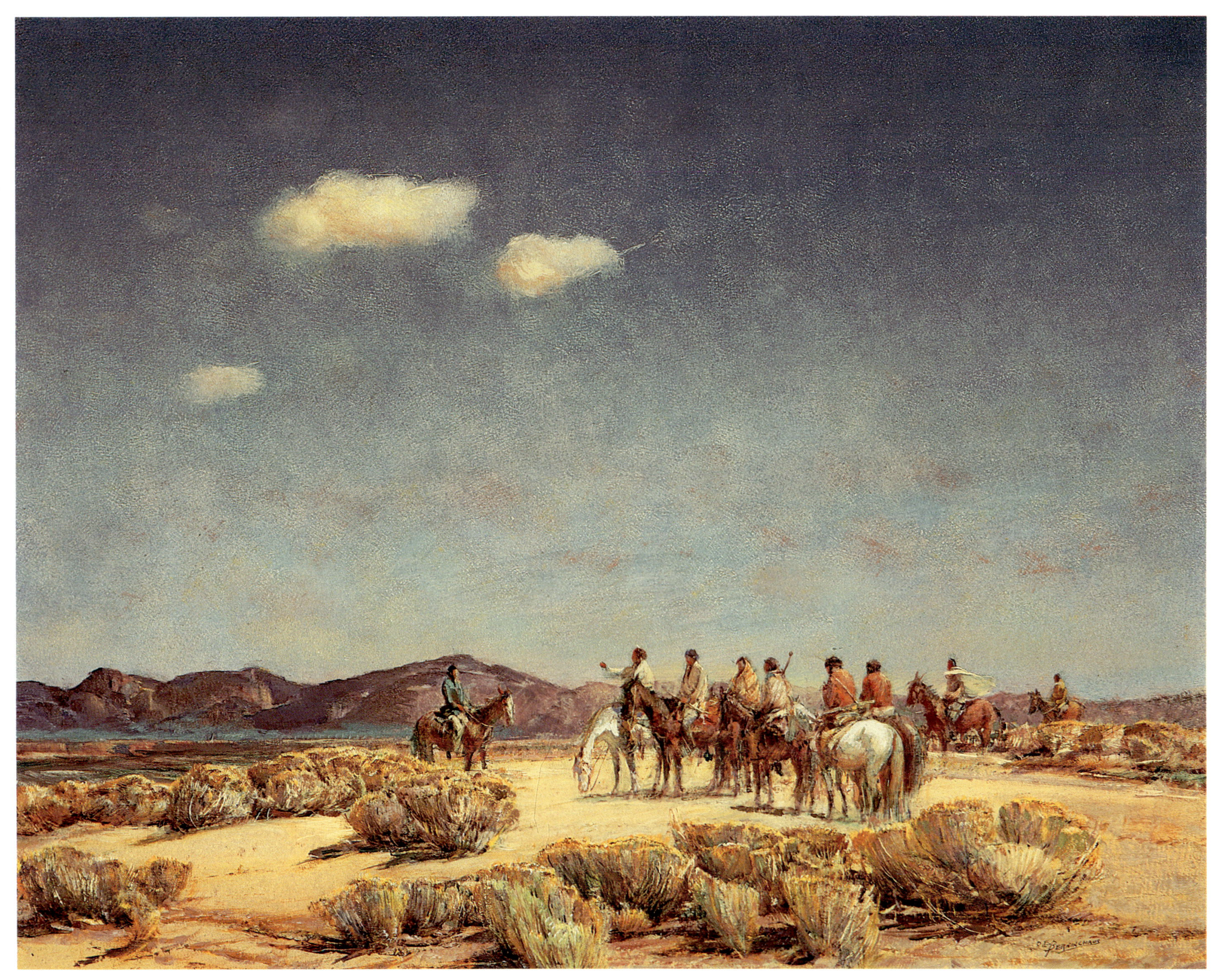

SOME RABBIT HUNTERS ON THE MESA, c. 1930. 16×20 inches, oil on canvas. Private collection.

The transportation series for Boatmen's Bank also included *Opening the West*, *The Itinerant River Merchant*, *Through Missouri by Covered Wagon* and *The J.M. White*. These paintings, along with the two shown in this book, covered the principal means of transportation in the early days of our country. Throughout the bank's history, the corporate family and officers have had a policy of collecting fine art, and today the collection is worth several million dollars. Among the works in the collection are those of Frederic Remington, Charles Russell and George Caleb Bingham. The Berninghaus series was completed in 1938, and is presently hanging in the executive suite of the Boatmen's National Bank in St. Louis, Missouri.

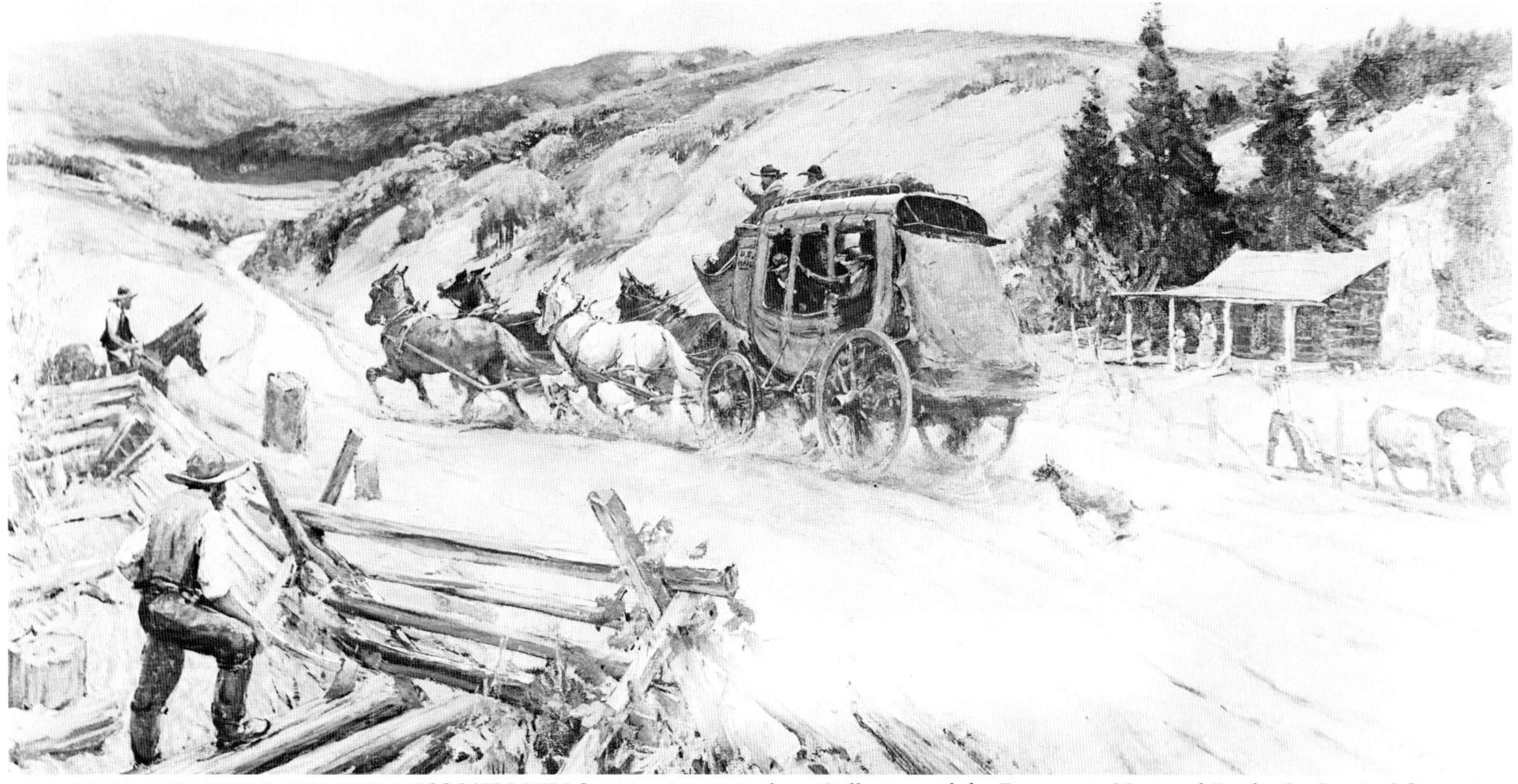

STAGECOACH THROUGH THE MISSOURI HILLS, 1938. 24x36 inches. Collection of the Boatmen's National Bank, St. Louis, Missouri.

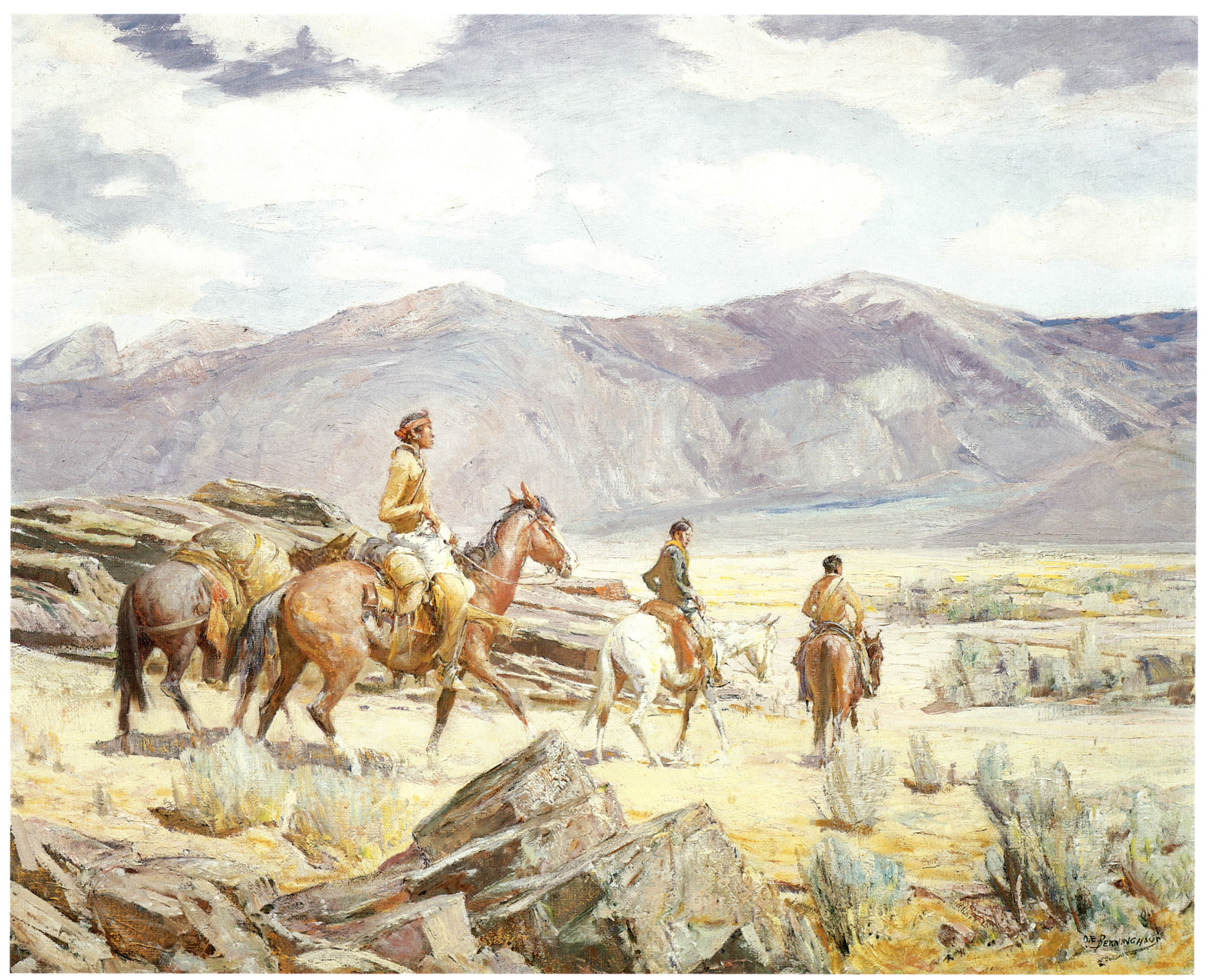

INDIANS RETURNING TO TAOS AFTER A TRADING EXPEDITION, c. 1948. 30×36 inches, oil on canvas.
Robert E. McKee, Jr. Collection. Photo courtesy of the Gerald Peters Gallery, Santa Fe, New Mexico.

As a citizen of Taos, Berninghaus was always involved in civic affairs. Although he had a busy schedule of his own, he always found time to help out with various local projects. There was a time in the mid 1940s when a dispute arose over the number of signs cluttering the main street of Taos, and a group of citizens was pressuring the city fathers to have all the "eyesores" removed by ordinance. Businessmen naturally objected, and the controversy raged. Berninghaus was called upon to illustrate how the street would look with or without signs. He did two sketches, which were viewed by council members at a meeting that lasted for many hours. In the end, the signs prevailed, and Berninghaus turned the sketch with the signs into an oil painting. His sense of humor was never far from the surface—the misspelling of Penney's was deliberate, and it helped to lighten a very tense meeting! The sign controversy did not end in the 1940s, but continues to be a bone of contention among the environmentalists, aes-thetes and businessmen in Taos. Today, the camera has been substituted for the work of a "Berninghaus."

Oscar often had fun with his art, and paintings such as *Taos Plaza* must have given him a few hours of relaxation from his more serious works. In *Taos Plaza*, one can find Mabel Dodge Lujan, Lady Dorothy Brett, John Dunn, Gerson Gusdorf and even the exact license plate number of Helen Blumenschein's car!

In the 1930s, the government created a program to help the serious economic situation that existed at the time—the Works Progress Administration (WPA). Through this program artists would submit sketches for murals that would be placed in public buildings, and *The Sooner Run* is one that Berninghaus proposed for a project in Oklahoma. Evidently it was not accepted, as there is no record of the actual painting of the mural, and this sketch presently is owned by a transplanted Oklahoman.

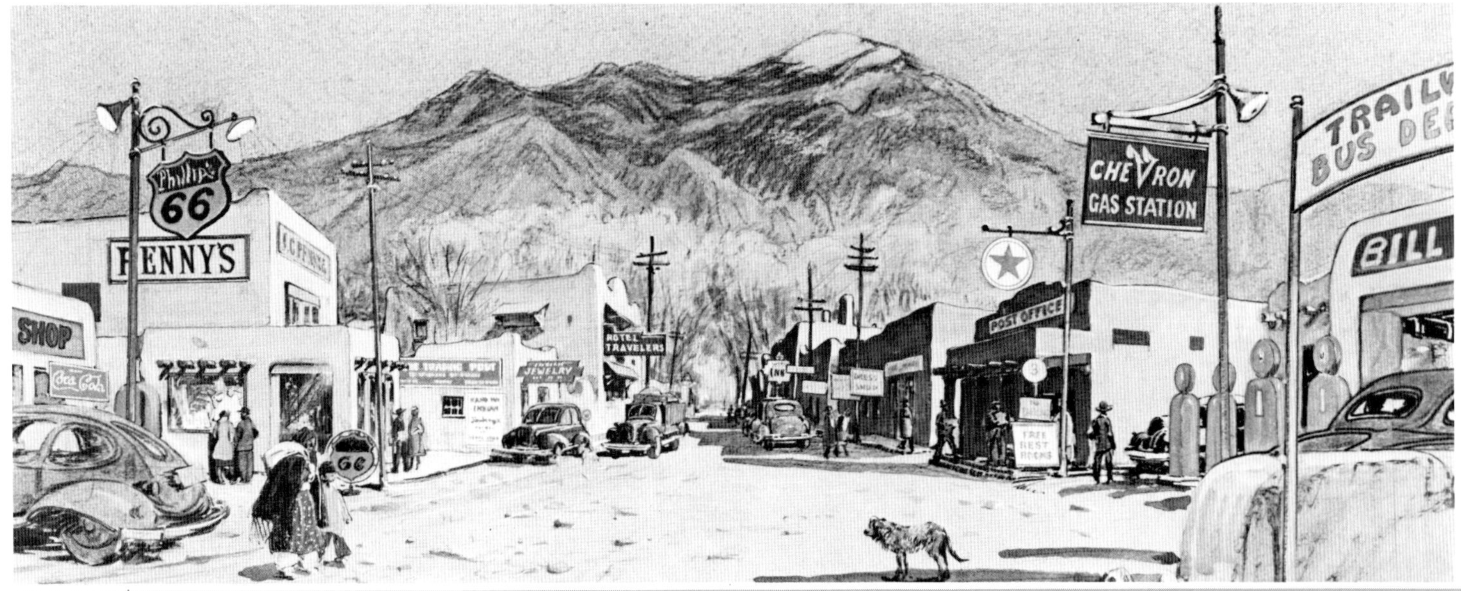

NORTH PUEBLO ROAD, 1946.
18 x 30 inches, watercolor.
Private collection.

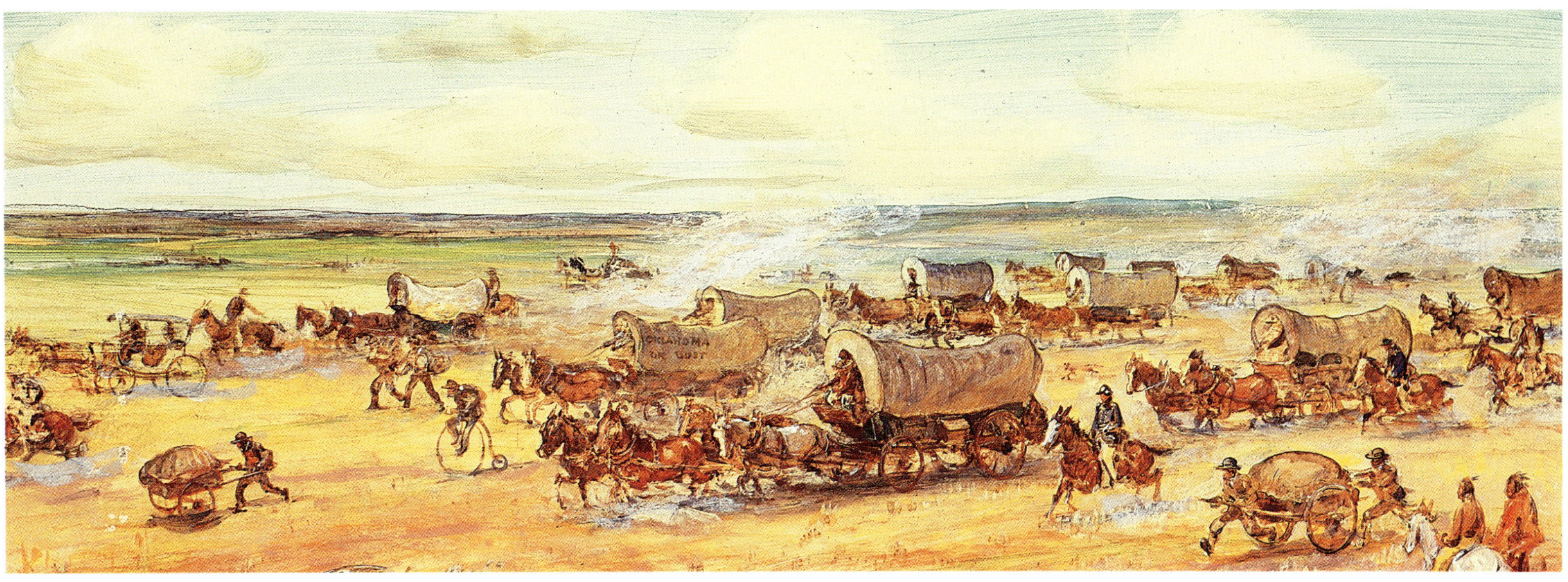

OKLAHOMA SOONER RUN,
c. 1930's. 8×21½ inches,
oil on board.
Private collection.

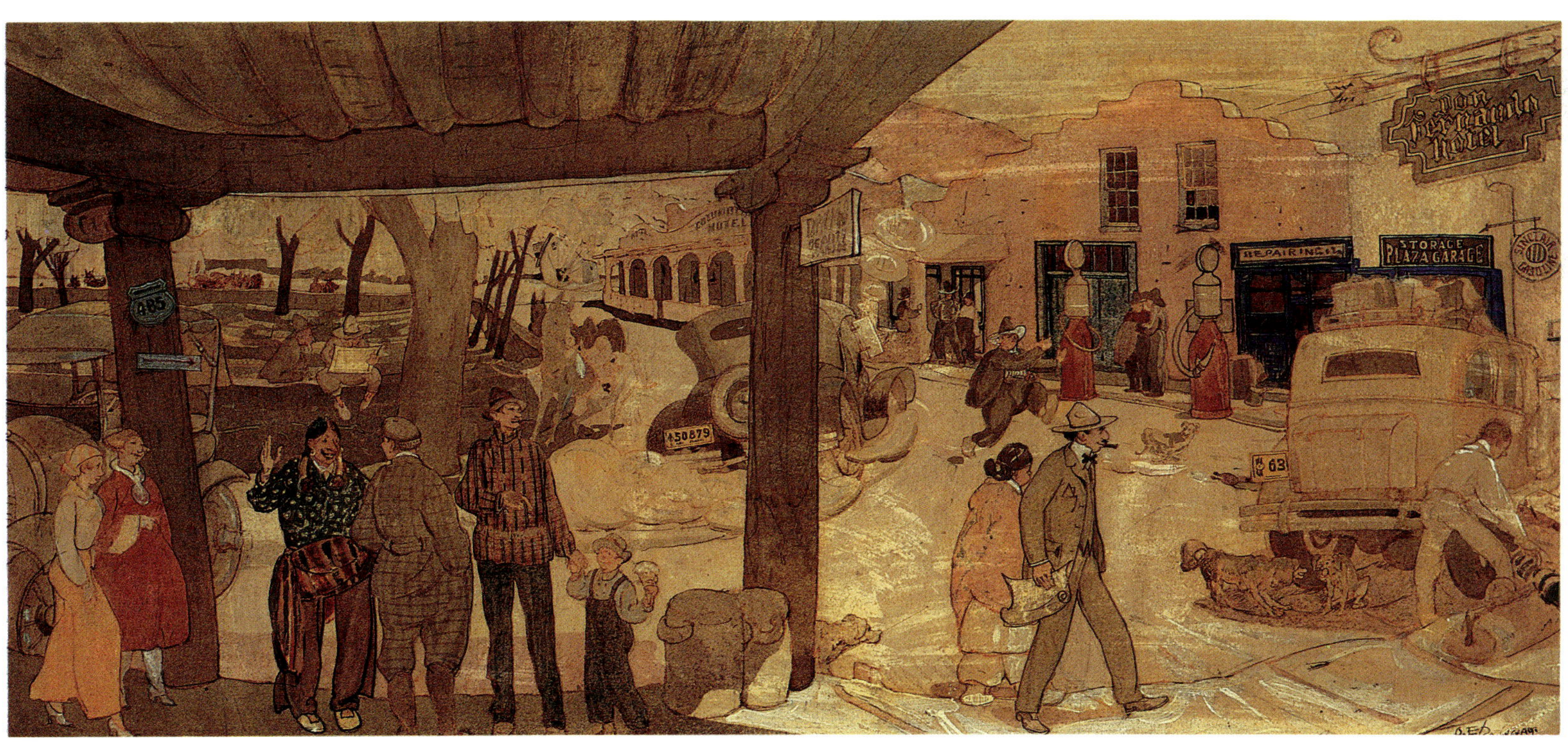

TAOS PLAZA, 1931
14×30 inches, gouache on
masonite. Private collection.

OSCAR E. BERNINGHAUS
THE SUMMIT

Age was beginning to take its toll on the founding members of the Taos Society of Artists. Three of them had died in 1936—E. Irving Couse, N.A., born in 1866, had financed his early art education through manual labor in construction and house painting; W. Herbert Dunton, born in 1878, was known as "Buck" Dunton, the painter of cowboys and the glory of the Old West; and Walter Ufer, N.A., who was born in 1876 and had studied art in Dresden and Munich before coming to Taos in 1914. Ufer was a convincing portrayer of the Southwest, using heavy paints to achieve a realistic style. Charles Berninghaus recalls that he and his father were at the hospital in Santa Fe waiting to donate blood to Ufer when he died.

Times were changing, and the influences of the modern world were slowly moving in on the village of Taos and the Taos Pueblo Indians. Many of the old ways were giving way, due to government programs, and Berninghaus could see these changes and felt that someday a great deal of the beauty of the Indian lifestyle would be gone forever. It was his intent to capture on canvas scenes such as *Haytime and Showers*—a visual history of the customs that had sustained the Indians for so long a time. *Haytime and Showers* is another outstanding example of Berninghaus' mastery of color and composition. The impending violence of the storm adds an atmosphere of urgency to the stacking of the hay, because in the high country the weather can change from one moment to another. Autumn can become early winter overnight, and the Indians want to be sure there will be feed for the livestock during the coming months. Yet, the canvas tells

of the family and a genuine understanding of the world in which they live. At one time, a critic wrote that "Berninghaus was not personally interested in anthropology or ethnology. Painting itself, not the subject matter or the preservation of vanishing cultures, was his primary concern." *Nothing* could be further from the truth, and in *Haytime and Showers* we find a veritable poem of both objective and subjective Indian life.

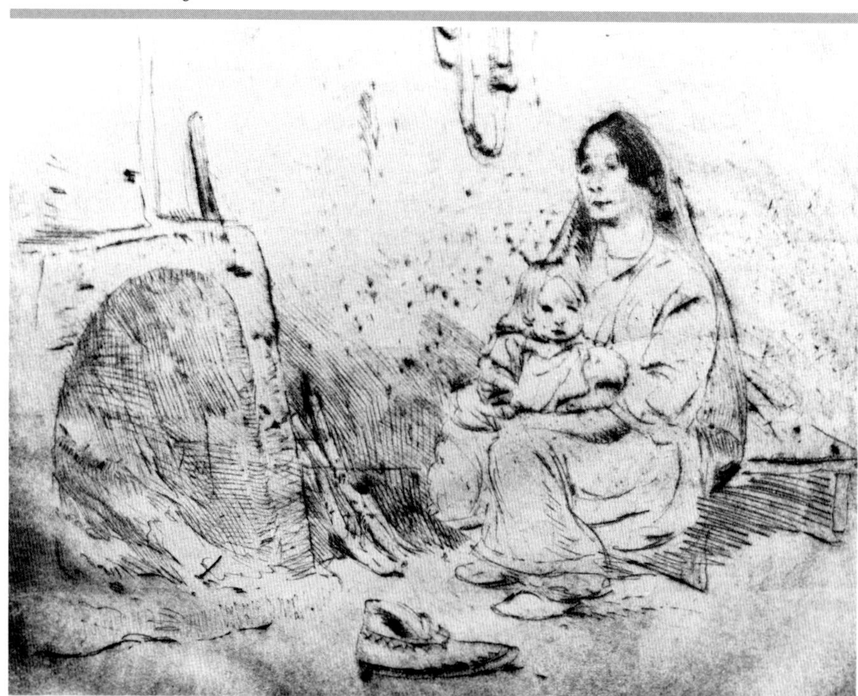

INDIAN MOTHER AND CHILD, c. 1925. 5x6 inches, etching. Private collection.

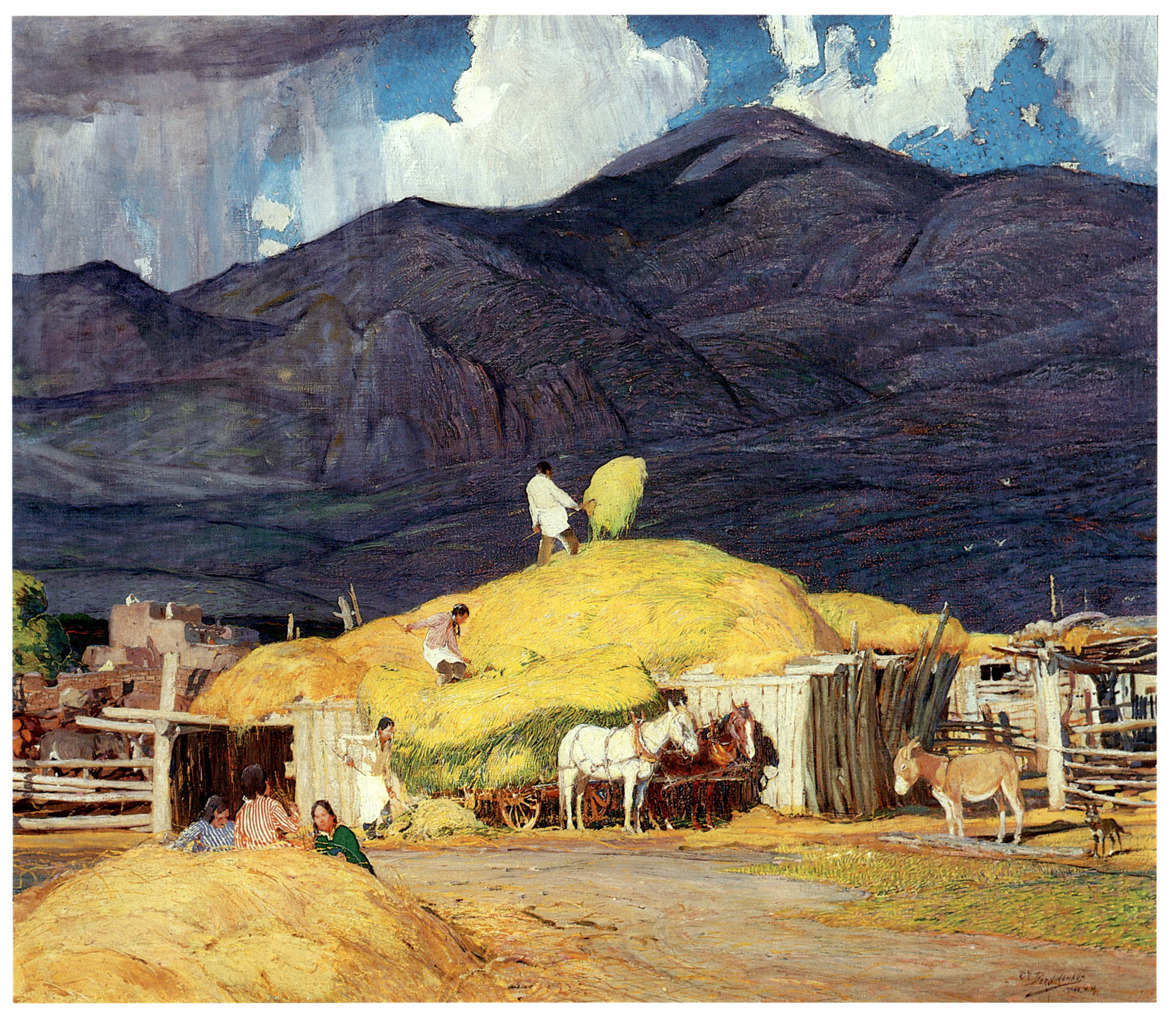

HAYTIME AND SHOWERS, c. 1940. 35x40 inches, oil on canvas. Private collection.

Of all the ceremonials and rituals of the Taos Indians, one of the most impressive was *The Inspection of Arms*. The subject of this canvas gives us a full view of the Taos Pueblo with the snow-covered peaks of the Sangre de Cristo mountains as a backdrop to the north and east. Berninghaus completed the first *Inspection* canvas in 1937 and occasionally used a picture of it as his Christmas card. He sent one of these cards to Thomas Gilcrease in Tulsa, Oklahoma, accompanied by a letter describing the painting. "*Inspection of Arms, Taos Pueblo* is, as the title implies, a gathering together of all the able-bodied men of the Pueblo to have the arms for defense inspected. This usually takes place once a year, sometime in January. It is a custom carried out for many, many years;

how far back I have been unable to learn. It is at the call of the War Chief. As noted in the picture a large circle is formed and the War Chief and his assistants go from one to the other, inspecting each for whatever arms he may have for defensive purposes. These consist of all sorts of weapons: bows and arrows, clubs, spears and a variety of guns all the way from a small 22 to the more high-powered ones. The painting is, of course, in color and the canvas size is 20 by 24 inches. I painted it because of its documentary value, for in later years it may become of some historical value."

The inspection ceremony takes place usually at the break of day, and is accompanied by a number of dances, sometimes lasting throughout the day.

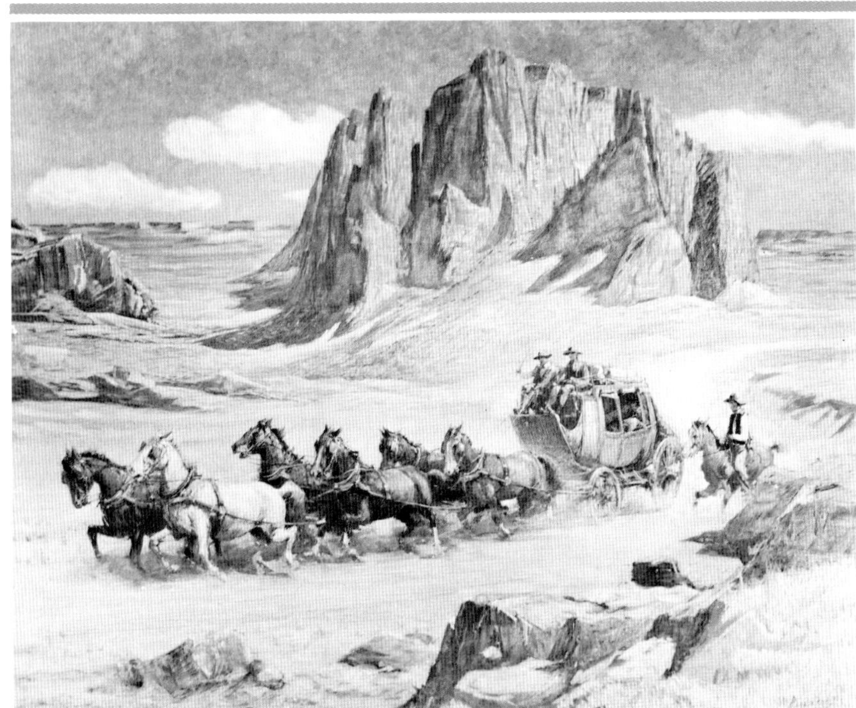

DESERT TRAVELERS, unlocated. Photo from artist's file.

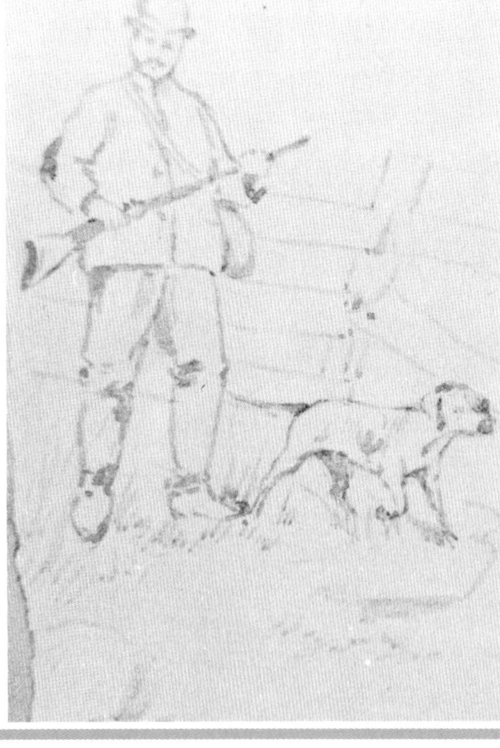

A HUNTER AND HIS DOG, c. 1920. 3 x 2 inches, pencil drawing. Private collection.

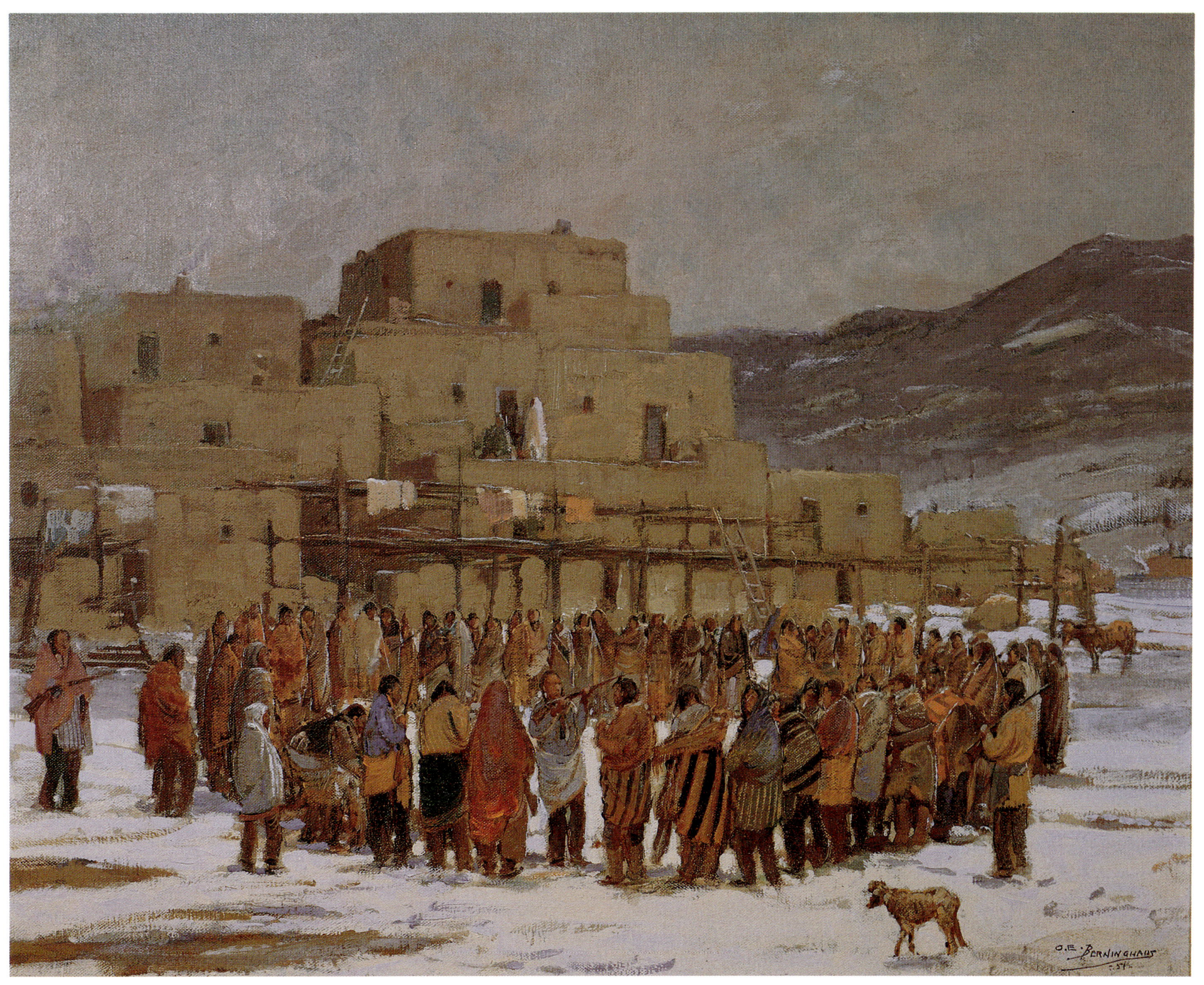

INSPECTION OF ARMS, 1951. 20x24 inches, oil on canvas. Private collection.

Autumn in Taos has always been Fiesta time, beginning with the San Geronimo days of late September. The valley is ablaze with color—the golden aspens, splashes of red from the oaks and yellows of the ancient cottonwoods. At sundown there is a different mood every few minutes with the changing light. There is literally a painting in almost any direction you look.

For the Taos Indians it is a time for prayer and ritual, a time for thanks to the Sun God for an abundant harvest. In one of their dances, a hundred men or more emerge from the Kiva in long lines and cross the small footbridge to the cottonwood trees. In their hands the dancers wave yellow-and-green branches, and there is the sound of the drum and singing voices. The "Sundown Dance" is both beautiful and stirring, even to the uninitiated.

It was the rituals and beautiful colors of autumn that inspired Berninghaus to paint *October*, truly a tribute to Indian Thanksgiving. For years the painting belonged to the Northside High School in Fort Worth, Texas, a gift of the school's principal, O.D. Wyatt. He paid about $500 for *October* in the early 1930s, and in 1983 the painting was sold to the Gerald P. Peters Gallery in Santa Fe, New Mexico, for $150,500.

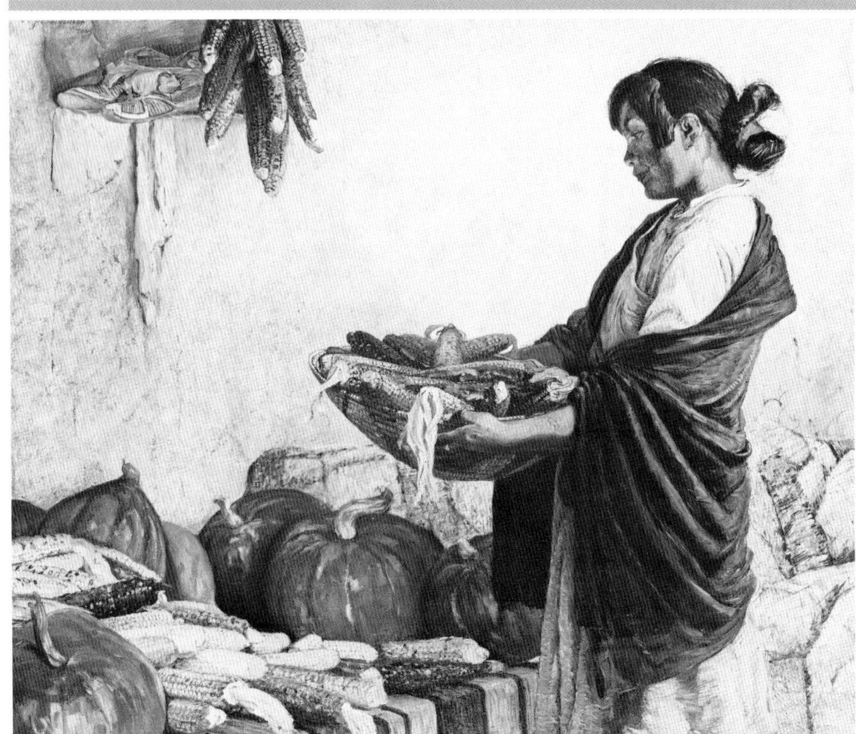

HARVEST, c. 1925. 25×30 inches, oil. Unlocated.
Photo from artist's file.

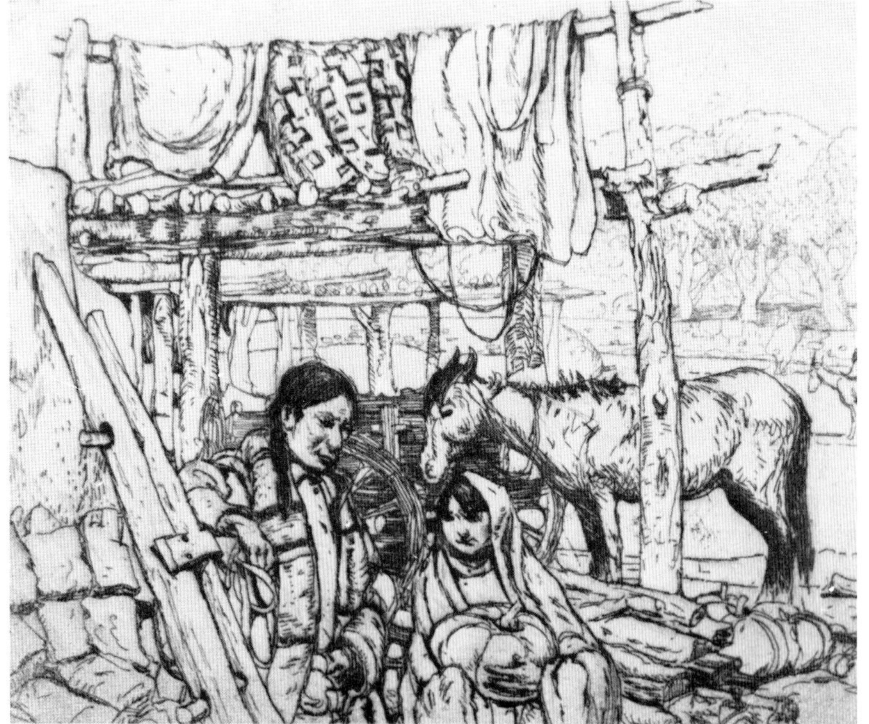

TAOS HARVEST TIME, c. 1930. 5×6 inches, etching.
Private collection.

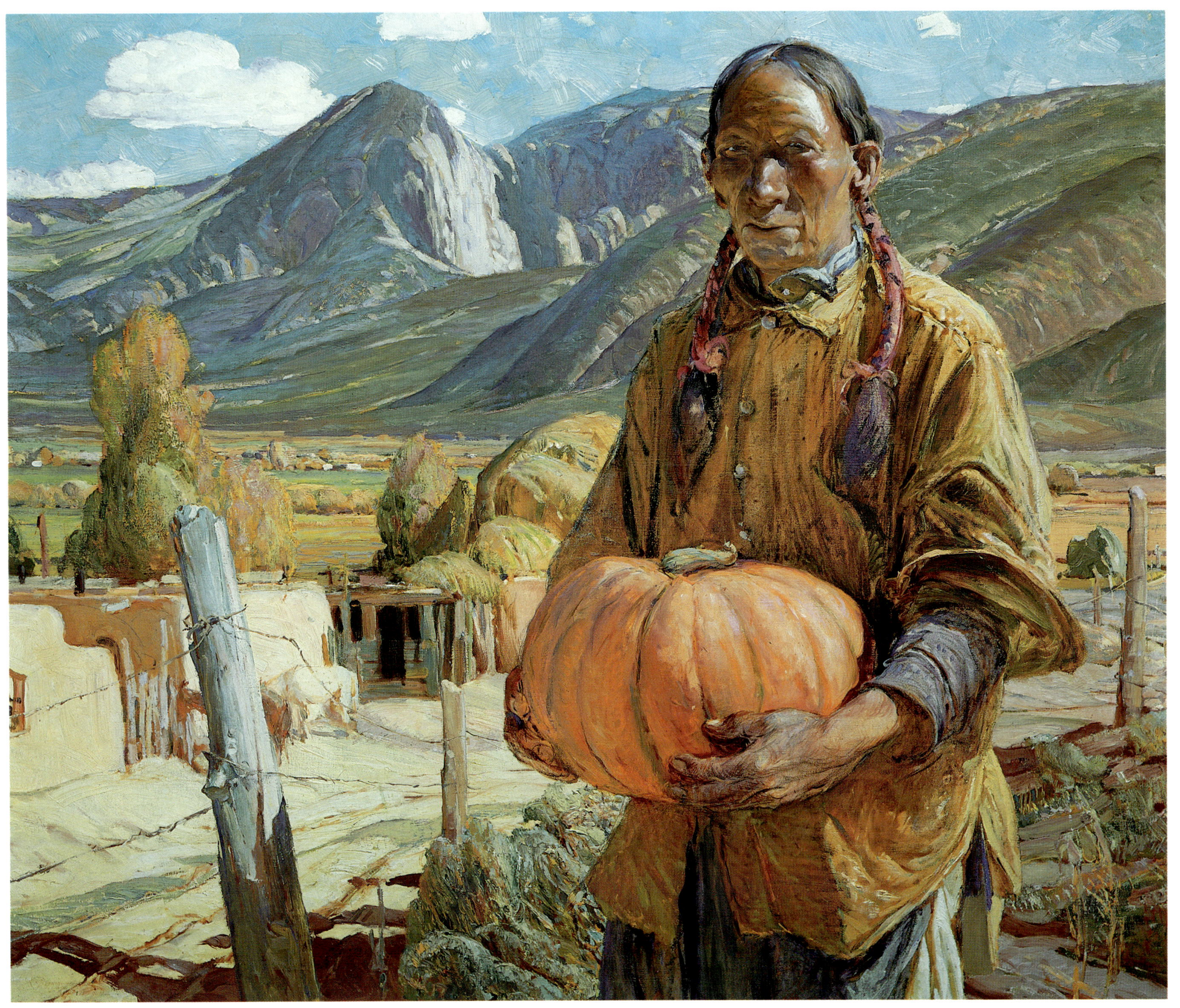

OCTOBER. 39x45 inches, oil on canvas. Photo courtesy of Gerald Peters Gallery, Santa Fe, New Mexico.

The Christmas season in Taos is an experience one can never forget. There is the cold, and sometimes the snow, and above all the air of celebration. Around the Plaza, the last-minute shoppers with wrapped gifts and heavy bags merge into the afternoon swirl of festivity. In the adobe homes, there is a warm wood fire, the ever present posole, chile and biscochitos. Eager children keep watchful eyes on the gifts, while arrangements of juniper, mistletoe and carved *santos* decorate the mantles.

On Christmas Eve, almost everyone goes to the Pueblo to witness the Indian ceremony of the Blessed Virgin. Thousands gather about the huge bonfires of pitchwood in the central Plaza, warming cold hands and awaiting the appearance of the image of Mary. The bells toll, the black smoke from the fires billows skyward and the procession pours out of the little chapel. First come the little children, dancing to the drums, then the priest and the statue of Mary carried under a white canopy. The Indians begin firing rifles as the parade passes the bonfires and then proceeds to the river. The procession circles the Pueblo, then returns to the chapel. The non-Indian crowd begins to break up—leaving for Christmas Eve dinners and parties with family and friends.

Christmas Eve was a special delight at the home of Oscar and Winnie Berninghaus. The fireplace was the center of attention for guests coming in from the cold Taos night. Oscar loved the season and had a tradition all his own. He would go from guest to guest, and with great care and interest inquire as to the exact drink wanted by each person, even to minute details like onion, olive or twist. Some would want scotch and water, others scotch and soda, bourbon and coke or perhaps a glass of wine. He made notes and disappeared into the kitchen. After a reasonable length of time, he would reappear with a large tray of Manhattans—for everyone! This little joke was typical of Berninghaus' dry sense of humor. Most of the guests knew what was going to happen—they had been there before!

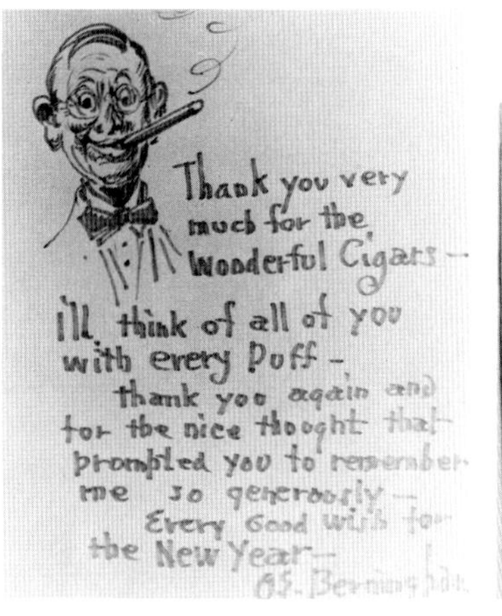

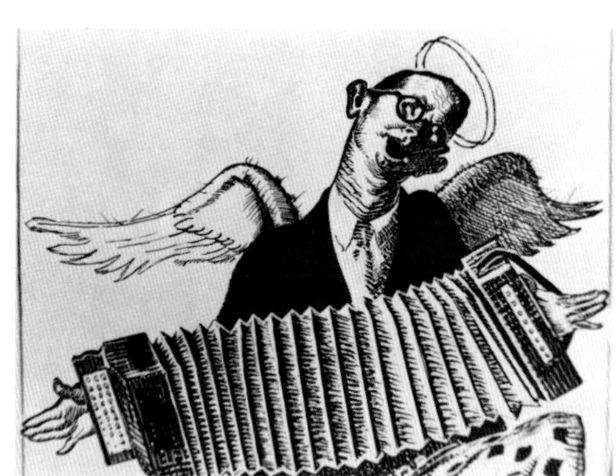

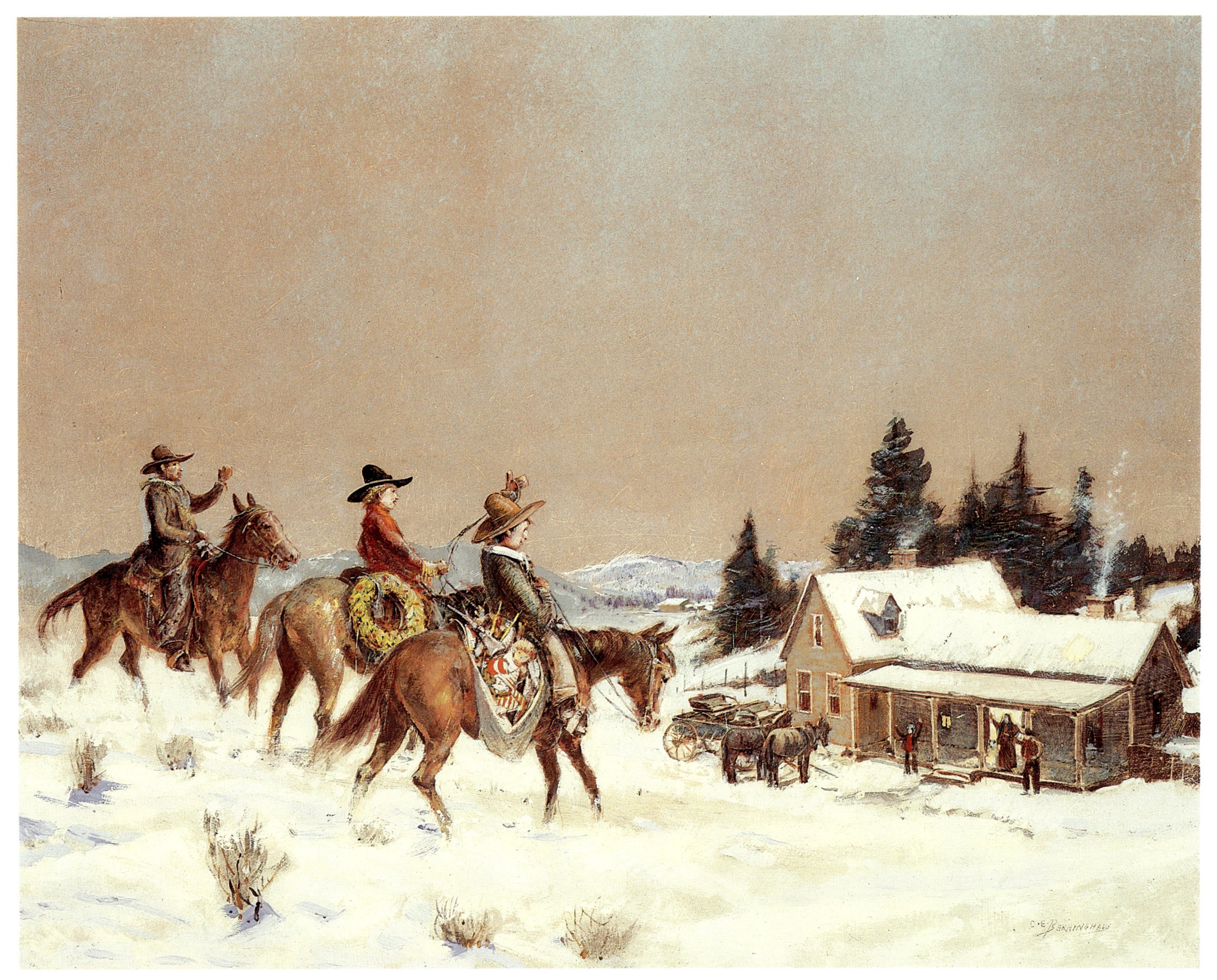

HOME FROM SHOPPING—CHRISTMAS EVE, c.1940. 16×20 inches, oil on masonite. Private collection.

By 1950, Oscar Berninghaus was spending a great deal of time in his studio, and less time outdoors. This is not to say he had reduced his painting schedule, although he was now 76 years old, but just that there were so many unfinished projects. The winters in Taos were very cold, and Oscar was beginning to consider his health a bit. It was cheerful to sit by the fire and visit with friends of all ages from the community. He always had time for visitors, and made everyone feel welcome—even if he was in the middle of painting.

Through the years, various art critics had written about the Taos artists, and Edmund Wuerpel was one of them. He was a long-time friend and neighbor of Berninghaus in St. Louis, but did not let this relationship keep him from straightforward reviews about any of the painters. Referring to the rigid discipline Oscar outlined for himself during the early years of his life, Wuerpel said: "Is it to be wondered that his work has remained conventional? There are definite phases in his work, periods of hardness in his technique, ultraconventionality in his arrangement, coldness and lack of light in his color. But always the honest endeavor to render truth—truth as he saw it at the moment. Current events changed, attitudes and requirements broadened. Men's minds underwent radical reversals in response to progressive changes. That was inevitable and Berninghaus changed too; even his attitude towards truth changed, but his method of revealing this truth remained fundamentally the same."

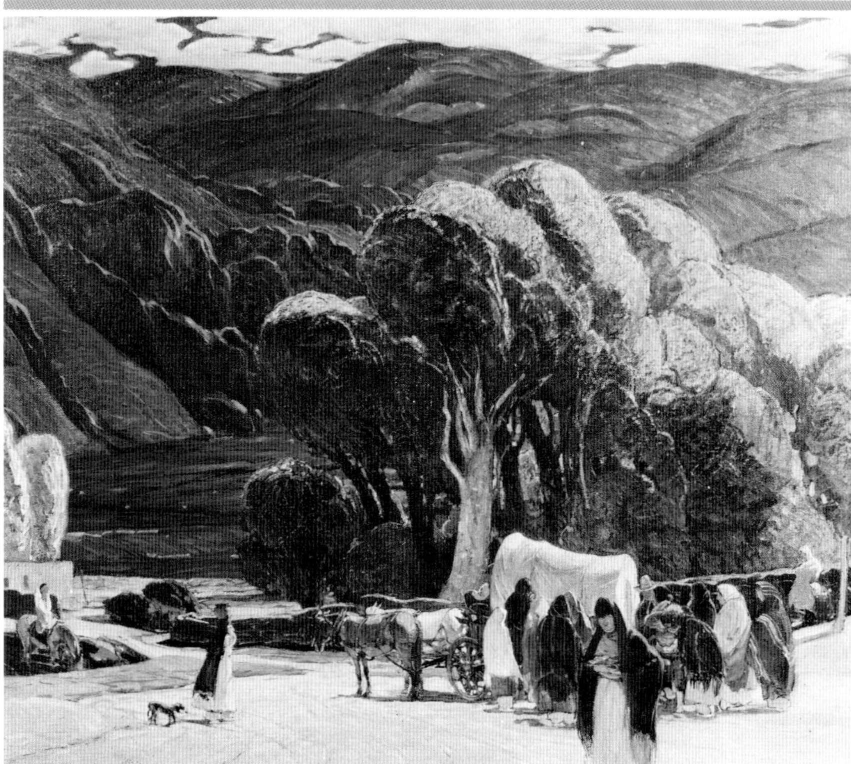

APACHE VISITORS. 35x40 inches, oil on canvas. Harrison Eiteljorg Collection, Indianapolis, Indiana.

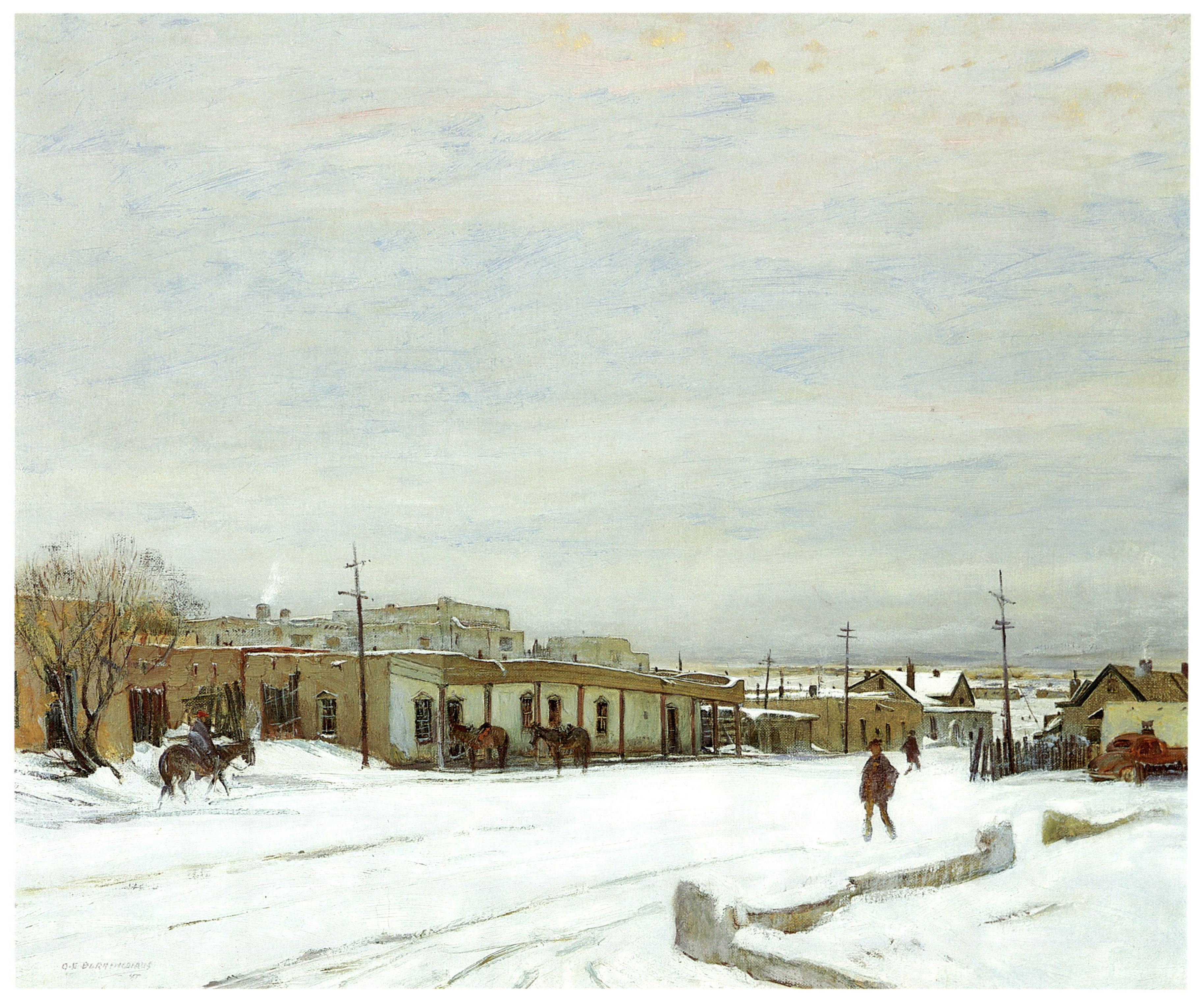

MIDDLE RANCHITOS ROAD, WINTERTIME, 1947. 20x25 inches, oil on canvas. Private collection.

In relation to the outside world, the village of Taos had changed very little since Oscar Berninghaus first came in 1899. It had acquired electric power, gas heat, radio and television, filling stations and some paved streets. For the most part, however, it remained a small town with its original charm. But the attitude of the art community was quite another matter because dramatic events over the past fifty years, including two World Wars, the atomic bomb, air travel and modern industry all brought changes in the basic concept of Western man. These changes were being expressed in the art world by Jackson Pollock, Grant Wood, Pablo Picasso and Salvador Dali, just to mention a few. The pop art of Jasper Johns and Andy Warhol was indeed far removed from the representational canvases of Taos. There were exceptions, such as Andrew Wyeth and Peter Hurd, who rejected the idea that soup cans, soft drink bottles and old newspapers were proper subjects for great art.

Berninghaus had watched the different movements come and go—the fauvists with their comfort and pleasure, the cubists and their struggle with changing forms, the Italian futurists obsessed with the speed and force of machines, the Dadaists and their dissatisfaction with self satisfaction and the surrealists and their time-warp mysteries. To Berninghaus they were all valid in their own way—he neither approved nor disapproved, nor did he change his approach because of them. He preferred to remain in his own world, a world of hope and promise filled with blue skies, mountains, trees and fresh air.

Indians, too, had changed by the 1950s, and Pueblo life was different. Little Joe Gomez, his model, more and more was wearing white man's attire. *Little Joe* is a splendid example of Berninghaus' versatility and awareness. Although the clothing is contemporary, the subject is *all* Indian with dignity and stature. This feeling of calmness and stability is achieved by a special emphasis on mass and the blurring of space, giving impact to the portrait.

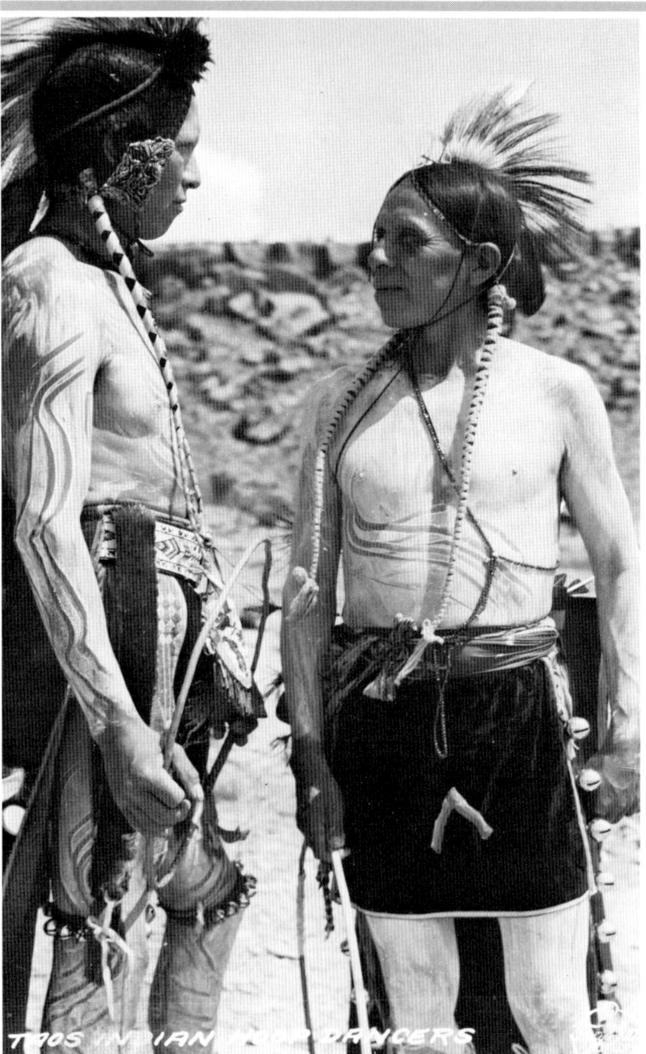

Little Joe Gomez, right. c. 1940.

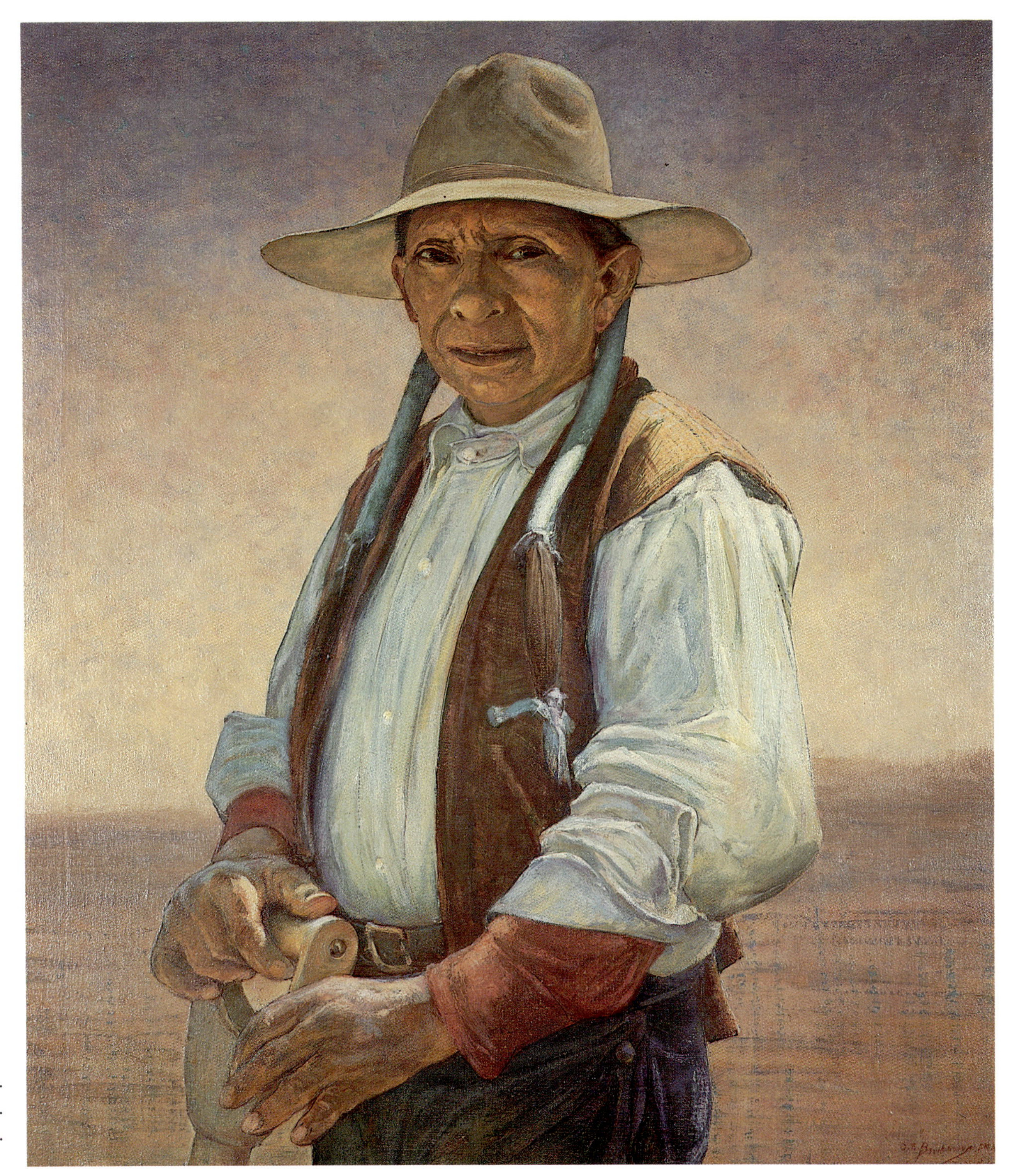

LITTLE JOE, 1941.
30×25 inches, oil on canvas.
Private collection.

Over the years, Oscar Berninghaus had employed almost all the techniques and materials available to an artist, from simple pen-and-ink drawings to the great oils that made him famous as a painter of American Indians and the Western frontier. He had mastered watercolors, both transparent and gouache, had painted on paper, canvas and masonite. His materials included charcoal, beeswax, gum arabic, synthetic resins and even egg tempera, an ancient material consisting of pigment and egg yolk. Berninghaus enjoyed working with monotypes, a very difficult and surprising task.

For a monotype (one print), he used a glass surface, onto which he painted the scene in oil. Then, before the paint had time to dry, he would overlay the painted glass surface with the receiving paper and press lightly with a roller. The real skill required for the monotype is in removing the paper without any lateral movement, which if done incorrectly will result in a blurred image. The ideal result is an actual transfer of color and composition with no indication of brushwork. Just one mistake, like pressing too hard on the paper, or pulling it off the painted surface too quickly, and the entire project is ruined.

No doubt Berninghaus had a few disasters of this type, but as was consistent with his nature, he persisted and achieved a beautiful result of mood and tone. He was generally known among his peers as being a real master of the monotype, and *Moonlight, Taos* and *Early Taos Home* help to prove that point.

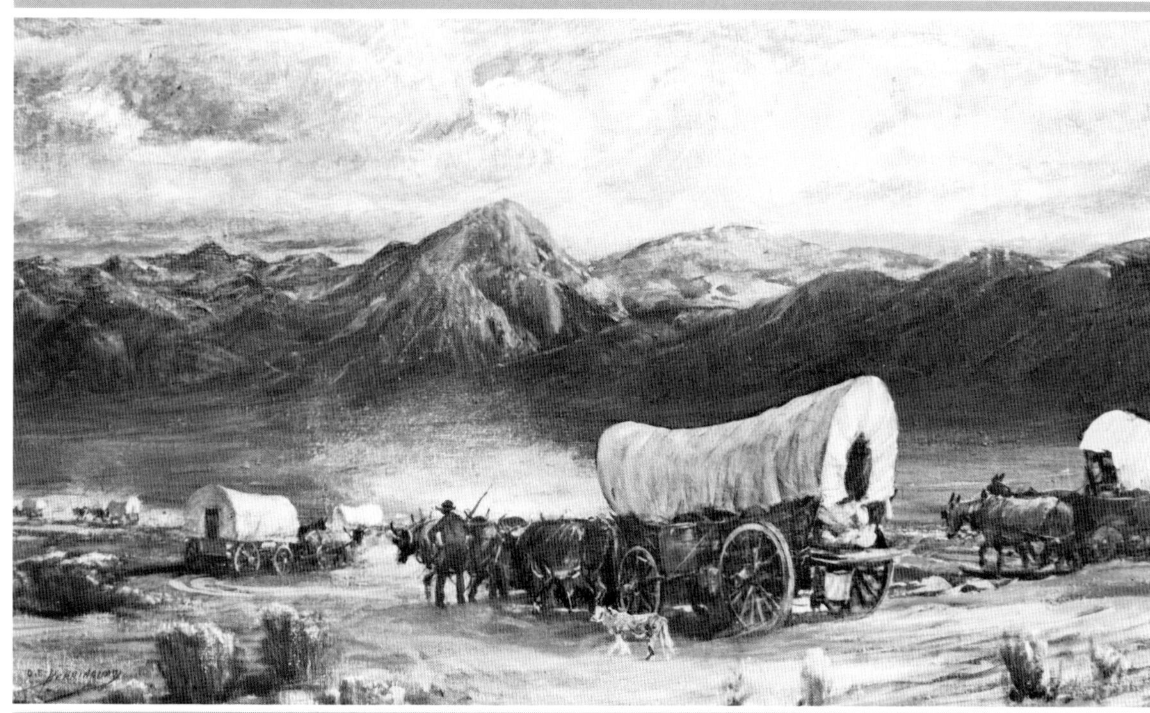

SHEEPHERDERS CHANGING CAMP, c. 1948.
25x30 inches, oil. Unlocated.
Photo from artist's file.

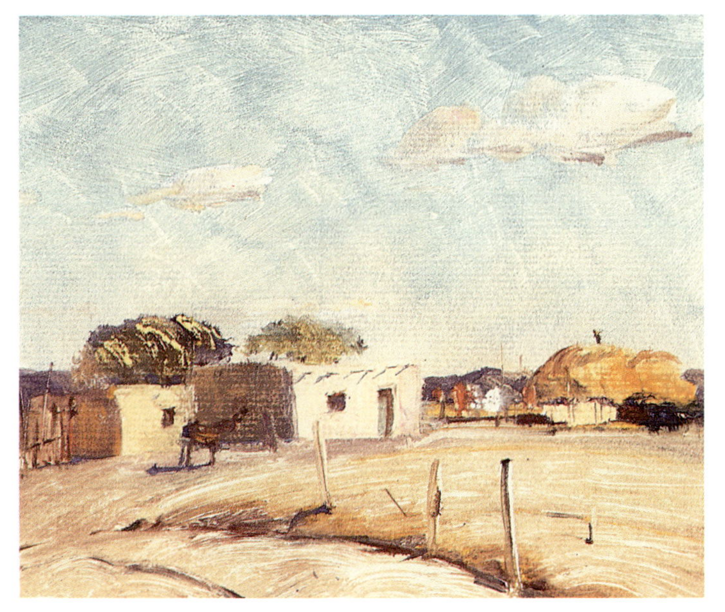

EARLY TAOS HOME, 1935.
5x6 inches, monotype.
Private collection.

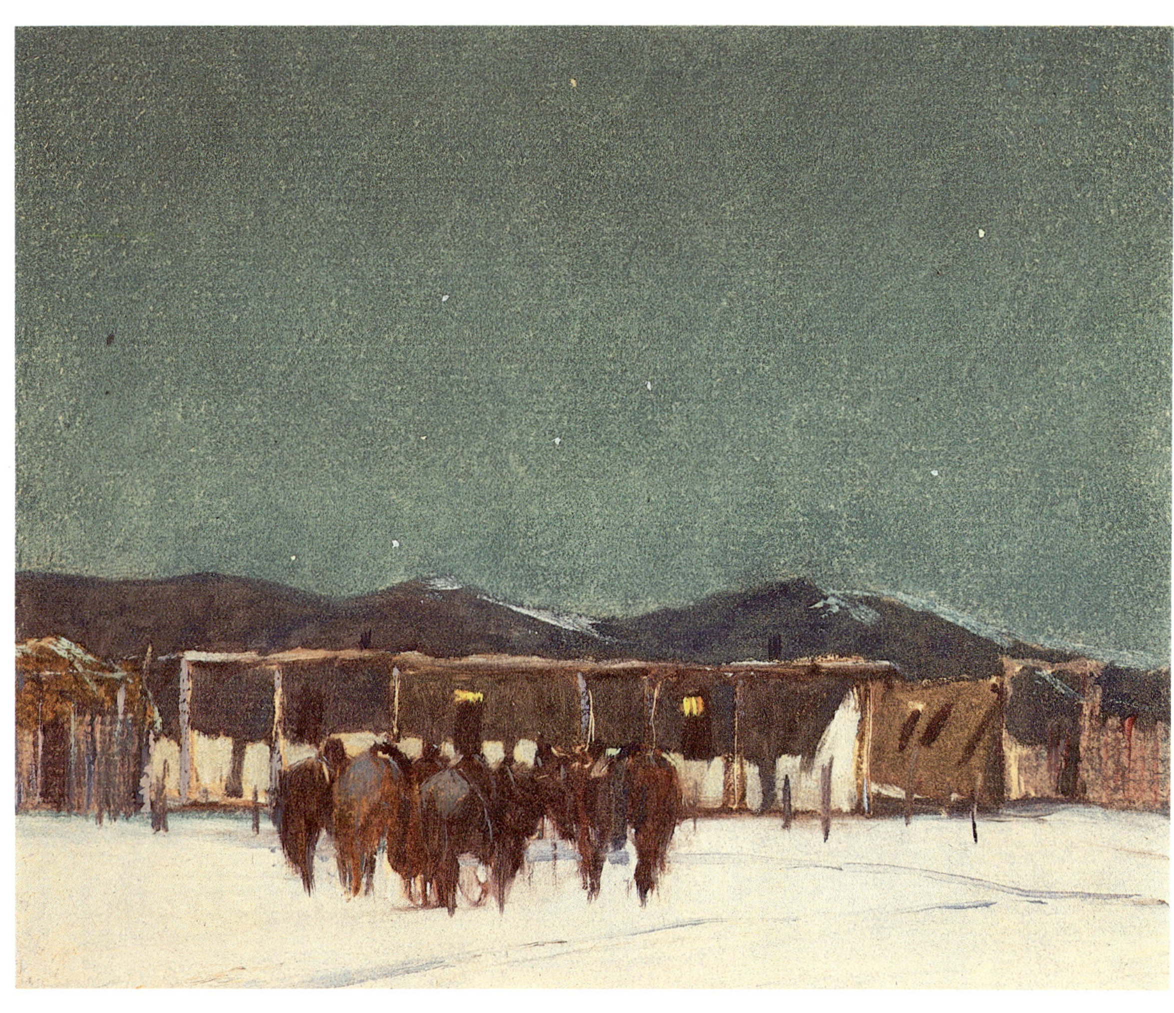

MOONLIGHT, TAOS, 1927.
5x6 inches, monotype.
Private collection.

Oscar Berninghaus died on April 27, 1952, three days after suffering a heart attack. He was 77 years old. Taos, New Mexico, which he had helped to make so famous, was shocked and saddened by his sudden illness and death. The entire community had respected and loved "Bernie," not only as a noted artist, but also as a citizen who had done so much during the years to develop Taos into one of the world's great art centers. The funeral service was held at his studio, and was attended by many of the old-timers in the art world, and by friends from the Taos Pueblo as well as the town's leading business people. On Tuesday, April 29th, he was buried at Sierra Vista Cemetery, and businesses were closed for one hour as a tribute to him. The life of Oscar Berninghaus had been a busy, productive one, and it was fitting that it should end in the little village he had loved and painted so much.

In an interview with *El Crepusculo,* the Taos newspaper founded in 1835 by Padre Martinez, Rebecca James told of her husband's last visit with Berninghaus on April 23rd, just one day before his heart attack: "You know, Bernie is simply remarkable. He was working on an enormous painting when I arrived, and he met me at the door, brushes and maulstick in his hand, spruce and spry as any youngster, and said: 'Come on, Bill, sit down awhile and we'll have a talk.' We talked about politics and taxes mostly. He told me about his trip East with Winnie, and said how happy he was to be home, that he would never leave Taos again, that he wanted to live here and no place else, wanted to die here, and no place else. And now he's gone, his brushes and maulstick, palette and paints laid down forever."

In another part of the article, Mrs. James wrote: "The body of his work is a magnificent document of the Southwest, painted as no one else has put down this country. It is suffused with tenderness, is straight and tough as a pine tree, strong as a verb."

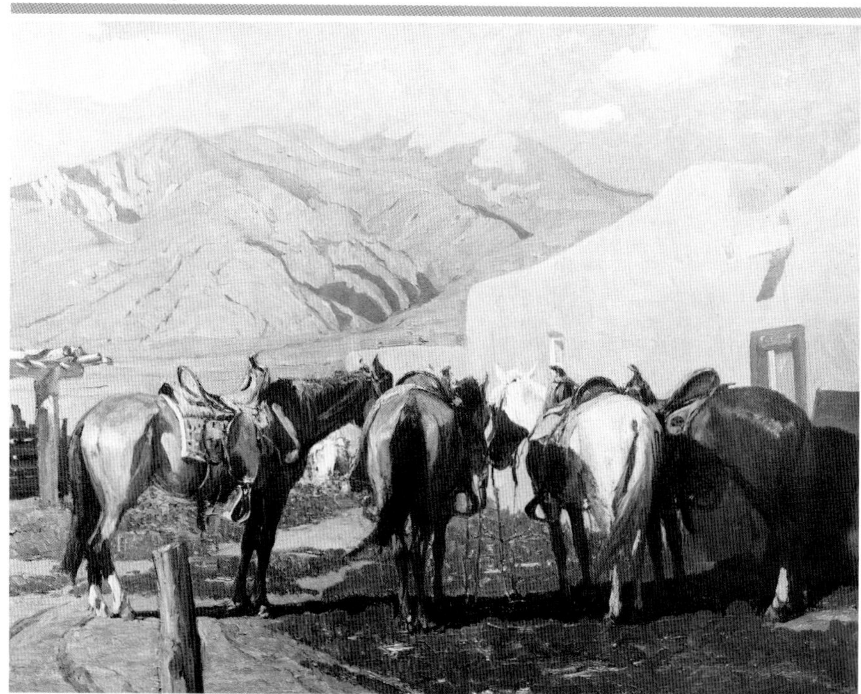

SADDLED PONIES, c. 1920. aka: *MEXICAN PONIES.* aka: *THE VIGIL.* Unlocated. Photo from artist's files.

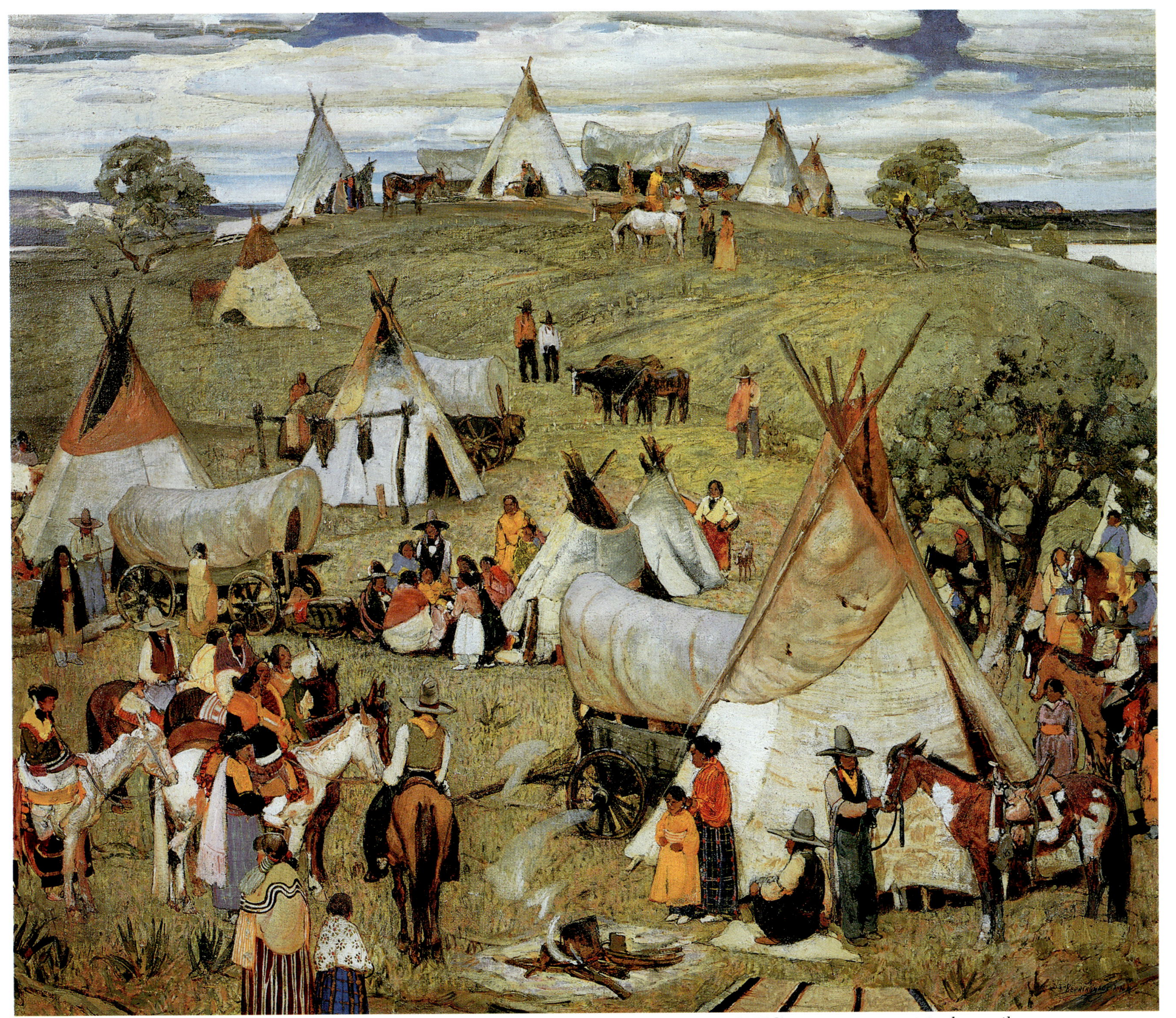

APACHE ENCAMPMENT AT BOULDER LAKE (JICARILLA APACHES), c. 1930. 35×40 inches, oil.
Photo courtesy of Gerald Peters Gallery, Santa Fe, New Mexico.

Almost all the major American newspapers and art publications carried the story of Berninghaus' death in early 1952. The *St. Louis Post-Dispatch* did an entire section on the life and times of the painter, complete with pictures and commentaries written by art critics who had known and worked with him. The *New York Times* mentioned his passing, as did papers in San Francisco, Los Angeles, Chicago and Boston. Berninghaus had been a giant of American art, and his death drew national attention.

One critic said, "It is hard to write of such a man. There was nothing picturesque in that rather slight, shy figure in a business suit of gray, on whose grayish-brown eyes the rimless spectacles conferred an owlish look." Of Oscar Berninghaus, the artist, he said, "No painter of the West has so caught and fixed its moods. The brilliant sky with the drift of lazy clouds, the misty mass of distant granite peaks, the rounded nearer hills, the shadows of purple, lavender and amethyst, the misty blues of the timbered hillside, these are not superficial things. They are the heart of the West. Also, they reveal the heart of Berninghaus. A man could live with a Berninghaus painting as he could live with the mountains."

Oscar Berninghaus the man was dead, but Oscar Berninghaus the artist was and is very much alive. He carved out a niche for himself in American art, as did the other Taos painters, that will live forever.

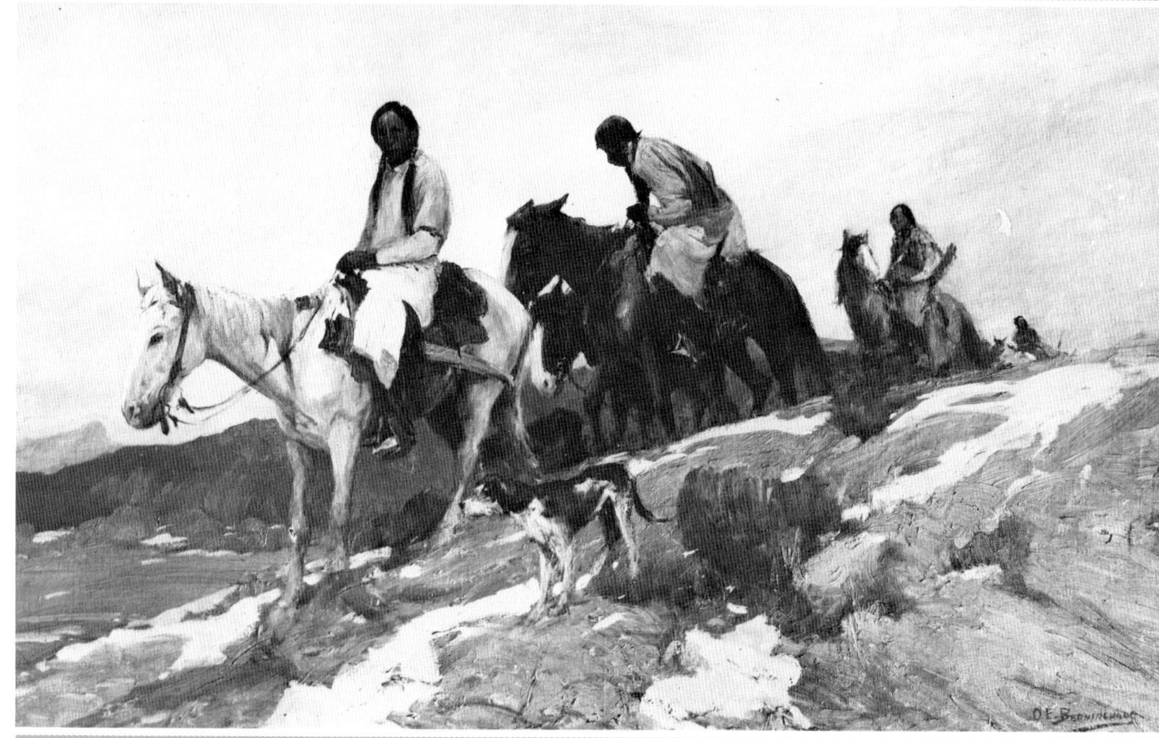

MOVING DAY, 1920.
30x40 inches, oil.
Harrison Eiteljorg Collection.

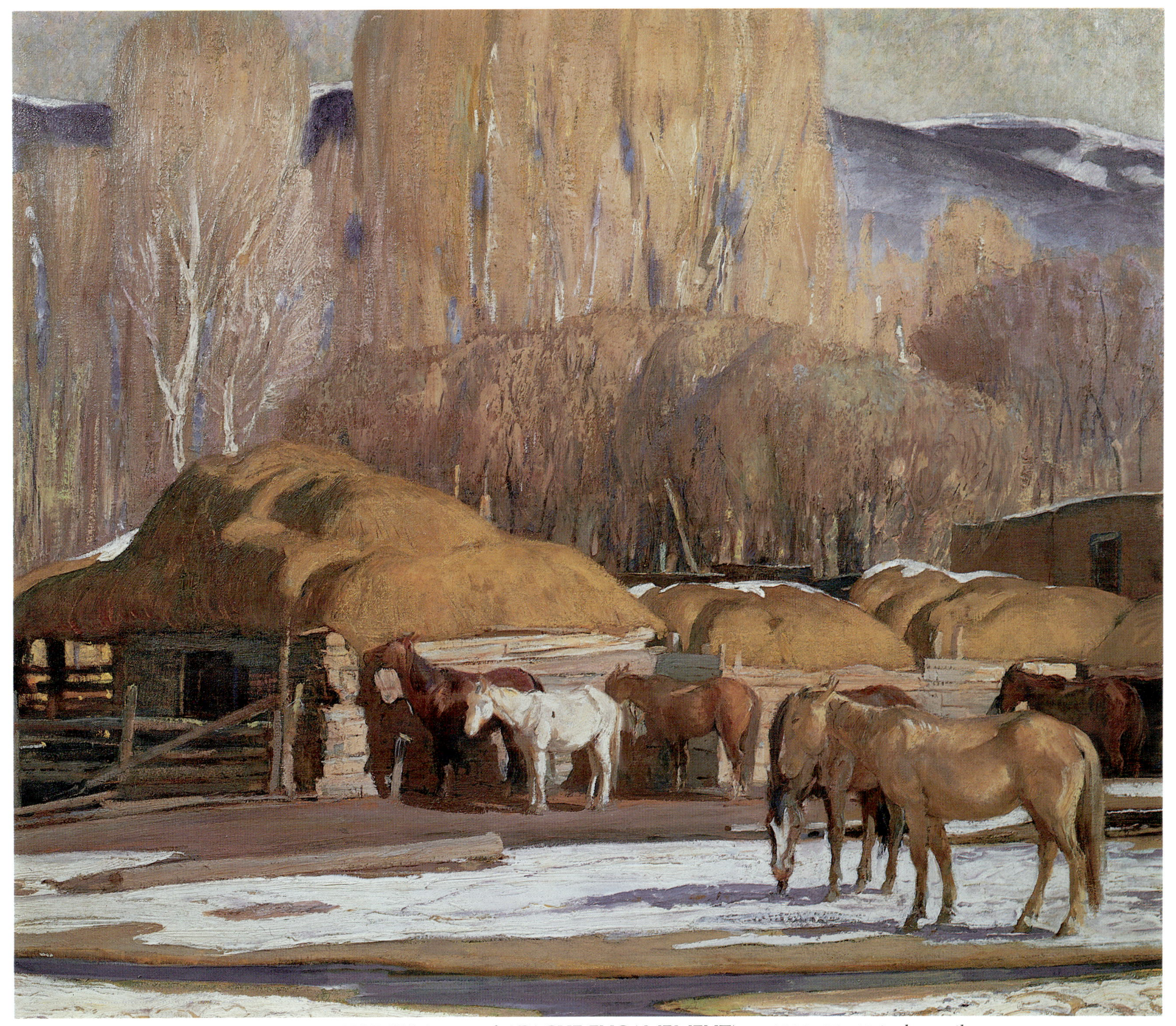

CORRALLED HORSES (verso of APACHE ENCAMPMENT), c. 1930. 35×40 inches, oil.
Photo courtesy of Gerald Peters Gallery, Santa Fe, New Mexico.

What was it that made Oscar Berninghaus such a fine American painter? Some say it was because of his incredible draftsmanship—the ability to draw. Others allude to his special handling of color, mass and form, and an eye for subject material. Perhaps all these comments are valid, and certainly these components are the essentials of any first-rate painter. However, the dominant factor in the success of Berninghaus appears to be courage—the courage to stick to what he believed, and continue looking neither to the right nor to the left. In this respect, Berninghaus could be considered narrow-minded, but let us not forget that most great empires were built by narrow-minded individuals, and in many instances given away by more broad-minded leaders who simply debated themselves out of business. He did not debate the subject of art—he painted and left the debating to others. In his own humorous way, he also realized the wisdom of the old adage: "If something works, don't try to fix it." He had captured the imagination of the American art world with his Indians, horses, breathtaking landscapes, blue skies and vast mountain ranges. It worked—why change it? As writer Rebecca James said: "He stuck to his ponies, his sage, his skies, Indians, Spanish Americans, mountains, streams and valleys because he loved them, believed in them and was still painting them with utmost fidelity the day before his heart gave out."

Of himself, Berninghaus wrote to an old friend, Edmund Wuerpel, in 1951 just months before he died: "I belong to the vintage of yesterday and having faith in it, I still paint that way. At the same time I respect the present-day movement, the modern, providing it is basically sound and good. I believe the powers that be have endowed each and every one of us with certain talents, ambitions and skills, some with more, some with less. And it is our obligation to do the best we can with the allotment assigned to us. I have tried to do the best I could with mine."

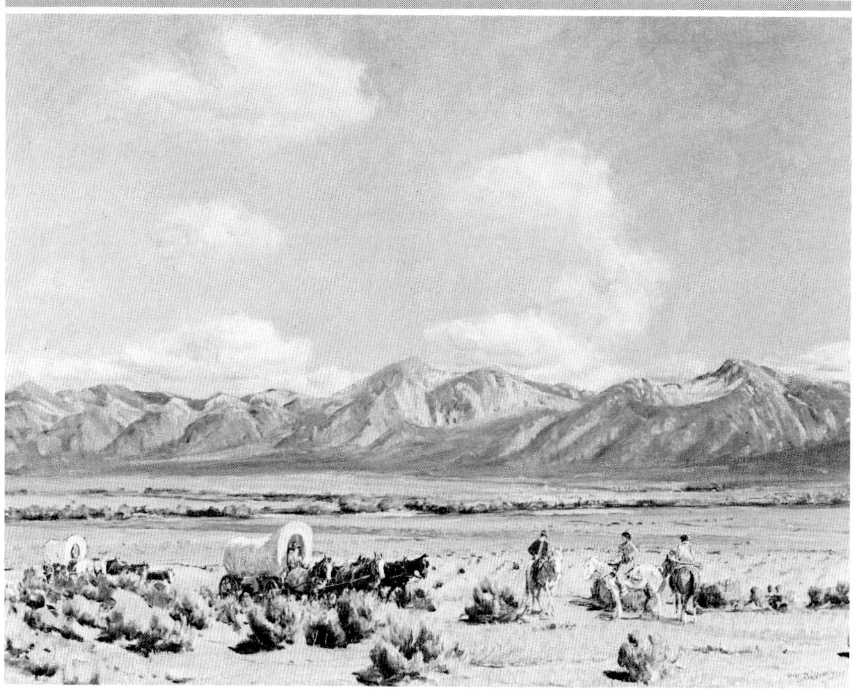

HOMESTEADERS SEEKING GREENER PASTURES, c. 1940. 25×30 inches, oil. Unlocated. Photo from artist's file.

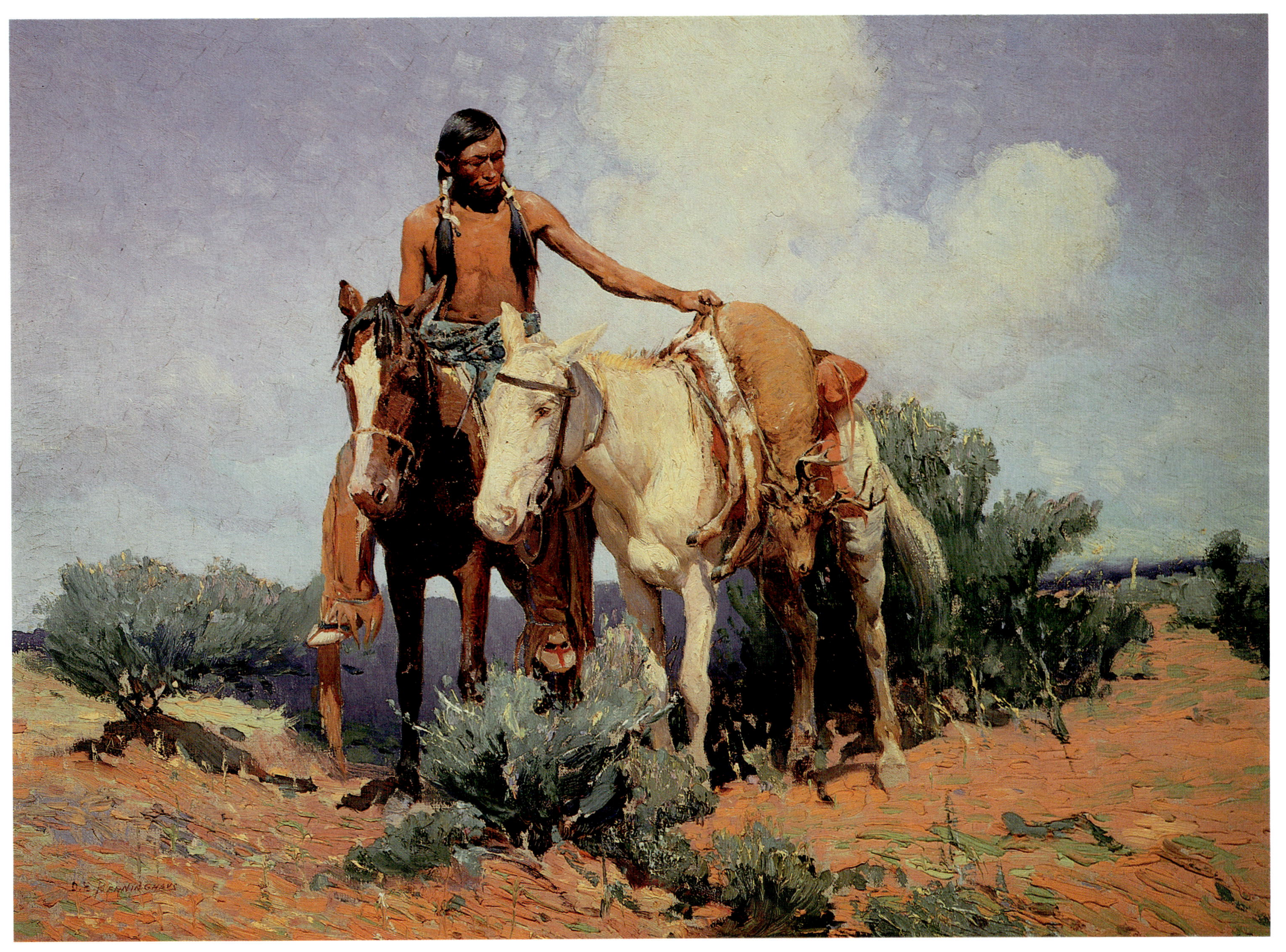

HIS FIRST BUCK. 22×30 inches, oil on canvas. Private collection.

They came to Taos and discovered themselves. Painters who found a paradise of color and form—a special light that could change faster than it could be captured—ever evasive and beautiful, if you could get it just right. And they did on canvas—from the bursting brass of mountain sunrises to the delicate shades of purple twilight. For subjects, the plain was alive with horsemen, wagons, Indians, merchants and colorful characters from all over the world. For more than half a century, they ate, drank, talked, painted, wrote and lived in this mecca of intellectual diversity—Taos. For some, especially the artists, it was a dream come true with the rich brown tones of the Indian Pueblo and its people. Some imagined the Indian living in perfect harmony with nature, and they painted a tone poem of woodwinds and strings and yellow aspens—blue skies and the rich, warm glow of campfires, reflecting from the bronze bodies and faces. For some, it was the great mountain, the sentinel that stood vast and silent, overlooking the ever changing drama of human toil on the plain below. They painted the action, the summer heat and snows of winter. Their canvases, even today, almost burst with the colors of Taos autumns and springtimes. Looking at these great paintings, you can almost hear the clear, concise genius of Vivaldi in the *Four Seasons.*

For yet others, it was the face of the Indian and his ever kept secret—where did he originate? Was his past across the Bering Straits from China or the depths of the great Blue Lake to the north? Even today, no one really knows. The early Spaniards, the French trappers, the Anglos from the East—they all wondered and theorized, but the enigma of the Indian remained intact—exciting and puzzling. On canvas, they captured that certain look, something older than time, something that stirred deep emotions and gave their paintings a special place in American art.

Some of the founding artists of Taos, like O.E. Berninghaus, saw and painted the Indian in transition. In their canvases one can see the influence of the advancing Western world. There might be a tourist with camera in hand, the Spanish cross, the wagon, Western clothing, schools and automobiles. They all saw and painted Taos differently—but they all painted Taos.

Now they are all gone, these founding artists. And yet they all live, in the rich canvases that hang in the world's great museums, galleries and private homes. They made Taos an art center and achieved greatness for themselves. They came to Taos, and Oscar Edmund Berninghaus was one of them.

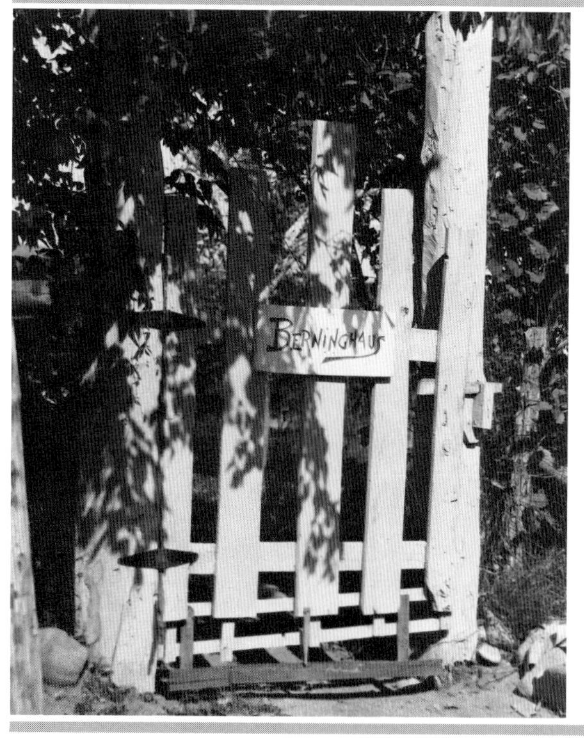

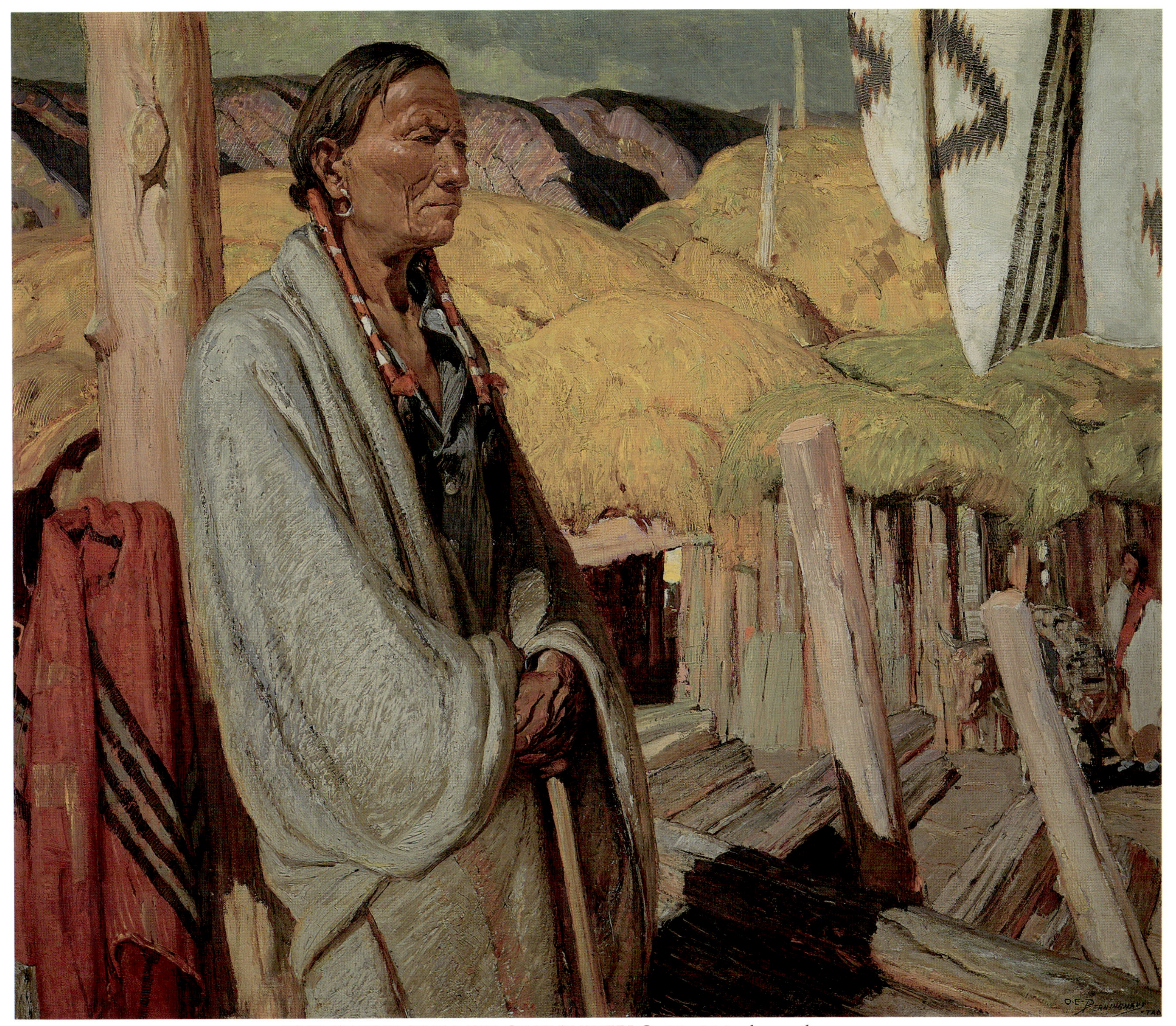

ONE OF THE OLD MEN OF THE PUEBLO. 30x36 inches, oil on canvas.
Photo courtesy of Gerald Peters Gallery, Santa Fe, New Mexico.

REFERENCES

Chronology:

1874 Oscar E. Berninghaus born, October 2, St. Louis, Missouri

1890 Leaves school, takes job with Compton and Sons, Lithographers

1893 Becomes apprentice to Woodward and Tiernan Printing Company

1894 Attends night classes, Art Department, Washington University, St. Louis

1899 First visit to Taos, Territory of New Mexico

1900 Oscar Berninghaus and Emelia Miller married, November 8, St. Louis

1900-1925 Spends each summer in Taos

1902 Dorothy Lydia Berninghaus born, July 8, St. Louis

1904 St. Louis World's Fair

1905 Julius Charles Berninghaus born, May 19, St. Louis

1913 Emelia Berninghaus dies, August 2, St. Louis

1914 Major commissions from Anheuser-Busch

1915 Taos Society of Artists officially formed, Berninghaus one of six founding members

1919 Buys home on La Loma in Taos

1921 Five lunettes installed in Missouri State Capitol, Jefferson City

1925 Family establishes home in Taos

1926 Elected as associate member of the National Academy of Design, New York

1929 Becomes designer of floats, Veiled Prophet Pageant, St. Louis

1932 Oscar Berninghaus and Winnifred Shuler married, January 31, Raton, New Mexico

1936 Paints series of Western scenes for Boatmen's National Bank, St. Louis

1942 World War II necessitates cancellation of Veiled Prophet Pageant

1942-1945 Contributes talents to war effort

1952 Oscar E. Berninghaus dies, April 27, Taos, New Mexico

Bibliography:

Bickerstaff, Laura M., *Pioneer Artists of Taos*, Denver: Sage Books, 1955

Luhan, Mabel Dodge, *Taos and Its Artists*, New York, Duell, Sloan and Pearce, 1947

Grant, Blanche C., *When Old Trails Were New*, The Story of Taos, Glorieta, New Mexico: The Rio Grande Press, Inc., 1983 (First published in 1934)

Nelson, Mary Carroll, *Legendary Artists of Taos*, New York: Watson-Guptill Publications, 1980

Broder, Patricia Janis, *Taos, A Painter's Dream*, Boston: New York Graphic Society, 1980

White, Robert R., *The Taos Society of Artists*, Albuquerque, New Mexico: University of New Mexico Press, 1983

Primm, James Neal, *Lion of the Valley*, Boulder, Colorado, Pruett Publishing Company, 1981

New Mexico Historical Review, April 1966, University of New Mexico Press

Grant, Blanche C., *The Taos Indians*, Glorieta, New Mexico: The Rio Grande Press, Inc. 1976. (First published in 1925)

Missouri Historical Review, January 1985, Columbia, Missouri, The State Historical Society of Missouri. *The Taos Connection*, New Mexican Art in Missouri's Capitol, by Bob Priddy

New Mexico Quarterly, Summer 1951, University of New Mexico Press

Articles from the following newspapers:
    St. Louis Post-Dispatch
    St. Louis Globe-Democrat
    St. Louis Star Times
    El Crepusculo de la Libertad, Taos, New Mexico
    The Taos News
    The Taos Star
    New York Times
    Chicago Tribune
    Kansas City Star
    Kansas City Times
    Tulsa Daily World
    Los Angeles Times
    The Denver Post
    The Daily Oklahoman
    Albuquerque Journal
    Albuquerque Tribune
    Santa Fe New Mexican
    Las Cruces News
    Arizona Republic
    Fort Scott Tribune

Art Clubs and Associations:

Salamagundi Club, New York

St. Louis Artists' Guild (Board member 1918---)

Two by Four Club, St. Louis

Taos Society of Artists (held all offices), 1915-1927

Society of Western Artists (Secretary 1911-1913)

Painters Group of the Middle West

The Deuce Club

Associate, National Academy of Design, 1927

Selected List of Prizes:

Dolph Prize, St. Louis, Missouri-1907, *Marquette and Joliet on the Mississippi*

Chicago Fine Arts Building Prize-1913, Society of Western Artists

Bascom Prize, St. Louis Artists' Guild-1915, *Taos Pueblo Indian, New Mexico*

Brown Prize, St. Louis Artists' Guild-1917, *The Sagebrush Trail*

Chamber of Commerce Prize, St. Louis Artists' Guild-1918, *Thirteenth and Locust Streets*

Sedalia State Fair Art Exhibit-1919

Popular Vote Prize, St. Louis Artists' Guild-1919 and 1921

Carl Wimar Prize, St. Louis Artists' Guild-1919, *Day of the Fiesta*

Grand Prize, St. Louis Art League-1920

Grand Prize, St. Louis Art League-1924, *Autumn Days*

Carl Wimar Prize, St. Louis Artists' Guild-1921

Sedalia State Fair Art Exhibit-1921

Silver Medal, Kansas City Art Institute Exhibition-1922

Ranger Fund Purchase Prize, National Academy of Design-1925, *Their Son*

Altman Prize, National Academy of Design-1926, *A Hunter of Taos*

Second Prize, Chicago Gallery of Art-1927 and 1930

Purchase Prize, Davis Exhibitions, San Antonio, Texas-1929, *Cotton Picking*

Honorable Mention, Davis Exhibition, San Antonio, Texas-1929, *Winter in the Panhandle*

St. Louis Globe-Democrat Prize, Missouri Artists Exhibitions-1929, *Taos Indians, Family Group*

CATALOGUE OF KNOWN PAINTINGS

The paintings listed in this catalogue are those located by press time, and represent only a portion of the works of O.E. Berninghaus. A concentrated effort is being made to locate all of his works, and the family would appreciate hearing from other collectors. Contact may be made through the publisher, and confidentiality is assured, unless otherwise indicated.

Explanation of abbreviations:

l.l. Signature location lower left. (O.E. Berninghaus unless otherwise noted)

l.r. Signature location lower right.

n.d. No date.

Five-digit number refers to catalog identification system.

Some credit lines have been shortened or abbreviated in the interest of space.

Paintings are listed alphabetically, roughly by subject.

Many lesser works, such as drawings and studies, are catalogued but not printed in this book.

ADOBE HOUSE AND BURROS, 12x18 inches, watercolor.
Signed: l.r. c. 1930. Private collection. 23002

ADOBE HOUSE, MAN AND HORSE, 8x9½ inches, monotype.
Signed: l.r. c. 1930. Private collection. 33003

ADOBES AND MOUNTAINS, 8½x10¼ inches, monotype.
Signed: l.l. 1950. Private collection. 35001

ALBERT "LOOKING ELK" MARTINEZ, 12x10 inches, watercolor.
Signed: l.r. 1925. Private collection. 22010

SENORA ALBERT MARTINEZ, 12x10 inches, watercolor.
Signed: l.l. 1925. Private collection. 22011

YOUNG AMERICANS, 8x5 inches, oil.
Signed. n.d. Boatmen's Bank, St. Louis. 19136

AMIZETTE, 25x30 inches, oil on canvas.
Signed: l.r. 1918. Bent Gallery, Taos, NM. 11002

AMIZETTE, HONDO CANYON, 12x14 inches, oil on board.
Signed: l.r. 1924. Private collection. 12035

APACHE ENCAMPMENT AT BOULDER LAKE, 35x40 inches, oil on canvas.
Signed: l.r. c. 1930. Private collection. 13031

APACHE VISITORS, 35x40 inches, oil.
Signed ? n.d. Eiteljorg collection. 19132

APACHE ENCAMPMENT, 7x10 inches, watercolor/pastel.
Unsigned. 1927. Private collection. 22006

APACHE INDIANS, 16x20 inches, watercolor.
Signed: l.r. n.d. Stark Museum of Art, Orange, TX. 29002

APACHE CAMP, 8x7½ inches, monotype.
Signed: l.r. n.d. Private collection. 39001

APACHES VISITING TAOS, 35x40 inches, oil on canvas.
Signed: l.l. c. 1922. Stark Museum of Art, Orange, TX. 12029

ON APPROACH, 24½x52½ inches, oil.
Signed: l.l. c. 1910. Private collection. 11043

SOUTH LITTLE ROCK, ARK., 5x8½ inches, watercolor.
Signed: l.r. c. 1899. Private collection. 20002

ARMS INSPECTION DAY, 20x24 inches, oil.
Signed: ? 1946. Private collection. 14053

CROSSING THE ARROYO, 16½x20 inches, oil.
Signed: l.r. n.d. Weimer collection. 19120

ASPEN FOREST, 40x30 inches, oil on canvas.
Signed: l.l. c. 1940. Private collection. 14004

FISHERMAN IN ASPEN FOREST, 30x36 inches, oil on canvas.
Signed: l.l. 1950. Private collection. 15008

ASPEN FOREST, 25×30 inches, oil.
Signed: l.r.   c. 1948. Private collection. 14063

ASPEN FOREST (working sketch), 11×8 inches, watercolor.
Unsigned. 1948. Private collection. 24012

ASPENS—FALL SEASON, 24×20 inches, oil on canvas.
Signed: l.l. 1928. Private collection. 12004

ASPENS IN THE FALL, 25×30 inches, oil.
Signed: l.r. c. 1940. Plaza de Retiro, Taos, N.M. 14013

FISHING AMONG THE ASPENS, 25×30 inches, oil on canvas.
Signed: l.l. 1950. Private collection. 15001

ASPENS, 20½×16½ inches, watercolor.
Signed. 1948. Private collection. 24007

ATTACK, OVERLAND STAGE, 1860, Size unknown, oil on
canvas.
Signed: l.r. c. 1914. Private collection. 11024

ATTACK ON THE WAGON TRAIN, 30¼×25¼ inches, oil.
Signed: l.r. n.d. Private collection. 19043

EARLY LEAD MINING IN WASHINGTON COUNTY, 6×12 feet,
oil on canvas mural.
Signed: l.r. 1920. Missouri State Capitol. 12054

OLD ST. GENEVIEVE, FIRST PERMANENT SETTLEMENT, 6×12
feet, oil on canvas mural.
Signed: l.r. 1920. Missouri State Capitol. 12055

*HERCULANEUM–WHERE SHOT MAKING WAS AN
INDUSTRY*, 6×12 feet, oil on canvas mural.
Signed: l.r. 1920. Missouri State Capitol. 12056

THE ATTACK ON VILLAGE OF ST. LOUIS IN 1780, 8×16 feet,
oil on canvas mural.
Signed: l.r. 1920. Missouri State Capitol. 12053

SURRENDER OF THE MIAMIS TO GENERAL DODGE IN 1814,
8×16 feet, oil on canvas mural.
Signed: l.r. 1920. Missouri State Capitol. 12052

AUTUMN DAYS, 35½×40 inches, oil.
Signed: l.r. 1925. Galleries Sternberg, Chicago. 12003

AUTUMN VILLAGE, 10×12 inches, oil on panel.
Signed: l.l. n.d. Private collection. 19031

BALBOA, PACIFIC OCEAN, 22×46 inches, oil on canvas.
Signed: l.r. c. 1914. Saint Louis Art Museum, St. Louis, MO.
11011

BASEBALL GAME, TAOS, 25×30 inches, oil.
Signed: l.l. c. 1930. Private collection. 13029

BEER GARDEN SCENE, 6×16 inches, watercolor.
Unsigned. c. 1920. Private collection. 22001

BEER GARDEN SCENE, 5×15 inches, watercolor.
Unsigned. c. 1920. Berninghaus collection, Germany. 22013

BERNINGHAUS RANCH, TAOS, N.M., 9×13 inches, oil.
Signed: ? c. 1940. Mr. and Mrs. Daniel Liberman. 14059

THE BLANKET TRADERS, 16×20 inches, oil on masonite.
Signed: l.r. n.d. Robert Anderson collection. 19002

CANAL BOAT, 22×46 inches, watercolor.
Signed: l.l. c. 1914. Saint Louis Art Museum, St. Louis MO. 21005

BRAVE OF THE TAOS MOUNTAINS, 16×20 inches, oil on board.
Signed: l.r. n.d. Butler Institute of American Art. 19000

HIS FIRST BUCK, 22×30 inches, oil on canvas.
Signed: l.l. n.d. Private collection. 19030

THE OLD BUCKSKIN, 25×30 inches, oil.
Signed: l.r. n.d. Eiteljorg Collection. 19133

BUILDING THE STEEL BARGES, size unknown, oil.
Signed. 1919. Private collection. 11044

BULLFIGHT, MEXICO, 45×51 inches, oil.
Signed: l.l. 1932. Private collection. 13003

A PARTY IN THE BUNKHOUSE, 16×20 inches, oil on canvas.
Signed: l.r. 1949. Private collection. 14047

PROSPECTOR ON BURRO, 5x6 inches, etching.
Unsigned. c. 1920. Private collection. 32007

CAMINO DEL PUEBLO NORTE, TAOS, 15x27 inches,
watercolor.
Signed: l.r. O.E.B. 1946. Private collection. 24013

THE CAMP, 12½x8½ inches, oil.
Signed. n.d. Boatmen's Bank, St. Louis. 19137

A CAMP IN THE CANYON, BEVO, 22x46 inches,
watercolor/ink.
Signed: l.l. c. 1914. Saint Louis Art Museum, St. Louis, MO. 21006

MOVING CAMP, 4½x8¼ inches, watercolor.
Signed: l.r. n.d. Private collection. 29000

GRAND CANYON VIEWPOINT, 11½x6½ inches, watercolor.
Unsigned. c. 1920. Private collection. 22008

UNTITLED GREETING CARD, 15¾x15¾ inches, oil.
Signed: Winnie and Bernie. 1947. Museum of Fine Arts, Santa Fe,
NM. 14031

CARD TO REBECCA JAMES, 5½x8¾ inches, watercolor.
Signed: Winnie and Bernie. 1949. Museum of Fine Arts, Santa Fe,
NM. 24011

CEMETERY IN NEW MEXICO, 9x13 inches, oil on board.
Signed: l.r. c. 1940. McNay Art Museum, San Antonio. 14016

CEREMONY OF THE RABBIT HUNT, 30x40 inches, oil on
canvas.
Signed: l.r. 1921. Museum of Western Art, Denver, CO. 12013

CHAMISO ALONG THE ROADSIDE, 25x30 inches, oil.
Signed. 1917. The Thomas Gilcrease Institute of American History
and Art, Tulsa, OK. 14025.

CHARLEY'S PLACE, 16x20 inches, oil.
Signed: l.l. 1919. Private collection. 11030

CHILI TIME, NEW MEXICO, 12x18 inches, watercolor.
Signed: l.l. c. 1930. Private collection. 23003

CHRISTMAS EVE, 16x20 inches, oil on masonite.
Signed: l.r. c. 1940. Private collection. 14005

GUADALUPE CHURCH PLAZA, 20x24 inches, oil on canvas.
Signed: l.r. 1947. Stark Museum of Art, Orange, TX. 14033

CHRIST CHURCH CATHEDRAL, 30x33³/₈ inches, watercolor.
Signed: l.r. 1913. Saint Louis Art Museum, St. Louis, MO. 21004

COMMERCE ON THE LEVEE (study), 8x14 inches, watercolor.
Unsigned. c. 1934. Private collection. 23017

COMMERCE ON THE LEVEE IN THE EARLY 80s, 8x12 feet, oil
on canvas.
Signed: ? 1936. Sverdrup, Parcel and Associates, St. Louis, MO.

CORN DANCE DAY, 20x24 inches, oil.
Signed: l.r. c. 1949. Museum of Fine Arts, Santa Fe, NM. 14030

CORNER OF MEXICAN SETTLEMENT, size unknown, oil.
Signed: l.r. 1918. Private collection. 11039

CORPUS CRISTI PROCESSION, 25x30 inches, oil on canvas.
Signed: l.l. n.d. Stark Museum of Art, Orange, TX. 19061

CORRALLED HORSES, 35x40 inches, oil on canvas.
Signed: l.r. c. 1930. Private Collection. 13031

INDIAN DRUMMER. COSTUME DESIGN, 8½x3 inches,
watercolor.
Signed: l.r. c. 1930. Private collection. 23007

BLACK MAN/COSTUME STUDY, 10x6½ inches, watercolor.
Unsigned. c. 1934. Private collection. 23010

COTTON PICKING, 30x40 inches, oil.
Signed. c. 1920. San Antonio Art League. 12010

COTTONWOOD RIVER RANCH, 35x40 inches, oil on canvas.
Signed: l.r. n.d. Los Angeles Athletic Club. 19020

THROUGH HOSTILE COUNTRY, 25¹/₈x30¹/₈ inches, oil.
Signed. 1930. The Thomas Gilcrease Institute of American History
and Art, Tulsa, OK. 13016

INDIAN COURTSHIP, size unknown, oil.
Signed: l.l. 1918. Private collection. 11034

COWBOY MESS CAMP, 22×44 inches, oil on canvas.
Signed: l.r. 1912. Saint Louis Art Museum, St. Louis, MO. 11014

COWBOY ON BURRO, 2 PACK ANIMALS, 5×6 inches, etching.
Signed: ?. c. 1925. Stark Museum of Art, Orange, TX. 32004

DANCE AT THE PUEBLO, 30×40 inches, oil on canvas.
Signed: l.l. n.d. The Anschutz Collection, Denver, CO. 19041

THE PUEBLOS AWAIT THE DANCERS, 30×40 inches, oil.
Signed: ?. 1947. Private collection. 14062

6 SCENES FROM THE DEERSLAYER, 5×11 inches each,
watercolor.
Unsigned. c. 1915. Stark Museum of Art, Orange, TX. 21008

DESERT TRAVELERS, size unknown, oil.
Signed: l.r. n.d. Private collection. 19126

DOMAIN OF THEIR ANCESTORS, 24×30 inches, oil on canvas.
Signed: l.r. n.d. Private collection. 19055

STOPPING FOR A DRINK, 11½×16 inches, oil on canvas.
Signed: l.l. 1950. Gerald Peters Collection, Santa Fe, NM. 15009

EARLY SPRING, NEW MEXICO, 16½×20½ inches, oil.
Signed: l.l. n.d. Private collection. 19019

PUFFING UP EMBUDO HILL, 12×16 inches, lithograph.
Signed: l.r. c. 1920. Private collection. 32003

EMELIA MILLER, 4½×3 inches, watercolor.
Signed: l.r. Bern 1895. Private collection. 20015

INDIAN ENCAMPMENT, 13½×9½ inches, oil.
Signed: ?. n.d. Private collection. 19109

THE ENCHANTED WOOD, 12×16 inches, oil on canvas.
Signed: l.l. n.d. The Anschutz Collection, Denver, CO. 19039

FARM SCENE, 23×46 inches, oil on canvas.
Signed: l.r. c. 1914. Saint Louis Art Museum, St. Louis, MO.
11018

NATIVE FARM, 7×8 inches, monotype.
Unsigned. c. 1940. Stark Museum of Art, Orange, TX. 34002

THE FEATHER, 20×30 inches, oil.
Signed. 1924. Gallery of the Masters, St. Louis, MO. 12006

FENCED LAND, 30×34¼ inches, oil on canvas.
Signed: l.r. n.d. Private collection. 19052

FERRY BOAT CROSSING RIVER, 19³⁄₈×43⁵⁄₈ inches,
gouache.
Unsigned. c. 1914. Saint Louis Art Museum, St. Louis, MO. 21003

SAN JUAN FIESTA, 35×40 inches, oil on canvas.
Signed: l.r. n.d. Stark Museum of Art, Orange, TX. 19074

FIRELIGHT PROCESSION, 20×24 inches, oil on canvas.
Signed: l.r. 1951. Stark Museum of Art, Orange, TX. 15012.

239 VEILED PROPHET FLOAT DESIGNS, 15×20 inches
approximately, watercolor.
Unsigned. 1929 to 1942. Missouri Historical Society. 23026

6 VEILED PROPHET FLOAT DESIGNS 15×21 inches, watercolor.
Unsigned. c. 1935. Private collections. 23020-25.

FLORIDA EVERGLADES, 22×46 inches, mixed media.
Signed. c. 1914. Saint Louis Art Museum, St. Louis, MO. 21001

INDIANS ALONG THE FOOTHILLS, 20×24 inches, oil.
Signed: l.r. n.d. Private collection. 19141

EDGE OF THE FOOTHILLS, size unknown, oil.
Signed: l.r. 1918. Private collection. 11040

IN THE PETRIFIED FOREST, 25×30 inches, oil.
Signed. n.d. Private collection. 19112

IN THE FOREST OF PUEBLO CANYON, 16×20 inches,
watercolor.
Signed. c. 1950. Private collection. 25001

FORGOTTEN, 22×30 inches, oil.
Signed: l.r. 1916. Cowboy Hall of Fame. 11004

FORGOTTEN, 24×36 inches, oil.
Signed. n.d. Private collection. 19146

CROSSING THE FOOTHILLS, 25×30 inches, oil.
Signed: l.r. n.d. Private collection. 19131

FREMONT, THE PATHFINDER, 22½×44½ inches, oil.
Signed: l.r. 1912. Saint Louis Art Museum, St. Louis, MO. 11012

FROLIC ON THE PLAINS, 36×41½ inches, oil.
Signed. n.d. Boatmen's Bank, St. Louis. 19138

FRONTIER COUNTRY STORE, 21×45 inches, oil on canvas.
Signed: l.r. c. 1914. Saint Louis Art Museum, St. Louis, MO.
11021

THE FRONTIERSMAN, 15×20 inches, gouache.
Signed: ?. c. 1940. Gallery of the Masters, St. Louis, MO. 24114

THE FRUIT VENDOR, 25×30 inches, oil on canvas.
Signed. c. 1925. The Thomas Gilcrease Institute of American
History and Art, Tulsa, OK. 12048

JAMES E. GARFIELD IN YOUTH, 20¼×7¾ inches, oil.
Signed: l.r. c. 1914. Saint Louis Art Museum, St. Louis, MO. 11019

JAMES GARFIELD, 5×11 inches, watercolor.
Signed: ?. c. 1915. Stark Museum of Art, Orange, TX. 21009

THE WIRE GATE, 12×16 inches, oil on board.
Signed: l.r. n.d. Stark Museum of Art, Orange, TX. 19080

GLORIETA, 30×34 inches, oil on canvas.
Signed: l.r. 1927. Private collection. 12022

GLORIETA PASS, 10×14 inches, oil on board.
Signed: l.l. 1940. Private collection. 14020

GLOW OF SOUTHWEST SUNSET, size unknown, oil.
Signed: illegible. 1924. Private collection. 12038

GRAND CANYON, ARIZONA, 30×40 inches, oil on canvas.
Signed: l.r.   1915. Santa Fe Railway. 11036

HER GRANDFATHER, 45×50 inches, oil on canvas.
Signed: l.r. c. 1925. Private collection. 12025

U.S. GRANT, 5×10¾ inches, watercolor.
Signed: l.c. c. 1915. Stark Museum of Art, Orange, TX. 21010

LOWER RANCHITOS HACIENDA, 21×27 inches, oil on canvas.
Signed: l.l. 1927. Private collection. 12002

AN HACIENDA IN TAOS, 25×30 inches, oil on canvas.
Signed: l.r. 1951. Private collection. 15002

HARVEST, 25×30 inches, oil.
Signed: illegible. c. 1920. Private collection. 12040

HARVEST STILL LIFE, 22×35 inches, oil.
Signed. 1946. The Thomas Gilcrease Institute of American History
and Art, Tulsa, OK. 14022

TAOS HARVEST TIME, 5×6 inches, etching.
Signed on mat. c. 1930. Private collection. 33002

GREEN HAY, 30×34 inches, oil on canvas.
Signed: l.r. 1936. Jefferson Bank, St. Louis. 13020

LANDSCAPE WITH HAYSTACK, 10×15 inches, oil.
Signed: l.l. n.d. Private collection, 19051

HAYTIME AND SHOWERS, 35×40 inches, oil on canvas.
Signed: l.r. c. 1940. Private collection. 14010

THE UNSUNG HERO, MOUNTAIN MAN, 25×30 inches, oil
on canvas.
Signed. 1951. University of Texas at Austin. 15020

8 SCENES FROM HIAWATHA, varied sizes, oil on canvas.
Signed: l.r. 1921. Stark Museum of Art, Orange, TX. 12030

BACK TO THE HILLS, 24×30 inches, oil.
Signed: ?. n.d. Private collection. 19107

LAST HITCHING RAIL, 9×12 inches, lithograph.
Signed: l.r. c. 1932. Private collection. 33005

HITCHING RAIL, TAOS PLAZA, 9×11¾ inches, lithograph.
Signed: l.r. n.d. Stark Museum of Art, Orange, TX. 39003

HITLER, 18×20 inches, watercolor.
Unsigned. c. 1942. Private collection. 24009

BERNINGHAUS HOME ON LA LOMA, 9×13 inches, watercolor.
Unsigned. 1920. Private collection. 22009

HOMESTEADER ON INDIAN LAND, 30×25 inches, oil
on canvas.
Signed: l.r. n.d. Private collection. 19123

HOMESTEADERS SEEKING GREENER PASTURES, 25x30 inches, oil.
Signed: l.r. c. 1940. Private collection. 14049

HONDO CANYON, 15½x19½ inches, oil.
Signed: l.l. 1925. Private collection. 14039

IN THE HONDO CANYON, 24x30 inches, oil.
Signed: l.l. 1951. Private collection. 15021

HORSE TRADERS, 24x30 inches, oil on canvas.
Signed: l.r. 1924. Private collection. 12020

HORSEMEN IN SAGEBRUSH, 16x20 inches, oil.
Signed: l.l. 1947. Private collection. 14006

CROWD AT THE HORSERACE, TAOS, 30x36 inches, oil.
Signed: l.r. c. 1944. Private collection. 14056

HORSES BY HAYSTACK, 20x24 inches, oil on canvas.
Signed: ?. n.d. Stark Museum of Art, Orange, TX. 19062

HORSES IN SNOW, 12x16 inches, oil on board.
Signed: ?. n.d. Stark Museum of Art, Orange, TX. 19063

HORSES, 14x18 inches, watercolor.
Signed: l.l. n.d. Stark Museum of Art, Orange, TX. 29004

HORSES, ADOBE BLDG., MOONLIGHT, 36x40 inches, oil on canvas.
Signed: l.r. c. 1914. Saint Louis Art Museum, St. Louis, MO. 11008

A HUNTER OF TAOS PUEBLO, 35x40 inches, oil on canvas.
Signed: l.r. 1926. Cranbrook School, Bloomfield Hills, MI. 12015

EARLY MORNING HUNTERS, 7x10 ⅝ inches, gouache.
Signed: l.r. 1902. Private collection. 20017

IGNACIO TRAIN DEPOT, 9x13 inches, oil on canvas.
Signed: l.l. 1900. The Anschutz Collection, Denver, CO. 10001

IGNACIO, 9x5½ inches, watercolor.
Signed: l.r. 1898. Private collection. 20007

IMMIGRANTS WEST, 13x18 inches, watercolor.
Signed: l.r. n.d. Private collection. 29014

CAMP OF THE IMMIGRANTS, 30x40 inches, oil on canvas.
Signed. 1944. Bartfield Gallery, NY. 14066

INDIAN FARMER OF TAOS, 35x40 inches, oil on canvas.
Signed: l.l. 1926. Private collection. 12049

THREE INDIAN RIDERS, 20x24 inches, oil.
Signed: l.r. 1948. Private collection. 14050

INDIAN ENCAMPMENT, 25x78 inches, oil on board.
Signed: l.r. n.d. Private collection. 19018

INDIAN GROUP, 15¾x20 inches, oil on board.
Signed: ?. n.d. Stark Museum of Art, Orange, TX. 19065

INDIAN POLICE, 14x10 inches, oil.
Signed. n.d. Boatmen's Bank, St. Louis. 19139

MOUNTED INDIAN, GALLOPING HORSE, 6¼x4¼ inches, gouache.
Signed: l.r. c. 1900. Private collection. 20016

INDIAN MOTHER AND CHILD, 5x6 inches, etching.
Unsigned. c. 1925. Private collection. 320002

INDIAN LADIES WITH POTS, 8x5 inches, monotype.
Unsigned. n.d. Weimer Collection. 39008

OLD PUEBLO INDIAN, TAOS, 10x8 inches, lithograph.
Signed: l.r. c. 1930. Private collection. 33001

INDIANS ATTACKING WAGONS, 13x24 inches, oil.
Signed: l.r. 1900. Private collection. 10002

INDIANS AND SPANISH SOLDIERS, 21x45 inches, oil on canvas.
Signed: l.r. c. 1914. Saint Louis Art Museum, St. Louis, MO. 11015

NEW MEXICO INDIANS, 23½x35½ inches, oil.
Signed: l.r. c. 1920. Missouri Athletic Club. 12034

INDIANS WATERING HORSES, 16x20 inches, oil.
Signed: c. 1920. Martin Kodner, St. Louis. 12044

INDIANS MOVING CAMP, 20x12 inches, oil.
Signed: ?. c. 1930. Mr. and Mrs. Sydney Schoenberg. 13030

INDIANS RETURNING TO TAOS, 30x36 inches, oil on canvas.
Signed: l.r. 1948. Robert E. McKee, Jr. 14019

INDIANS AND STAGE IN CANYON, 30x36 inches, oil.
Signed: ?. 1949. Private collection. 14058

INDIANS IN ASPEN FOREST, 25x30 inches, oil on canvas.
Signed: l.l. n.d. Private collection. 19001

INDIANS ON TAOS PLAINS, 30x36 inches, oil.
Signed: l.l. n.d. Private collection. 19050

INDIANS AT SUNSET, 21¾x28 inches, oil on canvas.
Signed: l.l. n.d. Jim Clark, Scottsdale, AZ. 19082

INDIANS OVERLOOKING THE MESA, 16x12 inches, oil
on board.
Signed: l.r. n.d. Nelson-Atkins Museum of Art. 19091

TAOS INDIANS, 12½x8½ inches, oil on canvas.
Signed: l.r. n.d. Boatmen's Bank, St. Louis, 19100

INDIAN AND HORSES, 9x13 inches, oil.
Signed: ?. n.d. Private collection. 19115

LANDSCAPE, INDIANS, HORSES, 6½x9 inches, oil.
Signed: signature destroyed. n.d. Weimer Collection. 19119

INDIANS ON THE MOVE, 22x40 inches, oil on canvas.
Signed: l.r. n.d. Private collection. 19134

INDIANS DRYING MEAT, 9x12 inches, watercolor.
Signed: l.l. c. 1900. Private collection. 20014

INDIANS AND THE STAGE/CANYON, 11x13 inches,
watercolor.
Unsigned. c. 1948. Private collection. 24014

INSPECTION OF ARMS, 20x24 inches, oil on canvas.
Signed: l.r. 1951. Private collection. 13011

JOE IN THE STUDIO, 36x32 inches, oil.
Signed: l.r. c. 1920. Museum of Fine Arts, Santa Fe, NM. 12023

LITTLE JOE, 30x25 inches, oil on canvas.
Signed: l.r. c. 1941. Private collection. 14001

JUST ENOUGH TIME, 35x40 inches, oil on board.
Signed: l.l. n.d. Private collection. 19086

KIT CARSON'S CABIN, 16x20 inches, oil.
Signed. c. 1920. Gallery of the Masters, St. Louis, MO. 12033

LACLEDE, SITE OF ST. LOUIS, 22½x44½ inches, oil on canvas.
Signed: l.r. c. 1914. Saint Louis Art Museum, St. Louis, MO.
11009.

IN THE VILLAGE OF LAVACITA, 16x20 inches, oil.
Signed: l.l. n.d. Private collection. 19048

LAZY DAY, 10x12 inches, watercolor.
Signed: l.r. 1928. Sternberg Galleries, Chicago. 22005

ST. LOUIS LEVEE, 10x15 inches, watercolor.
Unsigned. c. 1935. Mound City Gallery. 23019

ABE LINCOLN SPLITTING LOGS, 20¼x44⁵⁄₁₆ inches, oil.
Signed: l.l. c. 1914. Saint Louis Art Museum, St. Louis, MO. 11020

ABRAHAM LINCOLN, 5x11 inches, watercolor.
Unsigned. c. 1915. Stark Museum of Art, Orange, TX. 21007

LOG CABIN, FOUR HORSES, 16x20 inches, oil on board.
Signed: ?. n.d. Stark Museum of Art, Orange, TX. 19057

THE LOOKOUT, 25x30 inches, oil on canvas.
Signed: l.l. 1917. Private collection. 11029

1803, LOUISIANA TRANSFERRED, U.S. 10x12 inches,
watercolor.
Unsigned. c. 1920. Private collection. 22002

THE OVERLAND MAIL, 27½x39⁵⁄₈ inches, oil.
Signed: l.r. 1930. Philbrook Art Center, Tulsa, OK. 13012

WHY THE MAIL WAS LATE, 25x30 inches, oil.
Signed. c. 1940. The Thomas Gilcrease Institute of American
History and Art, Tulsa, OK. 14061

WHY THE MAIL WAS LATE (study), 15x20 inches, gouache.
Signed: ?. c. 1940. Private collection. 24115

MAKING CAMP, 9½×13¾ inches, oil.
Signed: l.r. c. 1930. Museum of Fine Arts, Santa Fe, NM. 13017

MARKET PLACE IN TAOS, 24×30 inches, oil on canvas.
Signed: l.l. n.d. Private collection. 19046

THE FUEL MERCHANT, 12¼×16 inches, watercolor.
Signed: l.l. 1940. Gerald Peters Gallery, Santa Fe, NM. 24010

MERRY CHRISTMAS, 22×46 inches, oil on canvas.
Signed: l.r.
c. 1912. Saint Louis Art Museum, St. Louis, MO. 11006

ON THE MESA OR INDIAN WITH PONIES, 9×13 inches, oil.
Signed: l.r. c. 1920. Private collection. 12013

ROADWAY ON THE MESA, 18¼×22⅛ inches, oil.
Signed. 1948. The Thomas Gilcrease Institute of American History
and Art, Tulsa, OK. 14023

ROAD ON THE MESA, 20×24 inches, oil on canvas.
Signed: l.r. 1948. Private collection. 14044

INDIANS ON THE MESA, TAOS, 16×20 inches, oil.
Signed. 1947. Gallery of the Masters, St. Louis, MO. 14046

SOME INDIANS SINGING ON MESA, 16×12 inches, oil on
board.
Signed: l.r. n.d. Nelson-Atkins Museum of Art. 19092

PUEBLO INDIANS ON THE MESA, 25×30 inches, oil.
Signed. n.d. Fenn Galleries, Santa Fe, NM. 19105

MEXICAN STREET SCENE, size unknown, watercolor.
Signed: ?. c. 1932. Private collection. 23004

CIUDAD JUAREZ MARKET, 9×7 inches, watercolor.
Signed: l.r. 1933. Private collection. 23005

TAXCO, 11×15 inches, watercolor.
Unsigned. 1932. Private collection. 23009

TAXCO, 11×15 inches, watercolor.
Unsigned. 1932. Private collection. 23011

THREE MEXICAN WOMEN, 6½×8 inches, watercolor.
Unsigned. c. 1933. Private collection. 23012

VILLAGE MARKET, OAXACA, 7×9 inches, watercolor.
Signed: l.l. 1932. Private collection. 23013

BULLFIGHT ARENA, 23¼×47¼ inches, gouache.
Signed: l.l.
c. 1932. Saint Louis Art Museum, St. Louis, MO. 23014

MEXICAN CORRAL, 16×20 inches, watercolor.
Signed: l.l. c. 1933. Stark Museum of Art, Orange, TX. 23015

GOING TO MARKET, MEXICO, 6½×9 inches, watercolor.
Unsigned. c. 1932. Private collection. 23016

OAXACA, MEXICO, STREET SCENE, 7×8 inches, monotype.
Signed: l.r. c. 1932. Private collection. 33006

OAXACA, MEXICO, OXCART, 7×8 inches, monotype.
Signed: l.r. c. 1933. Private collection. 33007

ACAPULCO, MEXICO, 7×8 inches, monotype.
Signed: l.r. 1932. Private collection. 33009

TAXCO, MEXICO, 7⅞×7 inches, monotype.
Signed: l.r. 1932. Wiggins Gallery, Roswell, NM. 33011

THE MIDNIGHT VISIT, 25×30 inches, oil on canvas.
Signed. n.d. Jefferson Bank and Trust, St. Louis, MO. 19056

MINER'S RETREAT, 16×20 inches, oil.
Signed. n.d. Woolaroc, Museum, Bartlesville, OK. 19033

MORNING IN MINING CAMP, 25×30 inches, oil on canvas.
Signed. 1950. University of Texas at Austin. 15019

MOONLIGHT, 16×20 inches, oil.
Signed: l.r. c. 1920. Private collection. 12001

MOONLIGHT IN TAOS, 24×20 inches, oil.
Signed. 1950. Woolaroc Museum, Bartlesville, OK. 15010

MOONLIGHT, TAOS, N.M., 9×13 inches, oil on board.
Signed: l.l. n.d. Private collection. 19016

MOONLIGHT, 16×20 inches, oil on canvas.
Signed: l.r. n.d. Private collection. 19029

MOONLIGHT OR THREE PONIES, 10×12 ⅛ inches, oil on canvas.
Signed: l.r. n.d. Stark Museum of Art, Orange, TX. 19058

MOONLIGHT, 10×11⅞ inches, oil on canvas.
Signed: l.l. n.d. Stark Museum of Art, Orange, TX. 19057

MOONLIGHT, 16×20 inches, oil on canvas.
Signed: l.l. n.d. Stark Museum of Art, Orange, TX. 19060

HOUSES IN THE MOONLIGHT, 16×20 inches, oil on board.
Signed: l.r. n.d. Stark Museum of Art, Orange, TX. 19064

MOONLIGHT IN RANCHITOS, 25×30 inches, oil on canvas.
Signed: l.l. and l.r. n.d. Stark Museum of Art, Orange, TX. 19067

MOONLIGHT (FIVE HORSES), 40×48 inches, oil on canvas.
Signed: l.l. n.d. Private collection. 19089

CORNER IN PUEBLO OF TAOS, 25×30 inches, oil on canvas.
Signed. n.d. Private collection. 19128

MOONLIGHT / TAOS, 20×24 inches, oil.
Signed: l.r. 1951. Private collection. 15023

MOONLIGHT, TAOS, 5×6 inches, monotype.
Signed: l.r. 1927. Private collection. 32001

MOONLIGHT MOUNTAIN LANDSCAPE, 7×8 inches, monotype.
Signed: l.r. c. 1920. Private collection. 32008

A MOOD OF THE MOUNTAIN, size unknown. oil
Signed: l.r. c. 1919. Private collection. 11041

TO THE MOUNTAINS, 10×15 inches, watercolor.
Unsigned. n.d. Private collection. 29007

MOVING DAY, 30×40 inches, oil.
Signed: l.l. 1920. Eiteljorg Collection. 12037

MOVING DAY, 24×30 inches, oil on canvas.
Signed: l.r. n.d. Gerald Peters Gallery, Santa Fe, NM. 19012

COMMUNICATION / ARIZONA POST OFFICE, 17⅝×60⅞ inches, mixed media.
Signed: l.r. c. 1935. National Museum / American Art. 23018

MIDDLE RANCHITOS ROAD, WINTERTIME, 20×25 inches, oil on canvas. Signed: l.l. 1947. Private collection.

NATURAL BRIDGE, 22×44 inches, oil on canvas.
Signed: l.r. c. 1914. Saint Louis Art Museum, St. Louis, MO. 11010

ON TO NEW LANDS, 11×14½ inches, oil on canvas.
Signed: l.r. c. 1920. Amon Carter Museum. 12009

HAPPY NEW YEAR CARD, 1½×3 inches, watercolor.
Signed. 1886. Private collection. 20010

NIGHT TRAVELERS, 16×20 inches, oil.
Signed: c. 1920. Gallery of the Masters, St. Louis, MO. 12043

NIGHT CAMP, 12×14 inches, oil on canvas.
Signed: l.r. n.d. Stark Museum of Art, Orange, TX. 19068

MIDSUMMER NIGHT, 9×13 inches, oil.
Signed: ?. n.d. Private collection. 19116

NIGHT SCENE, 8½×12⅜ inches, oil.
Signed: l.r. 1917. Museum of Fine Arts, Santa Fe, NM. 11003

NOCTURNE, 20×24 inches, oil canvas.
Signed: l.r. 1951. Stark Museum of Art, Orange, TX. 15013

OCTOBER, 39×45 inches, oil on canvas.
Signed. 1926. Private collection. 12050

OKLAHOMA SOONER RUN, 8×21½ inches, oil on board.
Unsigned. c. 1933. Private collection. 13015

ONE OF THE OLD MEN OF PUEBLO, 30×36 inches, oil on canvas.
Signed: l.r. n.d. Private collection. 19015

OLD FAITHFUL, YELLOWSTONE, 18½×42⅛ inches, oil.
Signed: l.r. c. 1914. Saint Louis Art Museum, St. Louis, MO. 11016

OREGON TRAIL, 30×40 inches, oil on canvas.
Signed. 1951. University of Texas at Austin. 15018

PACK TRAIN, 30×25 inches, oil.
Signed: l.l. n.d. Cowboy Hall of Fame. 19042

INDIANS WITH PACK HORSES, 30×25 inches, oil.
Signed: l.l. n.d. Cowboy Hall of Fame. 19045

INDIAN WITH PACK HORSE, 25×30 inches, oil on canvas.
Signed: l.r. n.d. Stark Museum of Art, Orange, TX. 19066

THE WHITE PACK PONY, size unknown, oil.
Signed: l.r. 1947. Private collection. 14051

A PASTORAL SCENE, 18×22 inches, oil.
Signed. n.d. Private collection. 19090

PATIENCE, 9×13 inches, oil.
Signed: ?. n.d. Private collection. 19111

PAVILION, FOREST PARK, ST. LOUIS, 18×22 inches, oil
on canvas.
Signed: l.r. 1920. Jefferson Bank and Trust, St. Louis, MO. 12027

PEACE AND PLENTY, 35×39½ inches, oil on canvas.
Signed: l.l. 1925. Saint Louis Art Museum, St. Louis, MO. 12028

HOT PEPPER DAY, 25×30 inches, oil on canvas.
Signed: l.l. c. 1930. Private collection. 13019

PHILMONT RANCH SCENE, 38 ⅞×167 inches, oil.
Signed: l.r. 1927. Philbrook Art Center, Tulsa, OK. 12016

PILOT KNOB, 5×8 inches, watercolor.
Signed: ?. n.d. Private collection. 29013

PLOWING THE FIELD, 16×20 inches, oil on board.
Signed: l.r. c. 1940. Private collection. 14045

PLOWING NEW GROUND, 16×20 inches, watercolor.
Signed: l.l. n.d. Stark Museum of Art, Orange, TX. 29005

THE FAITHFUL PONIES, 30×40 inches, oil on canvas.
Signed: l.r. 1918. Stark Museum of Art, Orange, TX. 11022

PICKING UP STRAY PONIES, 16×20 inches, oil.
Signed: l.r. n.d. Private collecton. 19125

TAOS INDIANS AND THEIR PONIES, 16×20 inches, oil.
Signed: l.r. 1922. Private collection. 12047

A PONY HERDER, 25×30 inches, oil.
Signed: ?. n.d. Private collection. 19142

SELF PORTRAIT, 19¾×15¾ inches, oil.
Signed: l.l. 1950. The Thomas Gilcrease Institute of American
History and Art, Tulsa, OK. 15011

POST OFFICE, TAOS, NEW MEXICO, 16×20 inches, oil.
Signed: ?. c. 1915. Gallery of the Masters, St. Louis, MO. 11026

PRIDE OF THE RESERVATION, 20½×16½ inches, oil.
Signed: l.r. n.d. Private collection. 19014

PUEBLO OF TAOS, 41×81 inches, oil on canvas.
Signed: l.r. 1914. Santa Fe Railway. 11037

TAOS PUEBLO, 16×20 inches, oil on canvas.
Signed: l.l. 1924. Private collection. 12005

TAOS PUEBLO IN MOONLIGHT, 30×40 inches, oil on canvas.
Signed: l.l. c. 1920. Private collection. 12036

PUEBLO INDIANS, MOONLIGHT, size unknown, oil.
Signed: illegible. c. 1920. Private collection. 12039

PUEBLO FAMILY, 9×12 inches, oil.
Signed. c. 1925. Private collection. 12047

IN THE PUEBLO OF TAOS, 22×28 inches, oil on canvas.
Signed: l.r. c. 1940. McKee Foundation, El Paso, TX. 14017

A CORNER IN THE PUEBLO, 16⅛×18 inches, oil.
Signed. 1946. The Thomas Gilcrease Institute of American History
and Art, Tulsa, OK. 14027

AFTER THE DANCE AT THE PUEBLO, 20½×24½ inches, oil.
Signed. 1946. The Thomas Gilcrease Institute of American History
and Art, Tulsa, OK. 14028

TAOS PUEBLO, WORLD WAR II, 30×36 inches, oil on canvas.
Signed: l.l. c. 1942. Stark Museum of Art, Orange, TX. 14036

PUEBLO INDIAN WOMAN OF TAOS, 40×45 inches, oil on
canvas.
Signed. c. 1942. Albuquerque (NM) High School. 14040

PUEBLO SCENE, NEW MEXICO, 20×24 inches, oil on canvas.
Signed: l.l. n.d. Private collection. 19008

PUEBLO-MORNING MARKET, 20½×24 inches, oil on canvas.
Signed: l.r. n.d. Private collection. 19027

PUEBLO INDIAN LIFE, 16×20 inches, oil on board.
Signed: l.r. n.d. Stark Museum of Art, Orange, TX. 19069

TAOS PUEBLO WOMAN, 26½×32 inches, oil.
Signed: ?. n.d. Private collection. 19117

PUEBLO MORNING MARKET, 20×24 inches, oil on canvas.
Signed: l.r. 1924. University of New Mexico. 12045

MORNING SHADOWS, TAOS PUEBLO, 12×16 inches,
watercolor.
Signed: l.l. c. 1920. Gerald Peters Gallery, Santa Fe, NM. 22007

PUEBLO SCENE, 5×6 inches, etching.
Signed: l.r. c., 1925. Stark Museum of Art, Orange, TX. 32005

PUEBLO CONVERSATION, 6×5 inches, etching.
Signed on mat. c. 1930. Private collection. 33012

RETURN TO THE PUEBLO, 16×20 inches, oil on canvas.
Signed: l.l. c. 1920. Mr. and Mrs. Lyle S. Woodcock. 12050

THE PUEBLO INDIAN, 16×20 inches, oil on canvas.
Signed: l.l. c. 1920. Mr. and Mrs. Lyle S. Woodcock. 12048

TAOS PUEBLO INDIANS, 16×20 inches, oil on canvas.
Signed: l.r. n.d. Private collection. 19147

IN HOT PURSUIT, 10×12 inches, oil.
Signed: ?. n.d. Private collection. 19108

THE PURSUIT, 24×36 inches, oil.
Signed: ?. n.d. Private collection. 19113

THE RABBIT HUNTER, 30×34½ inches, oil.
Signed: l.l. c. 1920. Private collection. 12026

TOO OLD FOR THE RABBIT HUNT, 35×40 inches, oil.
Signed. 1927. The Thomas Gilcrease Institute of American History
and Art, Tulsa, OK. 12031

SOME RABBIT HUNTERS ON MESA, 16×20 inches, oil on canvas.
Signed: l.r. c. 1930. Private collection. 13004

RABBIT HUNT, TAOS INDIANS, 20×24 inches, oil on canvas.
Signed: l.r. 1945. Private collection. 14003

RABBIT HUNT, TAOS VALLEY, 20×24 inches, oil on canvas.
Signed: l.l. c. 1941. Private collection. 14041

SOME INDIANS ON A RABBIT HUNT, 20×24 inches, oil
on canvas.
Signed: l.r. 1950. Private collection. 15003

RABBIT HUNTERS, 24×20 inches, oil on canvas.
Signed: l.l. 1950. Private collection. 15016

THE RABBIT HUNTER, 34⁷⁄₁₆×39½ inches, oil on canvas.
Signed: l.l. n.d. Museum of Fine Arts, Santa Fe, NM. 19035

RABBIT HUNT OR ON THE MESA, 20×25 inches, oil on canvas.
Signed: l.r. n.d. Private collection. 19044

THE RABBIT HUNT, 28×22 inches, oil on canvas.
Signed: l.r. n.d. Private collection. 19085

MORE RABBIT HUNTERS, 20×24 inches, oil.
Signed. n.d. Fenn Galleries, Santa Fe, NM. 19103

RABBIT HUNTING, 16×20 inches, oil.
Signed. n.d. Fenn Galleries, Santa Fe, NM. 19104

ALONG THE RACE TRACK, 16×20 inches, oil.
Signed. 1949. The Thomas Gilcrease Institute of American History
and Art, Tulsa, OK. 14029.

RACE AT THE PUEBLO, 12×16 inches, oil on board.
Signed: l.l. n.d. Private collection. 19026

SUNDAY RACE, 16×20 inches, oil on canvas.
Signed: l.l. n.d. Private collection. 19087

RACERS AT THE PUEBLO, 35×40 inches, oil on canvas.
Signed: l.l. n.d. Stark Museum of Art, Orange, TX. 19070

EARLY RAILROAD BUILDING, MISSOURI, 24×36 inches, oil
on canvas.
Signed: l.r. 1938. Boatmen's Bank, St. Louis. 13023

RAILROAD TRACK, 5×8 inches, watercolor.
Signed: Bern, l.l. c. 1898. Private collection. 20001

RAILROAD THROUGH ARKANSAS GAP, 4¹⁄₈ x 4¹⁄₂ inches, watercolor.
Signed: l.c. Bern. 1898. Private collection. 20011

RANCH HOUSE NEAR TAOS, 14x20 inches, oil on board.
Signed: l.l. 1949. Stark Museum of Art, Orange, TX. 14034

RANCHER'S HOME AND CORRAL, 16x20 inches, oil on board.
Signed: l.r. 1950. Stark Museum of Art, Orange, TX. 15014

RANCH HAND'S CABIN, 16x20 inches, oil on canvas.
Signed: reverse. n.d. Stark Museum of Art, Orange, TX. 19071

RANCH HOUSE WITH WHITE PORTAL, 30x35¹⁄₂ inches, oil on canvas.
Signed: l.l. n.d. Stark Museum of Art, Orange, TX. 19072

RANCH SCENE, 13⁷⁄₈ x19⁷⁄₈ inches, oil on board.
Signed: l.l. n.d. Stark Museum of Art, Orange, TX. 19073

RANCH HOUSE AND CORRAL, TAOS, 20x24 inches, oil.
Signed: l.l. 1951. Private collection. 15022

RANCHER'S HOME AND CORRAL, 25x30 inches, oil.
Signed: l.r. 1949. Private collection. 14064

RANCHITO FARM HOUSE, 20x24 inches, oil on canvas.
Signed: l.l. 1949. Stark Museum of Art, Orange, TX. 14035

LOWER RANCHITO, 20x24 inches, oil on canvas.
Signed: l.r. 1950. Private collection. 15005

RANCHITO NEAR TAOS, 12x16¹⁄₂ inches, watercolor.
Signed. n.d. Private collection. 29001

RANCHOS DE TAOS CHURCH, 28x28 inches, oil.
Signed: l.l. n.d. Private collection. 19049

RANCHOS DE TAOS, 16x20 gouache.
Signed: l.r. 1946. Private collection, 24015

BACK TO THE RESERVATION, 20x24 inches, oil.
Signed. c. 1940. Mr. and Mrs. Sydney Schoenberg, Jr. 14060

RICARDO AND HIS HORSES, 16x20 inches, oil on canvas.
Signed. c. 1919. Eugene B. Adkins collection. 11038

RIO GRANDE NEAR TAOS, 8x11¹⁄₂ inches, oil on panel.
Signed: l.r. c. 1905. Private collection. 10003

ITINERANT RIVER MERCHANT, 24x36 inches, oil on canvas.
Signed: l.r. 1938. Boatmen's Bank, St. Louis. 13026

BIG RIVER BELOW VINEYARD, MO., 4¹⁄₂ x7¹⁄₂ inches, watercolor.
Signed: l.l. Bern. c. 1900. Private collection. 20004

BIG RIVER, ORMDALE, 4¹⁄₂ x7¹⁄₂ inches, watercolor.
Unsigned. c. 1898. Private collection. 20005

MISSISSIPPI RIVERBOAT SCENE, 8x14 inches, watercolor.
Unsigned. c. 1920. Private collection. 22004

ROAD TO TAOS, 30x36 inches, oil.
Signed: l.l. n.d. Private collection. 19122

THE ROUNDUP, 30x40 inches, oil on canvas.
Signed: l.r. c. 1940. Museum of Western Art, Denver, CO. 14015

SADDLED AND WAITING, 19x28¹⁄₂ inches, oil on canvas.
Signed: l.l. n.d. Private collection. 19084

SADDLING UP, 9x13 inches, oil on canvas.
Unsigned. c. 1915. Jim Fowler, Scottsdale, AZ. 11005

SAND AND SAGE, 14x18 inches, oil.
Signed: l.r. c. 1940. Private collection. 14012

SAGEBRUSH AND INDIANS, 25x30 inches, oil on canvas.
Signed: l.l. c. 1940. Private collection. 14032

SAGEBRUSH AND SKY, 20x30 inches, oil on canvas.
Signed: l.r. c. 1940. Private collection. 14042

THE TRAIL THROUGH SAGEBRUSH, 20¹⁄₂ x16 inches, oil.
Signed: l.r. n.d. Weimer collection. 19121

A TRAIL ACROSS THE SAGEBRUSH, size unknown, oil.
Signed. n.d. Private collection. 19130

OUT IN THE SAGE, 16x20 inches, oil.
Signed: l.r. n.d. Private collection. 19143

THE SAGEBRUSH TRAIL, 24x30 inches, oil.
Signed: l.l. 1917. Gordon Fraser. 11033

SAN ANTONIO CHAPEL, TAOS, 25×30 inches, oil on canvas.
Signed: l.r. c. 1924. Private collection. 12014

SANTA FE TRAIL, 24×36 inches, oil on canvas.
Signed: l.l. n.d. Stark Museum of Art, Orange, TX. 19075

SANTA FE RAIL MENU COVER, 7×8 inches, watercolor/ink.
Signed: l.r. c. 1930. Private collection. 23001

SANTIAGO, THE WAR CHIEF, 30×33 inches, oil on canvas.
Signed: l.l. c. 1930. Harwood Foundation, Taos, NM. 13010

SANTIAGO BERNAL, 16×20 inches, oil.
Signed. n.d. Fenn Galleries, Santa Fe, NM. 19102

SATURDAY NIGHT, 24×30 inches, oil.
Signed. c. 1920. The Thomas Gilcrease Institute of American
History and Art, Tulsa, OK. 12021

SENTINEL IN GLORIETA FOREST, 25×30 inches, oil on canvas.
Signed: l.r. c. 1920. Private collection. 12032

THE SHEEPHERDER, 25×30 inches, oil.
Signed: l.r. 1946. Private collection. 14052

SHEEPHERDERS CHANGING CAMP, 25×30 inches, oil.
Signed: l.l. c. 1948. Private collection. 14055

RANCHOS WITH FLOCK OF SHEEP, 25×30 inches, oil
on canvas.
Signed: l.r. 1951. Private collection. 15007

SHORT CUT, 24¼×30¼ inches, oil.
Signed: l.r. c. 1935. Amon Carter Museum, Fort Worth, TX. 13008

THE SIGN FROM THE CHIEF, 30×24 inches, oil.
Signed. n.d. Woolaroc Museum, Bartlesville, OK. 19032

SNOW FALLING IN THE CAMP, 16½×20 inches, oil on canvas.
Signed: l.l. n.d. Private collection, 19025

SNOW SCENE, TAOS VALLEY, 16×20 inches, oil on board.
Signed: l.r. n.d. Stark Museum of Art, Orange, TX. 19076

THEIR SON, 35×40 inches, oil on canvas.
Signed: l.l. 1924. Private collection. 12007

A SON OF THE WAR CHIEF, size unknown, oil.
Signed: l.r. n.d. Private collection. 19124

SPRING PLOWING, 36½×40½ inches, oil.
Signed: l.r. n.d. Private collection. 19145

SPYING, 20×30 inches, oil.
Signed: l.r. c. 1912. Private collection. 11032

AT THE STABLE DOOR, 14×14 inches, oil on board.
Signed: l.l. c. 1940. Private collection. 14011

THE STAGE IN OPEN COUNTRY, 11⅛×14½ inches, oil.
Signed: l.l. c. 1930. Amon Carter Museum, Fort Worth, TX. 13009

THE STAGE IN INDIAN COUNTRY, 25×30 inches, oil on canvas.
Signed: l.l. n.d. Private collection. 19129

STAGE STOP, 2½×13½ inches, watercolor.
Signed: l.r. 1922. Private collection. 22003

THE SIX-HORSE STAGE, 20×30 inches, oil on canvas.
Signed: l.l. c. 1918. Mr. and Mrs. Lyle S. Woodcock. 11042

STAGECOACH, MISSOURI HILLS, 24×36 inches, oil on canvas.
Signed: l.r. 1938. Boatmen's Bank, St. Louis. 13025

MENACING INDIANS, STAGECOACH, 24×36 inches, oil.
Signed: l.r. 1950. Private collection. 15017

STORM CLOUDS OVER TRUCHAS, 20×24 inches, oil.
Signed: l.l. n.d. Private collection. 19127

STREAM AND INDIANS, 25×30 inches, oil on canvas.
Signed: l.r. c. 1930. Private collection. 13018

STREET SCENE IN TAOS, 11×15 inches, oil.
Signed: l.r. 1911. Weimer Collection. 11028

STREET IN MINING CAMP, 16×20 inches, oil on canvas.
Signed: l.r. n.d. Stark Museum of Art, Orange, TX. 19077

MY STUDIO IN TAOS, 7½×8 inches, oil.
Signed: ?. n.d. Private collection. 19110

SULTRY DAY, 7×8 inches, monotype.
Signed: l.r. n.d. Weimer Collection. 39009

SUNDAY STROLL, 5×8 inches, watercolor.
Signed: l.c. Bern. c. 1898. Private collection. 20003

SUNDAY STROLL, 4¾×9 inches, watercolor.
Signed: l.r. c. 1895. Museum of Fine Arts, Santa Fe, NM. 20012

SUNSET, 5×6 inches, monotype.
Unsigned. c. 1940. Stark Museum of Art, Orange, TX. 34003

SIGNAL OF SURRENDER, 17¾×11¼ inches, watercolor.
Signed: l.l. 1899. Gerald Peters Gallery, Santa Fe, NM. 20008

TAOS, NEW MEXICO. 52½×101½ inches, oil.
Unsigned. c. 1920. Hammer Galleries, NY. 12046

MOVIE NIGHT AT TAOS THEATER, 30×40 inches, oil on canvas.
Signed: l.r. 1939. Private collection. 13007

TAOS COUNTRY, 25×50 inches, oil.
Signed. c. 1939. Woolaroc Museum, Bartlesville, OK. 13014

TAOS STREET SCENE, 26×32 inches, oil.
Signed: l.l. 1946. Private collection. 14007

TAOS VALLEY VIEW FROM MESA, 25×30 inches, oil on canvas.
Signed: l.r. c. 1940. Private collection. 14009

TAOS TAPESTRY, 36×30 inches, oil on canvas.
Signed: ?. c. 1940. Stark Museum of Art, Orange, TX. 14037

TAOS VALLEY, 20×24 inches, oil on canvas.
Signed: l.r. 1951. The Museum at Texas Tech University. 15015

TAOS IDYLL, 36×40 inches, oil on canvas.
Signed: l.r. n.d. Eugene B. Adkins Collection. 19006.

TAOS INDIANS IN FRONT OF ADOBE, 10×12 inches, oil on
canvas.
Signed: l.l. n.d. Gerald Peters Gallery, Santa Fe, NM. 19010

SCENE OF TAOS, N.M. 20×16 inches, oil on canvas.
Signed: l.r. n.d. Gerald Peters Gallery, Santa Fe, NM. 19011

TAOS INDIAN, 14½×11¼ inches, oil.
Signed: l.l. n.d. Private collection. 19024

TAOS VALLEY, 13×20 inches, oil.
Unsigned. n.d. Museum of Fine Arts, Santa Fe, NM. 19036

TAOS SCENE, RENDERING LARD, 11×15 inches, oil.
Signed: l.r. n.d. Museum of Fine Arts, Santa Fe, NM. 19037

TAOS VALLEY, 25×30 inches, oil.
Signed: l.r. n.d. Museum of Fine Arts, Santa Fe, NM. 19038

TAOS INDIANS ON HORSEBACK, 20×16 inches, oil.
Signed: ?. n.d. Private collection. 19047

EDGE OF TOWN, TAOS, 12×16 inches, oil on board.
Signed: l.l. n.d. Private collection. 19053

TAOS INDIAN, 12½×9¼ inches, oil on board.
Signed: l.l. n.d. Private collection. 19054.

STREET SCENE IN TAOS, 11×14 inches, oil on canvas.
Signed: ?. n.d. Stark Museum of Art, Orange, TX. 19078

TAOS VALLEY RANCH, 30×40 inches, oil on canvas.
Signed: ?. n.d. Private collection. 19081

EDGE OF TOWN, TAOS, 8½×12 inches, oil.
Signed. n.d. Fenn Galleries, Santa Fe, NM. 19106

TAOS MOUNTAIN, 9×13 inches, oil.
Signed: ?. n.d. Private collection. 19114

TAOS LANDSCAPE, 12×16 inches, oil.
Signed: l.r. n.d. Private collection. 19135

EARLY TAOS HOME, 5×6 inches, monotype.
Signed: l.r. c. 1935. Private collection. 33013

EARLY TAOS, 6×5 inches, woodcut.
Signed: l.r. c. 1920. Stark Museum of Art, Orange, TX. 32006

TAOS, N.M., HOUSE AND BARN, 7×8 inches, monotype.
Signed: l.r. c. 1930. Private collection. 33008

TAOS MOUNTAIN, 7×8 inches, monotype.
Unsigned. c. 1930. Private collection. 33010

A STREET IN TAOS, N.M., 8½×9⅞ inches, lithograph.
Signed: l.r. n.d. Stark Museum of Art, Orange, TX. 39004

TAOS LANDSCAPE, 7¾×9⅞ inches, lithograph.
Signed: l.r. n.d. Stark Museum of Art, Orange, TX. 39005

TAOS GOATHERDER, 25×30 inches, oil on canvas.
Signed: l.r. n.d. Private collection. 19144

TAOS FARM LANDSCAPE, 13×17 inches, gouache.
Signed: l.l. n.d. Private collection. 29015

TAOS INDIANS, FAMILY GROUP, size unknown, oil.
Signed: l.l. 1929. Private collection. 12012.

TAXCO, 35×40 inches, oil on canvas.
Signed: l.r. c. 1933. Stark Museum of Art, Orange, TX. 13021

TAXCO SCENE, CATHEDRAL, 9×12 inches, oil.
Signed. c. 1932. Private collection. 13022

THRESHING TIME AT TAOS PUEBLO, 24×49 inches, oil.
Signed. 1939. Woolaroc Museum, Bartlesville, OK. 13013

THRESHING TIME, TAOS PUEBLO, 25⅝×30⅝ inches, oil.
Signed. 1944. The Thomas Gilcrease Institute of American History
and Art, Tulsa, OK. 14026

THRESHING WHEAT, 12½×28 inches, oil on board.
Signed: l.r. n.d. Stark Museum of Art, Orange, TX. 19079

THRESHING AT THE PUEBLO, 6×6 inches, lithograph.
Signed: l.r. O.E.B. c. 1930. Private collection. 33004

GOING TO TOWN, 6×8½ inches, watercolor.
Signed: ?. n.d. Private collection. 29011

TRADERS IN THE PUEBLO, 25×30 inches, oil on canvas.
Signed: l.r. 1941. Stark Museum of Art, Orange, TX. 14038

TRADERS IN THE PUEBLO, 25×30 inches, oil.
Signed: l.r. 1941. Private collection. 14054

OLD TRADING POST, IGNACIO, CO., 5×10½ inches,
watercolor.
Signed: l.r. Bern. 1899. Private collection. 20006

TRADING POST, IGNACIO, 12×9½ inches, watercolor.
Signed: l.l. 1899. Gerald Peters Gallery, Santa Fe, NM. 20009

AN UNCERTAIN TRAIL, 20×16 inches, oil.
Signed: l.l. 1915. Weimer Collection. 11027

THE RELIEF TRAIN, 11⁵⁄₁₆×20⅛ inches, chromolithograph.
Signed: l.r. 1912. Amon Carter Museum, Fort Worth, TX. 41000

TRANSPORTATION IN ALASKA, 21×45 inches, oil on canvas.
Unsigned. c. 1914. Saint Louis Art Museum, St. Louis, MO. 11013

UNTITLED: 3 INDIANS ON HORSES, 5×5¾ inches, etching.
Signed: ?. n.d. Museum of Fine Arts, Santa Fe, NM. 39002

IN OUR VALLEY, 20×24 inches, oil on canvas.
Unsigned. 1950. Private collection. 15006

THE VALLEY FROM TAOS, 20×16 inches, oil.
Signed: ?. n.d. Private collection. 19118

EVENING IN THE VALLEY, 14×18 inches, watercolor.
Signed: l.r. n.d. Stark Museum of Art, Orange, TX. 29003

THE VIGIL OR SADDLED PONIES, size unknown, oil.
Signed: l.l. 1920. Private collection. 12041

MOUNTAINS AND ADOBE VILLAGE, 5×5 inches, watercolor.
Unsigned. 1928. Weimer Collection. 22012

VISITORS IN CAMP, 16¼×23¼ inches, oil.
Signed: l.l. 1950. Private collection. 15004

WAGON TRAIN, 8¼×15½ inches, oil.
Signed: l.r. c. 1914. Stark Museum of Art, Orange, TX. 11023

THROUGH MISSOURI BY COVERED WAGON, 24×36 inches,
oil on canvas.
Signed: l.r. 1938. Boatmen's Bank, St. Louis, 13027

WATCHING THE WAGON TRAIN, 22×36¼ inches, oil
on canvas.
Signed: l.r. n.d. Gerald Peters Gallery, Santa Fe, NM. 19009

TRAIL OF THE WAGON TRAIN, 16×20 inches, oil on board.
Signed: l.l. n.d. Private collection. 19083

COVERED WAGON AT FAIR, 6 OXEN, 21x46 inches, watercolor.
Signed: c.r. c. 1914. Saint Louis Art Museum, St. Louis, MO. 21002

COVERED WAGON TRAIN / OXEN, 5x13½ inches, watercolor.
Unsigned. c. 1935. Private collection. 23008

SCOUT AND WAGON TRAIN, 24x20 inches, watercolor.
Signed: l.l. n.d. Stark Museum of Art, Orange, TX. 29006

THE LONG WAIT, 16x20 inches, oil on board.
Signed: l.r. c. 1930. Private collection. 13002

WAITING, 10x12 inches, oil on canvas.
Signed: l.r. 1928. Sangre de Cristo Art Center. 12008

WAITING FOR THEIR MASTERS, 15½x16 inches, oil.
Signed: l.r. 1922. Philbrook Art Center, Tulsa, OK. 12019

WAITING, 16x20 inches, oil on canvas.
Signed: l.l. 1926. Private collection. 12024

RETURN OF THE WARRIORS, size unknown, oil.
Signed: l.r. c. 1920. Private collection. 12042

WATER, CANOES, MEN, INDIANS, 22x36 inches, oil on canvas.
Signed: l.r. c. 1914. Saint Louis Art Museum, St. Louis, MO. 11017

WATER, 30x36 inches, oil.
Signed: l.r. 1945. Private collection. 14008

WATERING HOLE, 8½x12½ inches, oil on board.
Signed: l.r. n.d. Private collection. 19023

THE WATERHOLE, 30x40 inches, oil on canvas.
Signed: l.l. 1916. Wiggins Gallery, Roswell, NM. 11001

GOSSIP AT THE WATERHOLE, 7x7½ inches, watercolor.
Signed: ?. n.d. Private collection. 29012

OPENING THE WEST, 24x36 inches, oil on canvas.
Signed: l.r. 1938. Boatmen's Bank, St. Louis. 13024

THE WHITE PACK PONY, 16x20 inches, oil.
Signed: l.r. c. 1940. Private collection. 11035

THE J.M. WHITE, 24x35½ inches, oil on canvas.
Signed: l.r. 1941. Boatmen's Bank, St. Louis. 14043

WINTER SCENE—ARMY CAMP, 20¼x44 ⁵⁄₁₆ inches, oil.
Signed: l.l. c. 1915. Saint Louis Art Museum, St. Louis, MO. 11007

WINTER IN THE PANHANDLE, 30x40 inches, oil.
Signed. c. 1920. San Antonio Art League. 12011

WINTER NIGHT, TAOS, 34¾x40 inches, oil.
Signed: l.r. 1928. Philbrook Art Center, Tulsa, OK. 12017

WINTER MOUNTAIN LANDSCAPE, 16x20 inches, oil on masonite.
Signed: l.r. 1936. Private collection. 13028

WINTER AFTERNOON, 13¼x19 inches, oil on canvas.
Signed: l.r. c. 1947. Private collection. 14018

WINTER IN THE VILLAGE, 20x24 inches, oil.
Signed: l.r. 1949. Private collection. 14048

WINTER HUNT, 22x28 inches, oil on canvas.
Signed: l.l. n.d. The Anschutz Collection, Denver, CO. 19040

WINTER IN TAOS, 20x24 inches, oil on canvas.
Signed: l.r. n.d. Carlsbad Art Museum, NM. 19088

A WINTER CAMP, 36x23¼ inches, oil.
Signed. n.d. Boatmen's Bank, St. Louis. 19140

WINTER NIGHT, 6x4⅞ inches, woodcut.
Signed: l.r. n.d. Stark Museum of Art, Orange, TX. 39006

WINTER MOVE, 16x20 inches, oil on canvas.
Signed: l.l. c. 1928., Mr. and Mrs. Lyle S. Woodcock. 12049

WOODHAULERS, 6x5 inches, woodcut.
Signed: l.r. n.d. Stark Museum of Art, Orange, TX. 39007

WOODWARD & TIERNAN CALENDAR, 10x7 inches, watercolor and pen.
Signed: m.r. Bern. 1900. Private collection. 20013

Oil paintings by O.E. Berninghaus in the collection of August A. Busch, Jr.

DeSoto Discovery of the Mississippi

Marquette Descending the Mississippi, 1673

Henry Hudson Bargaining with the Indians

The Captive-Indians crossing river

Indians on cliff signaling to Indian village below at river, wagon train approaching

Wagon loaded with household goods drawn by two oxen with dog and cow trailing

California Redwood Forest with wagon going through tree

Levee Scene, St. Louis, in Early Seventies

Attack on Stagecoach

Westward Ho! Westbound wagon train on the Salt Lake Trail

Western Railway Station, Union Pacific train in western Kansas about 1870

Surprise Attack, Cavalry entering an Indian village

Progress of Lewis and Clark Expedition, conversing with Indians at camp

Frontier Town, Wagon train arriving in a frontier town

Fording the River, with horse drawn flat boats

The Pioneers

Pack Train, pack train on mountain pass

General Grant Hauling Cordwood

Bevo Mill

Scene of buffalo swimming river with one buffalo on bluff

Scene of covered wagon rolling over prairie drawn by white horse with brown horse and man walking nearby

The Grand Canyon

Scene of water harbor with four-stack ocean liner. Also, freight cars with Anheuser-Busch, Inc., Budweiser on side of cars, six automobiles, horses, wagons and boats

Santa Claus in large sled drawn by six steers. Scene is of sled loaded with toys on a mountain road with houses in valley below on Christmas Eve

Santa Claus in sled filled with toys drawn by six mules with light shining through windows on Christmas Eve

The Sleighing Party

A Bauernhof

Girl in Donkey Cart at Grant's Farm

Cowboy Cooking Chow

Two Indians fanning fire

Two men in front of tent, one shooting at bear

Basket with corn, pumpkin and squash

INDEX

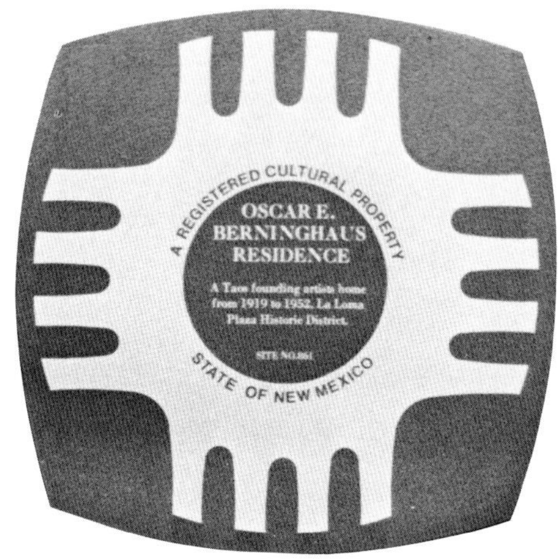

(Plaque: National Historic Register.)

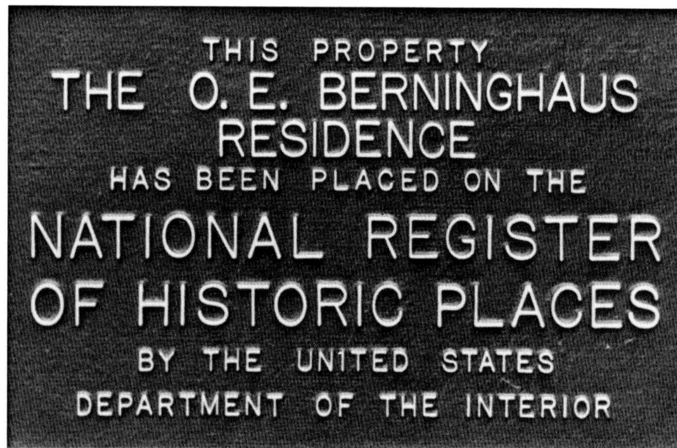

The O.E. Berninghaus home is presently owned by Taos artist,
Robert Daughters and his wife.